THE SOCIAL CONSEQUENCES OF PSYCHIATRIC ILLNESS

The Social Consequences of Psychiatric Illness

Edited by

LEE N. ROBINS, PH.D.
Professor of Sociology in Psychiatry
Washington University School of Medicine (St. Louis)

PAULA J. CLAYTON, M.D.
Professor of Psychiatry
Washington University School of Medicine (St. Louis)

and

JOHN K. WING, M.D., PH.D.
Director, MRC Social Psychiatry Unit
Institute of Psychiatry (London)

BRUNNER/MAZEL, *Publishers* • New York

Library of Congress Cataloging in Publication Data

Main entry under title:

The social consequences of psychiatric illness.

Includes bibliographies and index.

1. Psychology, Pathological—Social aspects. 2. Mental health services.
I. Robins, Lee N. II. Clayton, Paula J., 1934- III. Wing, John Kenneth.
[DNLM: 1. Mental disorders—Complications. 2. Social problems. WM100 S6755]
RC455.S595 362.2'042 80-11090

ISBN 0-87630-226-6

Published by
BRUNNER/MAZEL, INC.
19 Union Square
New York, N. Y. 10003

MANUFACTURED IN THE UNITED STATES OF AMERICA

Foreword

The field of psychiatric epidemiology has experienced a period of considerable growth and development in recent years. Part of the rapid expansion is due to internal developments within the field and part due to increased attention from outside the field. One measure of the greater attention from outside was reflected in the activities in the United States of the President's Commission on Mental Health. Soon after taking office, President Carter formed the President's Commission on Mental Health, which devoted considerable attention to documenting the magnitude and scope of mental disorders and their impact upon family life, community activities, and the national welfare. In the final report of the Commission, it recognized the need for further knowledge in the field of epidemiology and highlighted epidemiology as one of the areas requiring increased support for research and for research training. These actions on the part of the President's Commission reflect increasing attention by both the public at large and the policymakers to the magnitude and scope of mental disorders.

Advances in the field of psychiatric epidemiology were discussed at the World Psychiatric Association meeting held in St. Louis, and the proceedings are printed in this volume. Whereas most attention to social, economic, and familial factors has been on their possible role as antecedents to psychiatric illness, the organizers of the conference in St. Louis focused on social factors as consequences of psychiatric illness. This focus allowed for more specific types of research to be presented and for a broad scope of topics and methods to be discussed. For example, the impact of mental disorders upon the health care system was assessed quantitatively both in the United States and in England, with growing evidence suggesting increased morbidity and possible mortality of persons with psychiatric illness in general. While the degree of mortality may be debated, there is no disagreement as to the higher degree of utilization of general health care services by persons with diagnosed or even unrecognized mental illness. Similarly, the impact upon occupational systems, law enforcement, and family life is well-documented in various other papers.

Perhaps the most controversial area is the interaction between psychiatric disorder, life stress, and interpersonal relations. Most research and theory have focused upon life stress as antecedent to psychiatric disorder. Particularly since World War II, stress has been one of the unifying concepts in the social epidemiologic research, particularly in North America and the United Kingdom. The theoretical basis for this approach goes back to the ideas of Adolf Meyer and his associates who gave great emphasis to the role of the social environment in providing the background to the patient's adaptation to change. In this context, illness was viewed as part of the adaptive response of the organism to changes in the environment. Subsequent to Meyer's initial conceptualization, most attention has been given to the social and interpersonal components of the environment, particularly the issues of life change and social adversity that affect individuals in an urbanized, industrialized, and mobile society.

The problems of disentangling antecedents from consequences has been a significant methologic issue that has preoccupied many leaders in the field of psychiatric epidemiology. Among those participating in the conference, the Dohrenwends have been in the forefront of this research. The conceptualization of these factors is becoming more sophisticated. In addition to adverse life events, more attention is being paid to the role of social support systems, particularly social networks and social bonds as represented by immediate family members and other social groups. The complex interplay between these factors both as antecedents and consequences of mental disorder is ably unraveled in the excellent papers by the Australian group led by Scott Henderson, as well as in the work of the Dohrenwends.

Taken together, the papers in this volume represent the continuing sophistication and relevance of psychiatric epidemiology, not only to the mental health field in general but to those concerned with social policy and public welfare as well.

GERALD L. KLERMAN, M.D.

Contents

III. THE PSYCHIATRICALLY ILL AS PARENTS

IV. THE CONSEQUENCES OF PSYCHIATRIC DISORDER FOR LIFE STRESS AND INTERPERSONAL RELATIONSHIPS

V. PSYCHIATRIC DISORDER AND THE WORLDS OF WORK AND CRIME

Preface

The first of what has proved to be a triennial series of meetings sponsored by the World Psychiatric Association's Section of Epidemiology and Community Psychiatry in partnership with local professional societies was held in Aberdeen, Scotland, in 1969. The theme was psychiatric epidemiology and the book based on the proceedings provided a comprehensive summary which bears witness to the healthy state of the discipline (Hare & Wing, 1970). The second meeting was held in Mannheim, Germany, in 1972, and was concerned with the epidemiological basis for planning psychiatric services (Wing & Häfner, 1973). It was not possible to publish the proceedings of the third symposium, held in Opatija, Yugoslavia in 1975.

The fourth meeting, which formed the basis for the present book, took place in St. Louis, Missouri, in 1978. The topic chosen was the social effects of mental illness. The contributors were all outstanding in their particular fields of expertise and their papers demonstrate how a foundation of knowledge is gradually being built up upon which further progress can be made. This has not always been the case in psychiatric research. Replication of studies has been the exception rather than the rule and, when it was undertaken, tended to produce results at variance with those of earlier studies.

The St. Louis symposium, like its predecessors, was devoted to the presentation of material that would be likely to stand the test of time. The editors hope that readers will agree that this volume is not just another "book of the conference" but provides solid evidence that psychiatric epidemiology is continuing to make real contributions to our understanding of the interaction between man and environment.

The preparation of the papers from the symposium was made possible by support from the Division of Biometry and Epidemiology, National Institutes of Mental Health, United States Public Health Service.

THE EDITORS

REFERENCES

HARE, E. H. and WING, J. K. (Eds.) *Psychiatric Epidemiology*. London: Oxford University Press, 1970.

WING, J. K. and HÄFNER, H. *Roots of Evaluation*. London: Oxford University Press, 1973.

Contributors

Sylvia Adcock, National Health and Medical Research Council, Social Psychiatry Research Unit, The Australian National University, Canberra.

Sandra Arey, Ph.D., Children's Mental Health Unit, Department of Psychiatry, College of Medicine, University of Florida, Gainesville.

D. G. Byrne, Ph.D., National Health and Medical Research Council, Social Psychiatry Research Unit, The Australian National University, Canberra.

Paula J. Clayton, M.D., Department of Psychiatry, Washington University School of Medicine, St. Louis.

C. Robert Cloninger, M.D., Department of Psychiatry, Washington University School of Medicine; Jewish Hospital of St. Louis, St. Louis.

Brian Cooper, D.M., Department of Epidemiological Psychiatry, Central Institute of Mental Health, Mannheim, West Germany.

Serena Deutsch, M.A. Candidate, New York State Psychiatric Institute, New York.

Horst Dilling, M.D., Klinik Für Psychiatrie der Med. Hochschule Lubeck, West Germany.

Bruce P. Dohrenwend, Ph.D., Columbia University, College of Physicians and Surgeons, Social Psychiatry Research Unit, New York.

Barbara Snell Dohrenwend, Ph.D., Division of Sociomedical Sciences, Columbia University, School of Public Health, New York.

Paul Duncan-Jones, National Health and Medical Research Council, Social Psychiatry Research Unit, The Australian National University, Canberra.

L. Erlenmeyer-Kimling, Ph.D., Principal Research Scientist and Director,

Division of Developmental Behavioral Studies, New York State Psychiatric Institute, New York.

David P. Farrington, Ph.D., University of Cambridge, Institute of Criminology, England.

Margit Fischer, M.D., Chief Psychiatrist, Psykatrisk Hospital, Aarhus, Denmark.

Dennis Gath, D.M., University Department of Psychiatry, The Warneford Hospital, Oxford, England.

David Goldberg, D.M., Department of Psychiatry, The University Hospital of South Manchester, England.

Irving I. Gottesman, Ph.D., Department of Psychology, University of Minnesota, Minneapolis.

Janet R. Hankin, Ph.D., Program Director of Psychiatry Studies, Health Services Research and Development Center, The Johns Hopkins University, Baltimore, Maryland.

Scott Henderson, D.M., National Health and Medical Research Council, Social Psychiatry Research Unit, The Australian National University, Canberra.

Robert Jones, Department of Psychiatry, The University Hospital of South Manchester, England.

Gerald Klerman, M.D., Administrator, Alcohol, Drug Abuse, and Mental Health Administration, Rockville, Maryland.

Norman Kreitman, M.D., MRC Unit for Epidemiological Studies in Psychiatry, University Department of Psychiatry, Royal Edinburgh Hospital, Scotland.

Collins Lewis, M.D., Department of Psychiatry, Washington University School of Medicine, St. Louis.

J. Muhangi, M.D., Department of Psychiatry, University of Nairobi, Kenyatta National Hospital, Kenya.

Jerome K. Myers, Ph.D., Department of Sociology, Yale University, New Haven.

Juan C. Negrete, M.D., Department of Psychiatry, McGill University, The Montreal General Hospital.

Kathryn Strother Ratcliff, Ph.D., Research Instructor in Sociology in Psychiatry, Department of Psychiatry, Washington University School of Medicine, St. Louis.

Darrel A. Regier, M.D., M.P.H., Director, Division of Biometry and Epidemiology, National Institute of Mental Health, Rockville, Maryland.

Theodore Reich, M.D., Department of Psychiatry, Washington University School of Medicine, St. Louis.

John Rice, Ph.D., Department of Psychiatry, Washington University School of Medicine, St. Louis.

Lee N. Robins, Ph.D., Professor of Sociology in Psychiatry, Department of Psychiatry, Washington University School of Medicine, St. Louis.

Ruth Scott, National Health and Medical Research Council, Social Psychiatry Research Unit, The Australian National University, Canberra.

Sam Shapiro, Director, Psychiatry Studies, Health Services Research and Development Center, The Johns Hopkins University, Baltimore.

Michael Shepherd, M.D., Institute of Psychiatry, London.

Ute Sosna, Central Institute of Mental Health, Mannheim, West Germany.

Ming Tso Tsuang, M.D., Ph.D., Professor of Psychiatry and Psychiatric Epidemiology, University of Iowa, College of Medicine, Iowa City.

George J. Warheit, Ph.D., Department of Psychiatry, University of Florida, College of Medicine, Gainesville.

Myrna M. Weissman, Ph.D., Associate Professor of Psychiatry and Epidemiology, and Director, Depression Research Unit, Department of Psychiatry, Yale University School of Medicine, New Haven.

Siegfried Weyerer, Ph.D., Psychiatric Clinic of the University of Munich, West Germany.

John K. Wing, M.D., MRC Social Psychiatry Unit, Institute of Psychiatry, London.

Robin A. Wunsch-Hitzig, M.A., Research Scientist, New York State Psychiatric Institute, New York.

THE SOCIAL CONSEQUENCES OF PSYCHIATRIC ILLNESS

I

RESEARCH

1

Research on the Social Effects of Mental Disorders

DARREL A. REGIER, M.D., M.P.H.

The NIMH Division of Biometry and Epidemiology was pleased to be able to assist in sponsoring this important meeting in which many prominent psychiatric epidemiologists and social scientists have chosen to examine the social effects of psychiatric disorders. Such a focus is consonant with the mental health field's continuing concern about the stigma of mental disorder, a concern which was once again raised by the U.S. President's Commission on Mental Health (1978). Undoubtedly, such a stigma is partially attributable to what the layman believes to be the social effects of mental disorders—effects on the ability to work and to function in the roles of spouse and parent. There are also fears about possible chronic disability and dependency, and about the financial cost of psychiatric and associated medical and other human services to the individual, the family, and the community. Finally, there is concern that one mental disorder may lead to other disorders such as alcoholism, drug abuse and deviant criminal or delinquent behavior. These are some of the social effects which will be examined during this World Psychiatric Association Meeting.

It is clear that research is needed to replace fears, myths, and partial truths with scientifically developed information on the actual social consequences of mental disorders.

CHARACTERISTICS OF NEEDED RESEARCH

Much will be required of psychiatric epidemiologists and social scientists if research in these areas is to be productive. For most epidemiologists, there will need to be a departure from the conventional way of viewing psychiatric disorders as the dependent variables for which independent behavioral, environmental and genetic determinants are sought. The effect of such a reversal is to view the presence of a psychiatric disorder as only one of several independent vraiables which can lead to adverse social consequences.

One is thus led inexorably into the tangled webs of association between mental disorders and social conditions in an attempt to determine which came first and what are the causal linkages. Hence, mental disorders will be linked to social conditions which have been treated as predisposing or associated factors in previous research studies, and which must now be viewed as sometimes the *consequences* of mental disorders.

These are clearly not new issues. For example, controversies over social causation vs. social selection hypotheses have raged since the pioneer psychiatric epidemiological work of Faris and Dunham in the 1930s. However, over the past 40 years, we have increased our capacity considerably for dealing with some of these issues and many of the most thoughtful contributions have emanated from persons in this Conference.

There are three major research areas which we in the NIMH Division of Biometry and Epidemiology are supporting to further the development of work on these issues. First, there is support for increased research leading to improvements in the definition and classification of mental disorders. Second, there is a need to systematize a classification of social effects or consequences of psychiatric disorder, including operationalized categories for social role functioning and disability. Finally, there is support for improving our capabilities to describe and analyze the workings of the service system which provides care for persons with mental disorders, with particular attention to establishing methods for linking epidemiological and health services research activities.

Classifications, Nomenclatures and Standardized Interviews for Mental Disorders

Regardless of whether mental disorders are treated as independent or dependent variables, there is a prerequisite need for clear definitions of the disorders being studied. Classifications of natural phenomena are the basic tools of all scientific endeavors, and new classifications are often required before major advances can take place in a given scientific field.

In the past several years, there has been considerable progress in the fields of neurobiology, psychopharmacology, and psychopathology which has stimulated the emergence of the Feighner Criteria (Feighner et al.,

1972) and the Research Diagnostic Criteria (RDC) (Spitzer et al., 1978). In addition, cluster analysis and other statistical techniques have contributed to our knowledge of clinical syndromes. Clinical trials such as the collaborative depression studies sponsored by NIMH have been undertaken to assess the utility of these diagnostic criteria for predicting therapeutic responses to specific psychotropic drugs.

Empirical studies have also been undertaken to assess the comparability of international usage of the psychiatric nomenclature, as exemplified by the U.S.-U.K. study of schizophrenia and affective disorders (Cooper, et al., 1972). In addition, the International Pilot Study of Schizophrenia (IPSS) has advanced our understanding of the cross-cultural presence and nature of this disorder (World Health Organization, 1973). Building on the empirical approach of the Feighner and Research Diagnostic Criteria, the American Psychiatric Association Task Force on Nomenclature and Statistics has proposed a new psychiatric nomenclature, the Third Edition of the Diagnostic and Statistical Manual (DSM-III). This represents an attempt to adapt the nomenclature for statistical recording of mental disorders to fit emerging knowledge of psychopathology.

However, it remains for the international psychiatric community to assess the utility of these developments, and the NIMH is supporting discussion of this issue on several levels. Support has been provided for a joint WHO/Council for International Organizations of Medical Sciences (CIOMS) project which is developing definitions of psychiatric conditions and frequently used psychopathological terms. A field trial of the DSM-III is being supported by NIMH to assess its utility in clinical practice. In addition, the NIMH is now making plans to support an International Conference on the Classification of Mental Disorders with probable collaboration with the WHO.

As classifications and nomenclatures continue to develop, there is also a need to refine standardized psychiatric interviews which will make it possible to elicit information from patients and nonpatients in population surveys to determine the presence of specific disorders with a high degree of validity and reliability. There are several prominent instruments which attempt to elicit sufficiently detailed information to permit a specific diagnosis as opposed to a simple determination of "caseness." These interviews include the Present State Examination (PSE) developed by Dr. Wing and colleagues (1974) and the Clinical Interview Schedule (CIS) developed by Dr. Goldberg and colleagues (1970) at the Maudsley Hospital and the Institute of Psychiatry in London. In addition, there have been multiple instruments developed by the New York Biometrics Research Group of Drs. Spitzer and Endicott and colleagues, the latest of which is the Lifetime version of the Schedule for Affective Disorders and Schizophrenia (SADS-L) (Spitzer & Endicott, 1977). Finally, the Washington University, St. Louis, group of Drs. Robins, Helzer and Croughan have developed the Renard Diagnostic Interview (RDI) (Helzer et al., 1977).

Although these instruments represent major advances in our ability to identify specific psychiatric disorders with a high degree of validity and reliability, they present some difficulties for application to large-scale population surveys. Except for the Renard, all of these instruments require interviewers with a high degree of training and experience in evaluating psychiatric patients—a reality which renders their large-scale usage extremely unwieldy and expensive. In the U.S., it has now become necessary to have interviews which will enable translation of their output into DSM-III categories. Hence, although both the Renard and the SADS-L utilize many of the same categories and are based on the Feighner and RDC criteria respectively, neither covers the necessary range of disorders covered in the DSM-III.

With these limitations in mind, the NIMH has supported the development of a new instrument, the Diagnostic Interview Schedule (DIS), which will attempt to combine certain elements of the Renard and the SADS-L. Most of the development work is being done by Drs. Robins, Helzer and Croughan in collaboration with Drs. Spitzer and Endicott and the NIMH staff. The major specifications of the new DIS instruments are that it be structured so as to permit use of lay interviewers whose experience and training are similar to that of interviewers in other large-scale population surveys, and that it cover as wide a range of DSM-III categories as this data collection technique permits. The interview will obviously require validation studies conducted for each of the diagnostic categories included.

If we are successful in implementing such a one-stage diagnostic interview, it should accelerate the development of a new era in psychiatric epidemiology which commenced with the emergence of the previously mentioned structured psychiatric interviews. Indeed, the ability to use lay interviewers to determine the presence of specific mental disorders on a large scale is necessary in order to realize the potential of epidemiological methods as postulated by Morris some 20 years ago. These well-known functions included community diagnosis, the historical study of a community's health, monitoring the workings of the health system, estimating risks, completing the clinical picture, identifying syndromes, and ultimately searching for the causes of disorders (Morris, 1957). Two functions in particular, namely, the community diagnosis and determining the workings of the health system, are most dependent upon the development of such an instrument. And, as will be discussed later, these two functions must be carried out if the linkage between epidemiological and health services research is to be effected. Such a linkage is seen as key to understanding several major social effects of mental disorders.

A Classification of Social Effects

As we continue to refine our classifications, nomenclatures, and standardized psychiatric interviews to produce more homogeneous categories of mental disorder, we will also need to improve our systems for defining social effects or consequences of these disorders. Ideally, such a classification should be linked to diagnoses of mental disorder in a multiaxial classification system. There has already been some experience with this concept in the multiaxial classification of childhood disorders developed by Rutter and others (1975) under WHO auspices. Likewise, the DSM-III has a multiaxial format to permit classification of social functioning.

A recent Alcohol, Drug Abuse and Mental Health Administration (ADAMHA) Workgroup on Epidemiology, Health Services Research, and Statistics (1978) also came to the conclusion that a multiaxial classification system was essential if epidemiological work is to progress—particuarly in the alcohol and drug abuse fields. All three ADAMHA Institutes must be concerned with the social problems associated with emotional symptoms and with alcohol and drug use, even though such symptoms and substance use may not always constitute clear syndromes or disorders. Two of the most productive areas of epidemiological research in alcohol have been in the area of consequences: fetal alcohol syndrome research and research on traffic accidents. In both, alcohol use is viewed as the independent variable.

As a result of our review of the ADAMHA-sponsored epidemiological research on social problems and specific disorders, there was a specific recommendation that each Institute accelerate activities on the definition and multiaxial classification of ADM disorders and related problems with the goal of developing specific criteria for the following axes: 1) ADM disorders or syndromes; 2) quantity/frequency scales of related symptoms and drug or alcohol use behavior; and 3) social functioning and adverse consequences of ADM disorders or problems.

Several scales exist such as the Global Assessment Scale (GAS) of Endicott, Spitzer et al. (1976) and the social disability scales developed for a large WHO multinational study. However, additional and more systematized classifications must emerge if the goals of this conference are to be attained.

Health Services Research

From a Public Health Service perspective, one of the most important consequences of psychiatric disorder is the utilization of specialty mental health, general medical and other human services. The economic and other social consequences of service utilization are major concerns of health care planners, providers and patients alike.

However, there are several prerequisites if linkages are to occur across the fields of epidemiology and health services research. For epidemiology, there must be the capacity to preform community diagnostic surveys in which similar criteria are used for diagnoses as those used in clinical service setting. Psychiatric clinicians see no more value in epidemiological work based on determinations of "caseness" than internists would. Secondly, the capacity to relate both cross-sectional and cohort data on prevalence to utilization within a specified time period must be developed to determine the degree to which persons with disorders actually receive services.

Further requirements for health services research include the following: 1) It must be possible to link the receipt of services in different settings by individual patients, so that an accurate estimate of the proportion of affected persons receiving treatment can be made; 2) standardized units of service received (visits, bed days, and types of treatment) are required; 3) treatment outcome measures are urgently needed; 4) barriers and facilitators which mediate between the presence of a disorder and the utilization of services must be identified; and 5) utilization rates must be based on the same periods of time (e.g., annual) as those used for epidemiological surveys.

Although we have attempted to forge linkages between the available epidemiological and health services research data in the U.S., we are far from meeting the requirements described in this paper (Regier et al., 1978). From existing U.S. data, we have estimated a 15 percent annual period prevalence rate for ICD Section V mental disorders. Only one-fifth of persons with such disorders, or three percent of the population, receive specialty mental health services, whereas at least three-fifths receive some services in general medical facilities during one year. These data provide a broad general framework for linking epidemiological and health services research findings; however, we are attempting to stimulate the research community to accelerate development of more detailed studies in this area. With this goal in mind, we have designed a research program, entitled the Epidemiological Catchment Area (ECA) program, to facilitate this type of research.

The Epidemiology Catchment Area Program: Begun in Fiscal Year 1978, the ECA program is designed to utilize the DIS instrument for case identification of psychiatric disorders in a population of at least 200,000. Both noninstitutionalized and institutionalized population surveys are planned to determine the prevalence of specific mental disorders in a geographically defined population. Once the initial surveys are completed, the investigators will follow a cohort of approximately 3,000 persons over the next year to determine the development of new disorders (incidence), alterations in diagnosis and social functioning, and the utilization of specialty mental health, general medical, and other human services. Additional analyses of risk factors for specific disorders and barriers to care will be analyzed.

Although one pilot study commenced in the Fall of 1979, it is anticipated that at least five to ten of these research program sites will be needed both to obtain sufficient numbers of rare disorders and to assure attention to special population groups such as minorities, children, and the elderly.

CONCLUSIONS

1) The future for support of epidemiological research in the U.S. is particularly bright as health care policy makers recognize their increasing dependence on the results of basic and applied epidemiological research.
2) We will continue to participate actively in the international epidemiological research community to facilitate the synergistic development of the research fields I have just discussed by the relatively few available trained investigators in these fields worldwide.
3) Finally, we will attempt to stimulate promising new national and international research developments such as the DIS or other psychiatric case-identification instruments and facilitate their applications as rapidly as possible.

We anticipate an ongoing international dialogue on these research issues both bilaterally and through organizations such as the World Psychiatric Association and the World Health Organization.

REFERENCES

Cooper, J. E., Kendell, R. E., Gurland, B. G., et al.: *Psychiatric Diagnosis.* New York and London: Oxford University Press, 1972.

Endicott, J., Spitzer, R. L., Fleiss, J. L., et al.: The global assessment scale. *Arch. Gen. Psychiatry,* 33:766-771, 1976.

FARIS, R. E. L. and DUNHAM, H. W.: *Mental Disorders in Urban Areas: An Ecological Study of Schizophrenia and Other Psychoses.* Chicago: University of Chicago Press, 1939.

FEIGHNER, J. P., ROBINS, E., GUZE, S. B., et al.: Diagnostic criteria for use in psychiatric research. *Arch. Gen. Psychiatry,* 26:57-63, 1972.

GOLDBERG, D. P., COOPER, B., EASTWOOD, M. R., et al.: A standardized psychiatric interview suitable for use in community surveys. *British Journal of Preventive and Social Medicine,* 24:18-23, 1970.

HELZER, J. E., CLAYTON, P. J., PAMBAKIAN, R., et al.: Reliability of psychiatric diagnosis II. The test/retest reliability of diagnostic classification. *Arch. Gen. Psychiatry,* 34:136-141, 1977.

MORRIS, J. N.: *Uses of Epidemiology.* Edinburgh: E. S. Livingstone Ltd., 1957.

REGIER, D. A., GOLDBERG, I. D., and TAUBE, C. A.: The defacto U.S. mental health services system. *Arch. Gen. Psychiatry,* 35:685-693, 1978.

Report to the President from the President's Commission on Mental Health, Stock No. 040-000-00390-8. U.S. Government Printing Office, 1978.

RUTTER, M., SHAFFER, D., and SHEPHERD, M.: *A Multiaxial Classification of Child Psychiatric Disorders.* Geneva: World Health Organization, 1975.

SPITZER, R. L. and ENDICOTT, J.: *Schedule for Affective Disorders and Schizophrenia: Lifetime Version (SADS-L),* Edition 3. New York: New York State Psychiatric Institute, 1977.

SPITZER, R. L., ENDICOTT, J., and ROBINS, E.: Research diagnostic criteria. *Arch. Gen. Psychiatry,* 35:773-782, 1978.

The ADAMHA Workgroup on Epidemiology, Health Systems Research, and Statistics/Data Systems: *Report to the Administrator, Alcohol, Drug Abuse and Mental Health Administration (ADAMHA).* ADAMHA, 1978.

WING, J. K., COOPER, J. E., and SARTORIUS, N.: *The Measurement and Classification of Psychiatric Symptoms.* London: Cambridge University Press, 1974.

WORLD HEALTH ORGANIZATION: *Report of the International Pilot Study of Schizophrenia,* Vol. 1. Geneva: World Health Organization, 1973.

II

THE RELATION OF PSYCHIATRIC ILLNESS TO THE USE OF HEALTH SERVICES

Introduction by Michael Shepherd, M.D.

Although all four papers in this section have to do with health services, each is so different in design and purpose as to call for separate comment.

Drs. Hankin and Shapiro have carried out a thorough study of the complex and much-debated issue of the relationships between mental and physical disorder by the use of morbidity statistics derived from the records of a prepaid medical plan. While they are careful not to draw sweeping conclusions from their findings, it is necessary to underline the obstacles to extrapolating from so specialised a facility. Remembering my own visit to Columbia with Dr. Hankin in 1975, I can recall the answer given by the medical administrator to my enquiry about the role of social difficulties which can play so large a part in the presentation of psychiatric problems to primary care agencies: "We don't deal with the indigent here," was his comment. When Drs. Hankin and Shapiro refer to the "middle class suburban population" to whom psychiatric services are offered "when the condition is subject to significant improvement through short term therapy," they are describing a highly atypical population whose mental health, when identified in this way, may well be quite unrepresentative of the population at large.

It is well known that patients who come to health care agencies represent only a segment of morbidity for epidemiological enquiry, but during the past 30 years various studies have strongly pointed to an association between physical and psychiatric illness. Some workers have argued that these findings were largely manifestations of a high demand for medical care attributable to the patients' attitude to health and that the patients were labeled as neurotic largely because of the frequency of medical visits and multiplicity of ailments. In our own studies of psychiatric illness in general practice, to which Drs. Hankin and Shapiro refer, we have attempted to examine this issue both indirectly and directly. Our findings lend strong support to the concept of a true association between chronic psychiatric disorder and other forms of chronic ill health, the links being most marked with subjects suffering from cardiovascular and respiratory disease. These data, and the results of other studies, support the conclusions of Hinkle and Wolff that clustering of illness occurs in some individuals, with all forms of morbidity being involved.

No doubt Drs. Hankin and Shapiro will be extending their analysis to include the demand for psychiatric services by persons under medical care. If so, they will inevitably be confronted by the issues illustrated by Dr. Gath's detailed investigation of the psychiatric antecedents and outcome of hysterectomy. This study exemplifies a trend which has been well-developed in recent years, namely the carrying out of what used to be called clinical research with more attention paid to design and to the use of standardised measuring instruments, in this case a personality inventory, a mood-scale, a family relationships interview, and an assessment of psychiatric status.

As far as they go, the findings conform to expectations, but in the context of this conference it is unfortunate that the clinical rather than the social implications of the data have been emphasised. Twenty years ago, Querido conducted a six-month follow-up study of 1630 former general hospital inpatients to assess the forecasts made by clinicians compared with those made by an independent team consisting of a social worker and a psychiatrist who concentrated on "the social and/or psychic conditions which impair well-being." They found that regardless of the physical diagnosis the outcome of illness was significantly worse among "distressed" patients and that the predictions of the observing team, which included psychosocial factors, were correspondingly more accurate than those based on purely clinical considerations. Subsequent studies have refined this approach by applying it to individual disorders and it is to be hoped that Dr. Gath will make use of the social data which have been collected to put flesh on the clinical skeleton of his presentation.

Drs. Myers and Weissman raise issues of a different order. The material from the New Haven longitudinal study has been published in more detail elsewhere and poses questions concerning the sampling, the estimates of prevalence and the methods of assessment, all of them central to community-surveys of this type. However, since the authors have chosen to concentrate on the therapeutic implications of their findings, it is logical to focus on their views concerning the services necessary for the treatment of mental ill-health. They report that what they call "emotional problems" were referred chiefly to mental health professionals who dealt with three times as many such problems as non-psychiatric physicians. At the same time, the psychiatric patients made heavy use of the general medical services. They conclude: "Concern is raised that psychiatrically ill patients will overuse services. In fact, these data show that persons with psychiatric disorders may be transferred to the mental healh sector. This transfer, if coupled with early detection and appropriate treatment, could serve to reduce overall utilization of health care by the psychiatrically troubled."

The authors thus appear to assume that the mental health services constitute a more appropriate facility, presumably because intervention would be effective at this level. In so doing, however, they are developing an argument which runs counter to the mounting evidence which identifies the primary care centre as the most appropriate locus for the delivery of mental health care in the community. Much of the work on this issue has been conducted outside the United States, but it is relevant to refer to the Florida Health Study carried out by Dr. Schwab and his colleagues (1979) who paid particular attention to the health needs and the utilization of services by their survey population. They found, to their surprise, that whereas only about one-quarter of their psychiatric cases made use of the mental health services, almost 90% utilised the physical health services. They drew the conclusion that the primary care physician performed a much greater role in the provision of mental health care than had been appreciated. With so much interest currently being taken in the health/mental interface, this topic will clearly become a question demanding further study.

Finally, Professor Goldberg and Dr. Jones' paper raises the increasingly fashionable issues asociated with the economic analysis of mental illness. Cost benefit analysis has been defined by a distinguished economist as "the rather meaningless name given to investment analysis when the prospective *financial* return to the investor, whether private firm, citizen, government or even science foundation, is judged not to be the appropriate criterion." This rather negative concept would be exemplified in this paper by the "hard," i.e. financial, costs and benefits, which are distinguished from "soft," i.e. non-financial, costs and benefits. By both sets of criteria the British District General Hospital, it is claimed, emerges as a facility superior to the area mental hospital in the treatment of schizophrenia.

On the strictly economic side, the authors acknowledge the neglect of capital costs and concede that increased accuracy would have accrued from the employment of disease-costing instead of specialty-costing. They also refer to some of the difficulties imposed by the retrospective nature of the study and the attendant problems of design. There is, however, a broader issue raised by the study which has been well summarized by Professor Wiseman, the Director of the Institute of Social and Economic Research of the University of York, who has pointed out the confusion which has been introduced into the discussion of the "benefits of health services by economists, deriving from the fact that cost-benefit studies, based on the analogy with industrial production, identify 'benefit' with 'output' (i.e. utility to the person treated or the society of which he is a member)." "The latter," he adds, "may include the former but is clearly not identical with it." Attempts to evaluate "utility" are currently being made by the development of "social indicators" which, in the health sphere, consist in measures of the state-of-health ("state indicators"), measures of the need-for-health ("need indicators"), and measures of the effectiveness of health-affecting activities ("effectiveness" indicators). Together they make up the concept of the so-called "quality of life" and it is this which Professor Goldberg and Dr. Jones appear to be approaching with the notion of "soft" benefits which they attempt to separate from the "hard" elements of economic analysis.

This is certainly a more realistic approach than that of the straightforward financial approach exemplified by the statement of the Office of Health Economics in Britain which has argued that "The number of occupied mental hospital beds fell from 151,500 in 1954 to 119,000 in 1968. Taking the average costs for beds in mental hospitals, this fall represents a £24m/yr. to be set against £16m/yr. on psychotropic expenditure." Professor Goldberg and Dr. Jones firmly assert that their method of analysis "does not confuse value with price, but it does enable us to see what value costs." Nonetheless, the ethical overtones of the potential conflict between value and utility cannot be altogether dispelled.

In Britain the creation of a National Health Service has made it clear that the Government, the administrator and the citizen—who in the last resort has to pay—are all concerned with making the best use of available resources. These conditions have evoked a growing interest in the application of cost-efficiency studies, a trend which can be clearly discerned in every country which assumes responsibility for health-care, and which is becoming more apparent in the USA as the debate over health insurance warms up. At the same time, however, this trend has served to conceal an underlying dilemma which the late Richard Titmuss summarized in his essay on *The Ethics and Economics of Medical Care* as follows: "In drawing an analogy between the role of the doctor and the functioning of, say, washing machines, the consumer has to call in an expert. In concluding that medical care is not different from such commodities, he calls in an economist and fails to make three distinctions: first, between services and objects; secondly, between events that are a threat to life and health and those that are not; thirdly, between costs that can be estimated in advance and predicted over time and costs that cannot be so estimated and predicted. To disregard these distinctions means, in technical terms, that ordinal analysis applied to consumer demand equates mink coats with Caesarian operations. At some point they are assumed to exchange for one another."

In the present instance, one wonders what conclusions would be drawn if the results had indicated that the District General Hospital was more expensive but better. The problem is already with us in the field of psychogeriatrics where it impinges directly on the devotion of expensive health resources to an aged population whose quality of life is susceptible to very little improvement. If for no other reason than to promote discussion of this important issue, I am glad that Professor Goldberg and Dr. Jones have set the ball in motion.

REFERENCE

Schwab, J. J., Bell, R. A., Warheit, G. J., and Schwab, R. B.: *Social Order and Mental Health.* New York: Brunner/Mazel, 1979.

application of scientific studies in areas which can be clearly described in a way to ensure an assurance of responsibility [illegible] health care, and which [illegible] in the [illegible] as the debates over health insurance [illegible]. At the same time, however, this trend was resisted [illegible] contrast [illegible] the late [illegible] Johnson [illegible] in the [illegible] *The [illegible] Economic [illegible]* follows: [illegible] the [illegible] and the forthcoming [illegible] medical [illegible] the [illegible] expert [illegible] that [illegible] such contingencies [illegible] distinctions [illegible] between [illegible] and [illegible] that can be established in advance [illegible] the [illegible] and [illegible] to [illegible] consumer [illegible]

In the present instance [illegible] the [illegible] General Hospital [illegible] expensive [illegible] the problem [illegible] in the field of psychosomatics where it [illegible] health resources [illegible] to very little [illegible] Dr. Jones has set the ball in motion.

2

The Demand for Medical Service by Persons Under Psychiatric Care

Janet R. Hankin, Ph.D.
and
Sam Shapiro

Numerous studies indicate that persons with diagnosed mental, emotional, or psychological disorders use more medical services, aside from visits to specialists in psychiatry, than other persons (Fink et al., 1969; Regier et al., 1978; Shepherd et al., 1966). Researchers have used various case identification techniques to classify patients with and without mental disorder in earlier studies of utilization rates, including diagnosis by a general practitioner, scores on psychological distress inventories, and the use of mental health services. A variety of populations have been studied, including prepaid group practice enrollees, British National Health Service patients, random samples of community residents, and patients of private practitioners. While medical service utilization rates vary across the setting and with the method of case identification, the differential rates for persons with and without mental disorder are observed in every case. These results hold for both sexes and across all age groups (Andersen et al., 1977; Cooper et al., 1969; Cummings & Follette, 1968; Fry, 1960; Goldberg & Blackwell, 1970; Kessel, 1965; Kogan et al.,

Supported in part by NIMH Contract No. 278-76-0090 (OP) and The Health Services Research and Development Center Core Grant No. HS 01964 from the National Center for Health Services Research, Department of Health, Education, and Welfare.

We would like to acknowledge the assistance of John Stiney in the preparation of the tables for this paper.

1975; Liptzin et al., 1978; Locke et al., 1967; Locke et al., 1966; Rosen et al., 1970; Shepherd et al., 1959; Tessler et al., 1976).

From a medical economics standpoint, this observation has focused attention on the likelihood that a significant component of the additional utilization of medical services is a direct manifestation of psychiatric problems, and that the intervention of psychiatric treatment might partially pay for itself by reducing general medical care utilization. Longitudinal studies covering periods before, during, and after psychiatric treatment have attempted to address this question, and the answers are equivocal (Fink et al., 1969; Follette & Cummings, 1967; Goldberg et al., 1970; Kogan et al., 1975; McHugh et al., 1977). In a review of the literature on this issue, Jones and Vischi (1979) report that 7 of 11 studies suggest that nonpsychiatric utilization declines after psychiatric treatment has begun. However, they urge caution in drawing any definitive conclusions, since some of the studies have methodological limitations, while others are exploratory in nature.

The reasons for the decline in nonpsychiatric utilization after psychiatric intervention is not altogether clear, although it is suggested that psychiatric visits substitute for general medical care. Instead of visiting the primary care physician for counseling, support, and reassurance, the patient receives this care from psychiatric providers.

Another speculation is that the psychiatric treatment group has a large subgroup that has a need for general medical care because of concomitant physical disorders or because of a propensity to seek medical care, both preventive and therapeutic, due to a variety of dispositional factors (Tessler et al., 1976). Shepherd et al. (1966) studied nearly 15,000 patients in 46 general practices in London and found, "Those patients identified as suffering from psychiatric illness attended more frequently and exhibited higher rates of general morbidity and more categories of illness per head, than the remainder of patients consulting their doctors." In effect, the variables that explain the relatively high utilization of the psychiatric group would then be similar to those that account for high utilization in other subgroups. Under these circumstances, psychiatric care would be unlikely to have a substantial effect on general medical care utilization. The situation is, of course, more complex than can be accommodated by a single hypothesis, and it is important to continue to seek explanations if we are to enlarge our understanding of the association between psychiatric and general medical care.

This paper examines the issue by contrasting patterns of health-care-seeking behavior of utilizers of psychiatric care with those of non-utilizers of psychiatric care. A major variable is the diagnosis or symptom for which medical care was sought, and the utilization rates for acute and chronic conditions are compared. The approach usually taken in utilization studies is to focus on events during a 12-month or shorter interval that is close to or contains the period of psychiatric care.* This technique analyzes medical service utilization that occurs in close proximity to the acute phase of the psychiatric illness. In contrast, the data set to be reported here is concerned with aggregated experience over a three-year period. It thereby provides a basis for understanding underlying patterns of utilization among those who at some time seek psychiatric care. A longer time period would have been even more useful but this did not prove to be feasible.

THE SITE FOR RESEARCH

The Columbia Medical Plan is a prepaid group practice located in Columbia, Maryland, a new town situated between Baltimore, Maryland and Washington, D.C. The Plan opened in 1969 and offers comprehensive prepaid medical coverage to its enrollees. Benefits include preventive health services, diagnostic, treatment, and follow-up care, hospitalization, home care, ambulance services, and care in nursing homes. There is a $2.00 copayment for each nonpsychiatric visit and each prescription filled. During the period under study, 1973-1975, the average plan enrollment grew from 14,579 to 18,475 persons. The Plan serves a middle class, suburban population. As of 1975, 40 percent of the enrollees were under 18 years of age, 39 percent were 25-44, and less than 2 percent were 65 years old and over. The average annual utilization rate in 1975 for adults for all Plan services was 5.0 visits per enrollee, compared to a national utilization rate for adults of 4.6 visits.* Comparisons with the experience of other health settings suggest considerable similarity between the utilization patterns in these programs and the Columbia Medical Plan (Regier et al., 1978).

Psychiatric care is available to enrollees "when the condition is subject to significant improvement through short-term therapy" (Columbia Medical Plan). The definition of such conditions is not specified. Until

* There are two exceptions. Harvey-Smith and Cooper (1970) and Cooper et al. (1969) studied a three- and seven-period respectively.

* The rate of 4.6 visits is an estimate for persons aged 17-64 shown by the National Center for Health Statistics, U.S. Department of H.E.W. Since there are few persons over 65 enrolled in the Columbia Medical Plan, the rates for older persons were excluded. The 4.6 includes a correction for the estimated 11 percent of all physician contacts made by telephone which were included in the original NCHS rate but omitted from the CMP visit rate.

1975, the copayment for psychiatric care was $2 per visit for the first 15 visits and $10 per visit for each additional visit during the calendar year. In 1975 the copayment rose to $10 per individual, couple, and family session, $7.50 for each group session. The copayment increase had only a minimal effect on the psychiatric utilization rates. After the copayment increase was implemented, the number of psychiatric visits provided declined less than 1 percent while the number of patients seen dropped 7 percent. This decline was short-lived, and utilization rates began to rise in 1976 (Hankin et al., 1980). Thirty days of hospitalization are also covered. Therapists include psychiatrists, social workers, mental health counselors, and clinical psychologists. Referral from a nonpsychiatric provider is not required, and 71 percent of all new adult patients are self-referred (Hankin et al., 1978).

The data source for the study was the computerized data information system. This system provides data on all CMP enrollees and their utilization of Plan services. An encounter form is completed for every face-to-face contact between provider and patient which provides information on patient name, date, appointment status, place, first and second provider, purpose, laboratory and X-ray procedures ordered, problem/diagnosis, and disposition. Diagnostic and symptomatic information is coded by an automated data process which translates the text format into the desired code. This coding uses the Johns Hopkins Ambulatory Coding Scheme and a computerized dictionary of diagnostic and symptomatic terms based on the ICDA and Renner Symptom Codes (Steinwachs & Mushlin, 1978). Up to three diagnoses/problems are coded for each visit. Multiple diagnoses appear at only 15 percent of all visits.

The current study selected all patients aged 18 and over who were continuously enrolled in CMP from January 1, 1973, through December 31, 1975.* Patients were divided into two groups, those who had used Department of Psychiatry services sometime during the three-year interval (utilizers of psychiatric care) and patients who did not use Department of Psychiatry services during that time (non-utilizers of psychiatric care).**

Table 1 shows the age and sex characteristics of enrollees included in the present study. Almost 53 percent of the persons enrolled during the

* Throughout the analysis, age as of January 1, 1973, was used.

** This criterion for defining mental disorder does exclude persons who received a mental disorder diagnosis from a nonpsychiatric provider but did not receive care from the Department of Psychiatry. At CMP, this group is relatively small. From 1973 through 1975, only 106 persons (2.5 percent of all non-utilizers of psychiatric care) received a mental disorder diagnosis from a nonpsychiatric provider but did not receive care from the Department of Psychiatry.

three years were women, and about 77 percent were aged 18-44. Twenty-two percent of the enrollees used psychiatric services sometime during the three-year interval. Women were more likely to be utilizers of psychiatric services, and in both sexes, slightly higher proportions of those under 45 than over were seen by psychiatric providers.

TABLE 1

Total Enrollees in CMP and Proportion with Psychiatric Visit in Three-Year Period, by Age and Sex, 1973-1975

Age and Sex	Total	Percent of Total Enrollees	Utilizers of Psychiatric Care Number	Utilizers of Psychiatric Care Percent of Total Enrollees
Total	5509	100.0	1210	22.0
Females	2891	52.5	702	24.3
Males	2618	47.5	508	19.4
18-44	4238	76.9	957	22.6
45 or over	1271	23.1	253	19.9
Females				
18-44	2229	40.5	562	25.2
45 or over	662	12.0	140	21.1
Males				
18-44	2009	36.5	395	19.7
45 or over	609	11.1	113	18.6

Note: Data in this and subsequent tables are for persons aged 18 and over with continuous enrollment in the Columbia Medical Plan from January 1, 1973, through December 31, 1975. Age as of January 1, 1973, is shown in this and later tables.

Distributional data on psychiatry visits which appear in Table 2 reflect the short-term therapy orientation of the Department of Psychiatry. During the three-year period, almost two-fifths (39 percent) of the utilizers of psychiatric care visited the Department of Psychiatry only once or twice.

Nearly three-quarters of the patients made 10 or fewer visits. A small proportion (9 percent) made more than 25 visits during the three-year interval. Men made fewer visits than women on the average, with especially large differences appearing among those with more than 25 visits (12 percent versus 5 percent).

MEDICAL SERVICE UTILIZATION RATES FOR UTILIZERS AND NON-UTILIZERS OF PSYCHIATRIC CARE

Table 3 compares utilizers and non-utilizers of psychiatric care with respect to the frequency of their utilization of various types of services over three years. Examining total plan utilization, psychiatric plus non-psychiatric, utilizers of psychiatric care have almost twice as high a utilization rate as non-utilizers. Unlike the results of several earlier studies, no consistent differences between psychiatric service utilizers and non-utilizers are evident with respect to utilization of other types of services. This contrary finding may be a function of the three-year, as opposed to annual, utilization rate used in the current study.

TABLE 2

Number of Visits to the Department of Psychiatry for Males and Females during Three-Year Period, 1973-1975

Number of Visits to Department of Psychiatry	Percent of Utilizers of Psychiatric Care Total	Female	Male
1	24.5	21.8	28.0
2	14.1	13.7	14.7
3	7.7	7.8	7.5
4	7.1	8.0	5.8
5	4.9	4.1	5.8
6	3.6	4.3	2.8
7	3.9	3.7	4.1
8	2.9	3.1	2.5
9	2.6	2.6	2.8
10	1.9	1.9	2.0
11-15	8.7	7.9	10.0
16-25	9.0	9.3	8.7
26 or more	9.1	11.8	5.4
Total	100.0	100.0	100.0
Mean	9.12	10.08	7.80
Median	3.52	3.82	2.97

Nonpsychiatric visit rates for males and females over 45 tend to be higher for non-utilizers of psychiatric services than for utilizers. For men 18-44, utilization rates for the two subgroups are almost identical. However, among females at these ages, the nonpsychiatric utilization rate is about 20 percent higher for the utilizers of psychiatric care. Thus, over the three-year period, it is only among the women aged 18-44 that utilizers of psychiatric services showed a substantially greater utilization of

TABLE 3

Utilization of CMP Services in Three-Year Period, Utilizers and Non-Utilizers of Psychiatric Services by Age and Sex, 1973-1975

		Number of Visits to Specified Department Per Person				
				All Other Departments		
Characteristic	No. Enrollees	Total	Psychiatry	Total	Medicine	Other
W/Psych*	1210	23.3	9.1	14.2	6.6	7.6
W/O Psych	4299	12.8	—	12.8	6.1	6.6
Female						
18-44 w/psych	562	30.7	11.4	19.3	8.2	11.1
w/o psych	1667	15.6	—	15.6	6.2	9.4
45+ w/psych	140	18.4	4.9	13.5	6.8	6.7
w/o psych	522	16.1	—	16.1	8.1	8.0
Male						
18-44 w/psych	395	17.7	8.6	9.0	4.9	4.1
w/o psych	1614	8.7	—	8.7	4.9	3.7
45+ w/psych	113	12.3	4.9	7.4	3.9	3.5
w/o psych	496	12.8	—	12.8	7.5	5.3

*W/psych = with visit to Department of Psychiatry sometime during 1973-1975.
W/O psych = no visit to Department of Psychiatry during 1973-1975.

nonpsychiatric services. As anticipated, women have higher utilization rates than men, whether older or younger and whether utilizers or non-utilizers of psychiatric care.

Table 4 indicates a direct relationship between the levels of use of nonpsychiatric and psychiatric services. When the utilizers of psychiatric care are divided according to the intensity of use of psychiatric services, persons with only one or two psychiatry visits average 43 percent fewer nonpsychiatric visits than do those in the group with 3-10 psychiatric visits. In turn, the latter have a nonpsychiatric utilization rate that is 26 percent lower than the rate for the 11+ psychiatric visit group. The association between psychiatric and nonpsychiatric visit rates holds for both age groups among males and females.

An issue that arises in interpreting the large difference between the 1-2 psychiatric visit group and the 3-10 psychiatric visit group in their nonpsychiatric utilization is whether the former group contains more individuals who are well family members who are brought into therapy sessions once or twice in order to facilitate the treatment of the index patient. An examination of the type of therapy (e.g., individual, family, couple, group) indicates very similar distributions for persons with 1-2 psychiatric visits and those with 3-10 visits. The 11 or more psychiatric visit group is substantially different from the other two in that very few

TABLE 4

Nonpsychiatric Utilization Rates for Three Groups of Utilizers of Psychiatric Services, by Number of Visits to Psychiatry, and Age and Sex during Three-Year Period, 1973-1975

	Total	Age and Sex			
		Females		Males	
		18-44	45+	18-44	45+
Number of Visits to Department of Psychiatry During Three-Year Period					
1 or 2	10.4 (467)	16.0 (178)	8.8 (72)	6.5 (161)	5.5 (56)
3-10	14.9 (419)	19.7 (198)	16.5 (51)	8.8 (132)	8.6 (38)
11 or more	18.8 (324)	22.1 (186)	24.5 (17)	13.2 (102)	10.5 (19)

Note: Rates represent the average number of visits to all departments excluding the Department of Psychiatry during the three-year period. The numbers is parentheses refer to the number of patients having that number of visits.

were part of family or couple therapy sessions, but many (48 percent) were in group therapy as compared with less than 8 percent among the lower psychiatric utilizers.

CONDITION FOR WHICH MEDICAL CARE WAS SOUGHT

While these data indicate that the general medical service utilization rates of utilizers and non-utilizers of psychiatric care are similar, the utilizer groups may differ in the diagnosis or symptom for which medical care was sought. In a study of Blue Cross-Blue Shield members in Michigan, Liptzin, Regier, and Goldberg report higher utilization rates for almost every condition for persons with a mental disorder diagnosis. Their study is based on a one-year utilization experience of 2.2 million persons. The exceptions to the higher utilization rates among persons with diagnosed mental disorder occurred in the categories of Infective and Parasitic Diseases, Skin Diseases, and Injuries (Liptzin et al., 1978). A similar analysis was conducted using the current data set which reflects a three-year experience.

We classified each major ICDA category according to whether it contained primarily chronic conditions (C), acute conditions (A), or both chronic and acute conditions (M for mixed). In order to make this classification, we examined the distribution of visits for each diagnosis, within an ICDA category. Where a substantial majority of the visits were for acute conditions, the category was labeled acute. For example, Diseases of the Nervous System and Sense Organs were classified as acute, since almost all of the visits were for acute conditions such as eye inflammations, refractions, and otitis media. Diseases of the Digestive System were labeled as mixed, since the most frequently occurring conditions included hernias, gallbladder disease, ulcers, enteritis, and irritable bowel. Diseases of the Genitourinary System were categorized as mixed. The most frequent conditions seen for this category included urinary tract infections, cystic disease of the breasts, anovaluatory bleeding, dysfunctional uterine bleeding, and vaginitis. Finally, Diseases of the Musculoskeletal and Connective System were classified as chronic because the

TABLE 5

Utilization of CMP Services in a Three-Year Period. Utilizers and Non-Utilizers of Psychiatric Services, by Diagnosis and Reason for Visit, 1973-1975

Age and sex:	Male 18-44		Female 18-44		Male 45+		Female 45+	
Psychiatry visit:	w/	w/o	w/	w/o	w/	w/o	w/	w/o
ICDA Category								
Infective and parasitic (A)	.43	.36	.78	.56*	.78	.36*	1.02	.26*
Neoplasms (C)	+	+	.23	.13*	.26	.18	.45	.21*
Nervous system and sense organs (A)	.86	.82	1.41	.84*	1.93	1.45*	2.01	1.65*
Endocrine, nutrition, and metabolic (C)	+	+	.23	.13*	.26	.18	.45	.21*
Circulatory system (C)	.39	.37	.28	.27	.80	1.88*	.89	1.62*
Respiratory system (A)	.74	.59*	1.16	.79*	1.06	.57*	1.53	.78*
Digestive system (M)	.14	.15	.18	.13*	.17	.26†	.14	.27*
Genitourinary system (M)	.26	.19*	1.23	.84*	.21	.26	.97	.80
Skin and subcutaneous tissue (A)	.52	.52	.97	.74*	.94	.48*	1.14	.58*
Musculoskeletal and connective (C)	.08	.13*	.25	.13*	.14	.27*	.15	.31*
Accidents (A)	+	+	+	+	.12	.05†	.12	.06
Injuries (A)	.75	.69	.74	.51*	.68	.49*	.68	.58
Well care (A)	1.82	1.60*	6.22	5.78*	1.63	1.95*	3.62	3.00*
Symptoms (A)	1.71	1.35*	3.80	2.36*	2.16	1.77*	2.65	2.59

Notes: Rates shown are visits during three years per enrollee. Data exclude visits to Department of Psychiatry. Enrollees classified by whether they had visited the Department of Psychiatry during three-year period. Letter in parentheses indicates whether conditions are primarily acute (A), chronic (C), or mixed (M).

+ When the rate of utilization was low (less than .10 for both utilizers and non-utilizers of psychiatric care within a given age/sex category), the utilization rate is not shown because of large sampling variability.

† $p < .05$.

* $p < .01$. Significance tests for the difference between mean utilization rates of utilizers and non-utilizers of psychiatric care for these diagnostic categories are based on the normal approximation to the distribution of a Poisson sample mean.

most frequent conditions seen were arthritis and rheumatism, and osteomyelitis.*

Table 5 presents rates by diagnosis separately for utilizers and non-utilizers of psychiatric care. All diagnoses recorded during a visit are included.** Where utilization rates are low (less than .10 for both utilizers and non-utilizers of psychiatric care within a given age/sex category), the rates are not shown because of large sampling variability.***

A high degree of consistency among acute conditions is found in the direction of greater utilization by utilizers of psychiatric care (Table 5). This pattern holds for men and women in both age groups, with a single reversal: well care among men 45 and over. For mixed and chronic conditions, the pattern is ambiguous. For some of the comparisons, utilizers have higher rates, while in others, non-utilizers have higher rates. However, for women 18-44, utilizers have consistently higher rates for chronic and mixed disorders as well as acute ones.

Within acute conditions, the categories indicating the largest difference in utilization rates for utilizers and non-utilizers of psychiatric care are Nervous System and Sense Disorders, Respiratory System, Well Care, and Symptoms. For chronic conditions, the largest difference appears for older persons where non-utilizers have higher rates than utilizers of psychiatric care. Women tend to have higher utilization rates than men in almost all of the disease categories shown in Table 5, except for circulatory diseases.

There are two possible explanations for the higher utilization rates for acute conditions by utilizers of psychiatric care: The prevalence of diagnosed disease may be higher among the utilizers, or utilizers make more visits related to a diagnostic category. Table 6 examines the issue of prevalence in terms of the proportion of utilizers and non-utilizers

---

* Acute categories include Infective and Parasitic, Nervous System and Sense Disorders, Respiratory System, Skin and Subcutaneous, Accidents, Injuries, Well Care, Symptoms. Mixed include Genitourinary and Digestive Systems. Chronic include Neoplasms, Endocrine, Metabolic, Nutrition, Circulatory, and Musculoskeletal and Connective Tissue.

** Two types of codes were excluded from the analysis. At 2.1 percent of all visits, a procedure code was listed instead of a diagnostic. This category includes biopsies, minor surgery, and the like. Another 6.5 percent of the visits were excluded because they contained uncodeable entries (foot, right, chest, etc.) or uncoded entries (ICDA codes which appear less than 3 times a year at CMP).

** Using the .10 criterion for the utilization rates, the following categories were entirely eliminated from the analysis because of their infrequent occurrence: Diseases of Blood and Blood Forming Organs, Complications of Pregnancy, and Congenital Anomalies. Where subcategories of the ICDA diseases had utilization rates exceeding .10, they are shown in Table 5.

TABLE 6

Proportion of CMP Enrollees with a Diagnosis in a Specific ICDA Category in a Three-Year Period. Utilizers and Non-Utilizers of Psychiatric Care, 1973-1975

Age and sex:	Male 18-44		Female 18-44		Male 45+		Female 45+	
Psychiatry visit:	w/	w/o	w/	w/o	w/	w/o	w/	w/o
ICDA Category								
Infective and parasitic (A)	.24	.22	.38	.30*	.33	.20*	.41	.19*
Neoplasms (C)	+	+	.16	.14	+	+	.09	.14
Nervous system and sense organs (A)	.46	.47	.61	.49*	.61	.65	.63	.66
Endocrine, nutrition, and metabolic (C)	+	+	.12	.05*	+	+	+	+
Circulatory system (C)	.15	.13	.12	.11	.21	.37*	.19	.33*
Respiratory system (A)	.37	.32	.51	.40*	.44	.30*	.51	.38*
Digestive system (M)	+	+	.11	.08†	.11	.14	.08	.12
Genitourinary system (M)	.14	.10†	.54	.40*	.14	.10	.46	.40
Skin and subcutaneous tissue (A)	.28	.28	.43	.37*	.40	.27*	.45	.30*
Musculoskeletal and connective (C)	+	+	.15	.08*	.12	.15	.12	.17
Accidents (A)	+	+	+	+	+	+	.11	.06
Injuries (A)	.41	.40	.44	.32*	.35	.32	.41	.34
Well care (A)	.62	.57	.93	.89*	.69	.62	.84	.83
Symptoms (A)	.64	.61	.86	.73*	.71	.66	.74	.76

Notes: Rates are the number of diagnoses per enrollee. Enrollees classified by whether or not they visited the Department of Psychiatry during the three-year period. Letter in parentheses indicates whether conditions are primarily acute (A), chronic (C), or mixed (M).

+ When the proportion was low (less than .10 for both utilizers and non-utilizers of psychiatric care within a given age/sex category), the rate of diagnosis is not shown because of large sampling variability.

† T-Test significant at $p < .05$.

* $p < .01$.

receiving at least one diagnosis within each major ICDA category. Within each category, patients were counted once regardless of the number of specific diagnoses they received in that category or how many separate episodes of illness they had which received the same diagnosis.

For almost all of the categories of acute conditions, a higher proportion of utilizers of psychiatric care received at least one diagnosis within the ICDA category when compared to non-utilizers of psychiatric care. This finding holds for males and females and both age groups. The differences in proportions for utilizers and non-utilizers are statistically significant for women aged 18-44 across all acute ICDA categories. The pattern for chronic and mixed conditions is not consistent, except for

TABLE 7

Average Number of Visits by Diagnosis Among CMP Enrollees with at Least One Visit for the Condition in a Three-Year Period. Utilizers and Non-Utilizers of Psychiatric Care, by Diagnosis and Condition, 1973-1975

Age and sex: Psychiatry visit:	Male 18-44 w/	w/o	Female 18-44 w/	w/o	Male 45+ w/	w/o	Female 45+ w/	w/o
ICDA Category								
Infective and parasitic (A)	1.79	1.62	2.03	1.86†	2.36	1.84*	2.49	1.35*
Neoplasms (C)	+	+	1.66	1.54	+	+	2.15	1.92
Nervous system and sense organs (A)	1.85	1.73	2.30	1.81*	3.18	2.25	3.21	2.50
Endocrine, nutrition, and metabolic (C)	+	+	1.91	2.48*	+	+	+	+
Circulatory system (C)	2.68	2.79	2.40	2.44	3.78	5.12*	4.77	4.84
Respiratory system (A)	1.70	1.85	2.25	1.98*	2.40	1.89*	2.99	2.04*
Digestive system (M)	+	+	1.65	1.54	1.50	1.91	1.73	2.22
Genitourinary system (M)	1.89	2.02	2.28	2.11†	1.53	2.58*	2.11	2.01
Skin and subcutaneous tissue (A)	1.84	1.82	2.24	2.01*	2.32	1.77*	2.51	1.96*
Musculoskeletal and connective (C)	+	+	1.67	1.60	1.23	1.80*	1.24	1.77*
Accidents (A)	+	+	+	+	+	+	1.07	1.03
Injuries (A)	1.81	1.71	1.68	1.61	1.95	1.51*	1.67	1.71
Well care (A)	2.92	2.79	6.67	6.51	2.37	3.15*	4.34	3.62*
Symptoms (A)	2.67	2.23*	4.41	3.22*	3.05	2.67†	3.57	3.42

Notes: Enrollees classified by whether or not they visited the Department of Psychiatry during the three-year period. Letter in parentheses indicates whether the conditions are primarily acute (A), chronic (C), or mixed (M). Data in this table include the first visit during the three-year study period where the diagnosis was reported. Tests of significance for differences between pairs of visit rates exclude this index visit. The significance tests for the difference between the pairs of visit rates are based on the normal approximation to the distribution of a Poisson sample mean.

† $p < .05$.

* $p < .01$.

\+ When the proportion receiving a diagnosis was low (less than .10 for both utlizers and non-utilizers of psychiatric care within a given age/sex category, the average number of visits per diagnosis is not shown because of large sampling variability.

women 18-44, among whom the proportions for the psychiatric utilizers are higher. In the other age/sex groups, non-utilizers of psychiatric care have higher proportions of persons receiving a diagnosis of a chronic condition; the one exception is for males aged 18-44 with circulatory diseases. The picture for mixed conditions is inconsistent, except for women aged 18-44.

The remaining possible explanation of the higher utilization rates of utilizers of psychiatric care for acute conditions is that utilizers have a higher rate of visit per diagnostic category than non-utilizers. Table 7 shows the number of visits for a given category of illness including the index visit where the condition was diagnosed.* Utilizers of psychiatric care who receive a diagnosis for an acute condition average more visits per acute diagnostic category than non-utilizers of psychiatric care. A less distinct pattern emerges for persons receiving a diagnosis for a chronic or mixed condition; utilizers of psychiatric care tend to have slightly lower or similar average rates of visits per diagnostic category than non-utilizers.

DISCUSSION

The experience in a prepaid group practice serving a middle class suburban population has been examined in order to compare medical care utilization of utilizers and non-utilizers of psychiatric care over a three-year period. This study does not address the question of the impact of psychiatric care on subsequent medical service utilization. It is concerned with the underlying patterns of nonpsychiatric utilization of persons who turned to psychiatric treatment sometime during the interval. The period covered in this investigation includes the stage at which patients were actively seeking psychiatric care. During most of the three-year period, however, psychiatric utilizers were not receiving psychiatric care.

Twenty-two percent of adults continuously enrolled in the Columbia Medical Plan between 1973 and 1975 used psychiatric services at least once during that period. In the aggregate, as anticipated, there are large differences between the psychiatric utilizer and non-utilizer groups in total utilization of Plan services. However, there is little evidence of higher utilization of nonpsychiatric services by psychiatric patients.

When the use of only nonpsychiatric services is considered, a highly variable situation emerges in which age and the nature of the condition for which nonpsychiatric care is received play important roles. For women 18-44, nonpsychiatric utilization rates for utilizers of psychiatric care are higher than the rates for non-utilizers. For persons aged 45 and older, the reverse is true: Nonpsychiatric utilization rates are higher for non-utilizers.

The data indicate that the relatively high nonpsychiatric utilization by women 18-44 who are utilizers of psychiatric care is a function of the higher proportion among them receiving a diagnosis of both acute and chronic conditions. In addition, once they receive a diagnosis for an acute

* Data in Table 7 include the first visit during the three-year study period where the diagnosis was reported. Tests of statistical significance for differences between pairs of visit rates exclude this index visit.

illness, these patients average more visits per acute condition category than do women 18-44 who are non-utilizers of psychiatric care. In the other age/sex groups, the pattern of greater nonpsychiatric utilization among the utilizers of psychiatric care is consistent only for acute conditions.

We can speculate on the reasons for this difference in utilization for acute conditions. The seeking of medical care fulfills a variety of functions for the patient, including reassurance and social support (Mechanic, 1978; Shuval, 1970; Tessler et al., 1976). It has been hypothesized that patients suffering from psychological symptoms feel uncomfortable presenting these psychiatric complaints to the physician and instead present a variety of minor acute complaints (Balint, 1957; Mechanic, 1972). Another explanation of the observed illness behavior of utilizers of psychiatric care is that their psychiatric symptoms increase their vulnerability to acute illnesses and may lower their capacity to cope with minor illnesses. The decision to seek care for an acute condition is usually made by the patient, rather than the physician, and is thus dependent upon the patient's perception of the symptoms.

The situation for chronic and mixed conditions is less consistent. For some chronic conditions, psychiatric utilizers have higher nonpsychiatric utilization rates, while for other conditions, the pattern is reversed. The instance in which some consistency appears concerns chronic conditions among those over 45. In this age group, utilizers of psychiatric services generally average fewer visits for their chronic conditions than do non-utilizers. This may be related to an increased likelihood of substituting a psychiatric visit for nonpsychiatric care in a long-term illness where anxiety is an important factor. It may, however, reflect a lower level of compliance in return follow-up care for chronic conditions among psychiatric utilizers.

The findings related to both the acute and chronic conditions consistently indicate the need for close coordination between psychiatric and primary care services. The underlying relatively high visit rates to nonpsychiatric providers for acute conditions and symptoms among psychiatric utilizers may represent one manifestation of mental or emotional problems that will not effectively be addressed without such coordination.

The finding of lower levels of utilization for chronic conditions among psychiatric utilizers aged 45 and over provides other evidence for strengthening ties between psychiatric and general medical care. The reason for the lower levels needs further investigation, but one important explanation may be that it reflects a break in follow-up care from primary care providers.

REFERENCES

ANDERSEN, R., FRANCIS, A., LION, J. et al.: Psychologically related illness and health service utilization. *Med. Care,* XV *Supplement,* 59-73, 1977.

BALINT, M.: *The Doctor, His Patient and the Illness.* New York: International Universities Press, 1957.

COLUMBIA MEDICAL PLAN: Service Benefits. Columbia, Maryland, 1976.

COOPER, B., FRY, J., and KALTON, G.: A longitudinal study of psychiatric morbidity in a general practice population. *Br. J. Prev. Soc. Med.,* 23:210-217, 1969.

CUMMINGS, N. A. and FOLLETTE, W. T.: Psychiatric services and medical utilization in a prepaid health plan setting: Part II. *Med. Care,* 6:31-41, 1968.

FINK, R., SHAPIRO, S., GOLDENSOHN, S. S. et al.: *Psychiatric Treatment and Patterns of Medical Care.* Final Report to the National Institute of Mental Health. Project MH 02321. Department of Research and Statistics. Health Insurance Plan of Greater New York. July, 1969.

FOLLETTE, W. and CUMMINGS, N. A.: Psychiatric services and medical utilization in a prepaid health plan setting. *Med. Care,* 5:25-35, 1967.

FRY, J.: What happens to our neurotic patients. *The Practitioner,* 185:85-89, 1960.

GOLDBERG, I. D., KRANTZ, G., and LOCKE, B. Z.: Effect of a short-term outpatient psychiatric therapy benefit on the utilization of medical services in a prepaid group practice medical program. *Med. Care,* 8:419-428, 1970.

GOLDBERG, D. P. and BLACKWELL, B.: Psychiatric illness in general practice. A detailed study using a new method of case identification. *Br. Med. J.,* 2:439-443, 1970.

HANKIN, J. R., KOCH, F., BENDIT, E. et al.: *Development and Testing of Methodology to Assess Quality of Mental Health Care.* Final Report. NIMH Contract No. 278-76-0090(OP), Baltimore, Maryland, The Johns Hopkins Medical Institutions, Health Services Research and Development Center, 1978.

HANKIN, J. R., STEINWACHS, D. M., and ELKES, C.: The impact on utilization of a copayment increase for ambulatory psychiatric care. *Med. Care,* XVIII, 1980.

HARVEY-SMITH, E. A. and COOPER, B.: Patterns of neurotic illness in the community. *J. Roy. Coll. Gen. Practit.,* 19:132-139, 1970.

JONES, K. and VISCHI, T.: Impact of alcohol, drug abuse and mental health treatment on medical care utilization. *Med. Care,* XVII *Supplement,* 1-82, 1979.

KESSEL, N.: The neurotic in general practice. *The Practitioner,* 194:636-641, 1965.

KOGAN, W. S., THOMPSON, D. J., BROWN, J. R. et al.: Impact of integration of mental health services and comprehensive medical care. *Med. Care,* XIII:934-942, 1975.

LIPTZIN, B., REGIER, D. A., and GOLDBERG, I. D.: *Health and Mental Health Utilization in a Large Insured Population.* Unpublished manuscript. Rockville, Maryland, National Institute of Mental Health, 1978.

LOCKE, B. Z., FINUCANE, D. L., and HASSLER, F.: Emotionally disturbed patients under care of private nonpsychiatric physicians. *Psychiatric Research Report,* 22:235-248, 1967.

LOCKE, B. Z., KRANTZ, G., and KRAMER, M.: Psychiatric need and demand in a prepaid group practice program. *Am. J. Public Health,* 56:895-904, 1966.

MCHUGH, J. P., KAHN, M. W., and HEIMAN, E.: Relationship between mental health treatment and medical utilization among low-income Mexican-American patients: Some preliminary findings. *Med. Care,* XV:439-444, 1977.

MECHANIC, D.: Social psychologic factors affecting the presentation of bodily complaints. *New Eng. J. Med.,* 286:1132-1139, 1972.

MECHANIC, D.: *Medical Sociology,* Second Edition. New York: Free Press, 1978.

REGIER, D. A., GOLDBERG, I. D., BURNS, B. J. et al.: Epidemiological and health services research findings in four organized health/mental health service settings. Paper presented at the Annual Meetings of the American Psychiatric Association. Atlanta, Georgia. May, 1978.

ROSEN, B. M., LOCKE, B. Z., GOLDBERG, I. D. et al.: Identifying emotional disturbances in persons seen in industrial dispensaries. *Mental Hygiene*, 54:271-279, 1970.

SHEPHERD, M., COOPER, B., BROWN, A. C. et al.: *Psychiatric Illness in General Practice*. London: Oxford University Press, 1966.

SHEPHERD, M., FISHER, M., STEIN, L. et al.: Psychiatric morbidity in an urban group practice. *Proc. Roy. Soc. Med.*, 52:269-274, 1959.

SHUVAL, J.: *Social Functions of Medical Practice*. San Francisco: Jossey-Bass, 1970.

STEINWACHS, D. M. and MUSHLIN, A.: The Johns Hopkins ambulatory-care coding scheme. *Health Services Research*, 13:36-49, 1978.

TESSLER, R., MECHANIC, D., and DIMOND, M.: The effect of psychological distress on physician utilization. A prospective study. *J. Health Soc. Behav.*, 17:353-365, 1976.

U.S. DEPARTMENT OF H.E.W. National Center for Health Statistics. Current Estimates from the Health Interview Survey—1975. Series 10, No. 115, 1976.

3

Psychiatric Aspects of Hysterectomy

DENNIS GATH, D.M.

Psychiatrists and others have taken an interest in the psychiatric aspects of hysterectomy for many years (Meikle, 1977). The subject still calls for attention, for two reasons:

1) *Frequency of Hysterectomy*

In the United Kingdom, hysterectomy is a common operation. In Oxford, for example, the frequency increased by 50 percent between 1960 and 1970 (Oxford Regional Hospital Board, 1973), and in 1969 it was the second commonest operation of organ removal in females (Fairbairn & Acheson, 1969).

2) *Reported Frequency of Psychiatric Disorder After Hysterectomy*

There is a large and conflicting literature about the risk of psychiatric disorder after hysterectomy. Notable papers have been those by Lindemann (1941) Stengel et al. (1958), Ackner (1960), Patterson and Craig (1963), and Bragg (1965).

According to one review, 15 studies "purport to show that hysterectomy is followed by undesirable psychological reactions," whilst six find no such effect (Meikle, 1977). However, it is difficult to draw firm inferences from any of the early studies, since virtually all of them were re-

This study was carried out with the help of a grant from the Medical Research Council.

trospective, or uncontrolled, or based on small numbers or short follow-up, or on unsatisfactory criteria.

Interest in this subject has been restimulated by two investigations. From a retrospective study of hospital case notes in Dundee, Barker (1968) concluded "depression should be looked upon as one of the major post-operative complications of hysterectomy."

After a retrospective search through the casenotes of a general practice, Richards (1973) concluded that "hysterectomy involves a large morbidity in terms of depressive illness."

Both these studies suggested that a poor psychiatric outcome was associated with two factors: 1) a gynecological diagnosis of dysfunctional uterine bleeding; 2) a history of psychiatric disorder at any time before the hysterectomy.

It seemed to us that these findings should be further investigated by means of a prospective study using standardized methods of case-finding.

AIMS OF THE STUDY

The study was designed to answer four questions:

1) To what extent do women become psychiatrically disturbed after hysterectomy performed for excessive menstruation of benign origin?
2) Is the degree of psychiatric disturbance greater when there is little or no pathology in the uterus?
3) Is psychiatric disturbance after hysterectomy largely associated with psychiatric disturbance before the operation?
4) What other factors are associated with a poor outcome?

The first three questions call for comment. In question 1, we limited the gynecological group to those with excessive menstruation of benign origin for two reasons: 1) malignant disease was excluded because it poses psychological problems in itself, 2) some of the local gynecologists said that excessive menstruation of benign origin presented the most difficult problems of selection for surgery.

Question 2 was included because in a large proportion of hysterectomies, the histological diagnosis is "dysfunctional uterine bleeding," that is, no pathology is demonstrable in the uterus. As noted above, a poor psychiatric outcome after hysterectomy has been linked with this condition (Barker, 1968; Richards, 1973).

Question 3 raises the possibility that a history of psychiatric instability, recent or remote, may be a determinant of selection for surgery.

DESIGN AND METHOD

Design

This was a prospective study of a consecutive series of patients having hysterectomy for excessive menstruation of benign origin. The patients were otherwise unselected.

It was expected that after the operation this group could be divided into two roughly equal sub-groups on histological findings: 1) an organic group with fibroids or endometriosis in the uterus; 2) a dysfunctional group, with no demonstrable pathology in the uterus.

It was decided to make psychiatric and social assessments of all patients about four weeks before the operation, and six months after the operation and again 18 months after the operation. All assessments were to be made by interviewers who were blind as to the organic/dysfunctional diagnosis.

Comparison of the two gynecological groups at different stages of assessment would enable us to examine two hypotheses concerning question 2 in the previous section:

Hypothesis 1: pre-operatively, the degree of psychiatric disturbance would be found to be greater in the dysfunctional group than in the organic group.

Hypothesis 2: post-operatively, the degree of psychiatric disturbance would be increased in the dysfunctional group and reduced in the organic group.

Method

Information was collected by means of interviews with the women undergoing hysterectomy; interviews with their husbands; and extraction of data from gynecological casenotes. Only the patient interviews will be reported in this paper.

All interviews with patients were carried out in their homes. The enquiry was comprehensive and detailed, and generally lasted one and a half to two hours.

Pre-operative Interview

The pre-operative interview was made up of 11 sections:

1) Demographic and social.
2) Gynecological history.
3) Understanding and expectations of the operation.
4) Psychosexual functioning.

5) Physical health, past and present.
6) Psychiatric health, past and present.
7) Present State Examination (P.S.E.).
8) Family health.
9) Marriage and social adjustment.
10) Eysenck Personality Inventory.
11) McNair and Lorr Mood Scale.

Item 9, marriage and social adjustment, was assessed by means of the interview devised by Brown and Rutter (1966). Item 10, the Eysenck Personality Inventory or E.P.I. (Eysenck & Eysenck 1963) and Item 11, an adjective check list for measuring mood (McNair & Lorr, 1964), are self-administered scales. They were completed by the patients at the end of the interview.

The present paper presents mainly the results obtained with Item 7, the Present State Examination (P.S.E.). The principles underlying this standardized interview have been described by Wing et al. (1974). The interviewer follows a schedule of questions directed at eliciting information about psychiatric symptoms which are defined in a Glossary of Definitions. The questions relate to symptoms experienced during the previous four weeks. Abnormalities of speech, behavior and affect observed during the interview are recorded. The examiner decides whether each symptom is absent (0), present in moderate degree (1), or present in severe degree (2).

Post-operative Interviews

The interviews six months and 18 months after the operation were similar to the foregoing, but adapted to cover the post-operative period. Data will be presented here only for the second (18-month) follow-up.

Interviewers

The interviewers were four women aged between 30 and 40, all married with children. None was medically qualified but all had previous training in psychiatric social work or counselling.

The interviewers received several weeks training in the administration of the interview described above. In particular, they were given training in the use of the P.S.E. and the Brown-Rutter Schedule.

Pilot Study

Fifty patients were interviewed in a pilot study. The last 20 of these interviews were included in an inter-rater reliability study; agreement between the four interviewers was found to be uniformly satisfactory.

Final Gynecological Diagnosis

A senior gynecologist examined the histological reports on all specimens of uterus removed at operation and made a final diagnosis of organic or dysfunctional in every case.

RESULTS

A consecutive series of 156 patients were interviewed before hysterectomy. At follow-up six months and 18 months after the operation, 148 of these were interviewed.

On histological diagnosis, exactly half the 156 patients were found to have organic lesions in the uterus; the other half had no significant pathology and were classified as dysfunctional. The mean age of the organic group was 44.09 years (s.d. 5.82), and of the dysfunctional group 40.18 years (s.d. 5.75) ($p < 0.001$).

Question 1: *To what extent do women become psychiatrically disturbed after hysterectomy performed for excessive menstruation of benign origin?*

Total P.S.E. Score

Pre-operative findings. One technique for measuring whether the operation results in disorder is to assess how many new psychiatric cases occur post-operatively as defined by P.S.E. total scores rising from below 11 to 11 or over, a common cut-off point for "caseness." But first we need to see whether most subjects were already "cases" before the operation. If almost all were, there would be little opportunity for their number to rise post-operatively. In the series of 156 women (combined dysfunctional and organic groups) interviewed before hysterectomy, 85 (55 percent) were cases, and 71 (45 percent) were non-cases, as determined by a score of 11 or over.

The hysterectomy group can be usefully compared with a general population sample of 237 women (Bedford College Sample) in a defined district of London, recently described by Wing et al. (1978). Within this general population sample, 29 women (12 percent) were identified as cases, and 208 (88 percent) as non-cases. Clearly, the proportion of cases is much smaller than in the hysterectomy sample ($p < 0.001$).

To obtain a more comparable general population sample, we extracted from the Bedford general population sample a sub-group of 64 patients who were matched for age with the hysterectomy group. Of this general population sub-sample, 9 women (14 percent) were cases, and 55 (86 percent) were non-cases. Again the proportion of cases was much smaller than in the hysterectomy group ($p < 0.001$).

Presenting the data in another way, the mean total P.S.E. score for the hysterectomy group was 12.34 (s.d. 7.60), and for the age-matched general population sub-sample it was 4.33 (s.d. 6.20). Here again the difference was highly significant ($p < 0.001$).

Taken together, these findings indicate that, before the operation, there was a considerable degree of psychiatric morbidity in the hysterectomy group. Nonetheless, there were a sufficient number psychiatrically well at the time of the operation to see whether it had any effects on their later mental health.

Post-operative findings. Of the 71 women not cases before the operation, and thus at risk of developing a psychiatric disorder after the operation, only 10 became cases. While this rate is clearly not very high, it is not known whether it is higher than would be expected, since we lack data for control populations. However, it is noteworthy that these 10 cases make up less than one-fourth of all cases (45) found at follow-up. Thus, most illness observed after the operation *could not* be attributed *to* the operation. It is also noteworthy that a large proportion (55 percent) of those initially cases had *improved* by follow-up, suggesting that the operation may actually have *reduced* morbidity, although again we do not have comparable data for a control group to estimate the proportion of spontaneous remission one could have expected over the follow-up period. Improvements and cases of falling ill are shown diagramatically:

Before hysterectomy	*18 months after hysterectomy*
71 non-cases	10 cases
	58 non-cases
	3 not interviewed
85 cases	35 cases
(P.S.E. total score)	45 non-cases
	5 not interviewed

Application of the McNemar Chi Squared Test showed that significantly more patients improved than fell ill ($p < 0.001$).

Despite this evidence of significant improvement, after the operation the proportion of cases in the hysterectomy group was still significantly higher than that of the sample of 237 women in the general population mentioned above ($p < 0.001$), and significantly higher than that of the age-matched general population sample ($p < 0.05$).

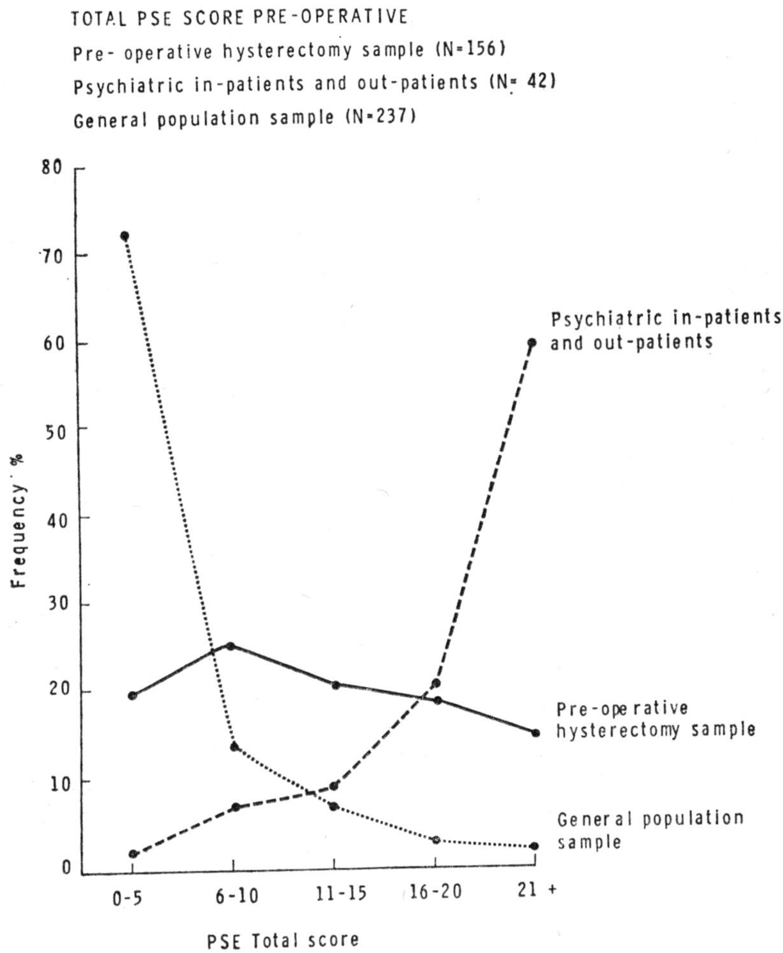

FIGURE 1

The fact that the hysterectomy group continued to include a large number of psychiatrically disturbed women after the operation is borne out by their mean total P.S.E. scores. For the hysterectomy sample, the mean total P.S.E. score fell from 12.34 (s.d. 7.60) before the operation, to 7.49 (s.d. 8.12) six months after the operation and 8.14 (s.d. 8.94) 18 months after the operation. Both post-operative means were significantly lower than the pre-operative mean ($p < 0.001$), both were also still significantly higher than the general population mean ($p < 0.001$).

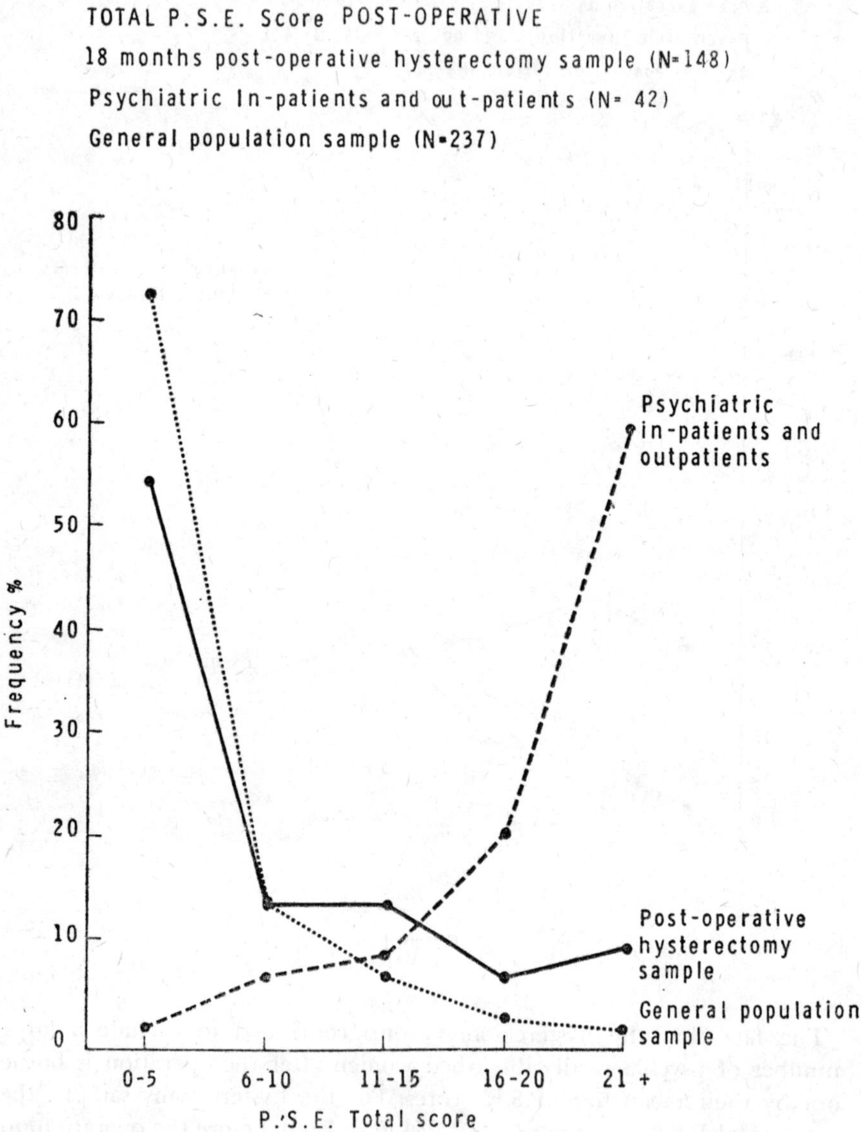
TOTAL P.S.E. Score POST-OPERATIVE
18 months post-operative hysterectomy sample (N=148)
Psychiatric In-patients and out-patients (N= 42)
General population sample (N=237)
80
70
60
50
40
30
20
10
0
Frequency %
Psychiatric in-patients and outpatients
Post-operative hysterectomy sample
General population sample
0-5
6-10
11-15
16-20
21 +
P.S.E. Total score

FIGURE 2

Comparison of hysterectomy group with psychiatric patients. Figure 1 shows the distributions over the complete range of P.S.E. total scores, of three samples: 1) the hysterectomy group assessed pre-operatively; 2) a group of 42 psychiatric inpatients and outpatients (Wing et al., 1978); 3) the general population sample of 237 women (Wing et al., 1978). The distribution of the hysterectomy group is clearly intermediate between that of the psychiatric patient population and that of the general population.

Figure 2 shows the same data, this time for the hysterectomy group assessed after hysterectomy. It can be seen that after the operation the distribution of the hysterectomy group is closer to that of the general population.

P.S.E. Index of Definitions

The Index of Definitions provides a more complex method of determining the confidence with which a functional psychiatric disorder may be regarded as present (Wing et al., 1978). This involves a set of rules which operates not only on the size of total score but also on the type, severity and combination of symptoms present. When levels of disorder of 5 or greater on the Index of Definition were regarded as cases, and lower levels as non-cases, only 11 cases changed from cases to non-cases or the reverse, as compared with their total P.S.E. pre-operative scores. These changes caused no important differences in the results: again there was a marked drop in the number of cases post-operatively, but again the level remained significantly higher than that in the two general populations described above, and they remained significantly less disturbed than a sample of psychiatric patients.

Psychiatric diagnosis. So far the P.S.E. Index of Definitions has only restated what we had already found from the total score. However, the Index of Definitions does have one great advantage over the total score: at level five and above, the CATEGO programme can be applied in order to allocate each case to a diagnostic class.

According to the CATEGO programme, the 90 patients who were cases before hysterectomy included 58 depressives, 30 with anxiety states, one hypomanic and one obsessional neurosis.

The 43 women who were cases after the operation were classified as 28 cases of depression, 13 anxiety states, and two as hypomania.

Other indices of outcome. After the operation, a large proportion of women showed improvement as judged by several other indices. For example, in the hysterectomy group as a whole, there was evidence of improved psychosexual functioning. Compared with pre-operatively, it was found that 18 months after the operation the frequency of reported enjoyment of sexual intercourse increased ($p < 0.001$).

Post-operatively, the frequency of sexual intercourse was significantly higher amongst non-cases than amongst cases, as determined by the P.S.E. Index of Definitions ($p < 0.01$).

Question 2: *Is the degree of psychiatric disturbance greater when there is little or no pathology in the uterus?*

In data collected both before and after the operation, no significant differences were found between the organic and dysfunctional groups on any important variables. Thus, there were no significant differences between the groups in:

1) Demographic and social features, such as marital status, social class, having a job. (The age difference reported above was the only exception.)

2) Psychiatric status as determined by the following five measures: P.S.E. total scores; P.S.E. Index of Definitions; Lorr and McNair Mood Scale; Eysenck Personality Inventory; history of psychiatric contact at any time before the operation.

3) Marriage adjustment.

4) Psychosexual functioning.

The finding of no important differences between the organic and dysfunctional groups, either before or after the operation, was unexpected. It was contrary to recent reports in the literature (Barker, 1968; Richards, 1973). It did not support the two psychosomatic hypotheses given above.

Question 3: *Is psychiatric disturbance after hysterectomy largely associated with psychiatric disturbance before the operation?*

We have already answered this question in relation to P.S.E. mental state before the operation. Several other pre-operative measures of psychiatric status were found to be related to psychiatric outcome:

History of contact with psychiatric services. Of the 156 women interviewed before the operation, 22 (14 percent) had a previous history of psychiatric contact. This proportion was significantly greater than the 4 percent found amongst 539 women aged 40-55 in the general population of Dundee ($p < 0.001$) (Ballinger, 1977).

In our series, it was found that a history of psychiatric contact discriminated significantly between cases and non-cases, as determined by the P.S.E. Index of Definitions, both before the operation ($p < 0.01$) and after the operation ($p < 0.05$). In other words, having a history of pre-operative psychiatric disturbance carried an increased risk of post-operative psychiatric disturbance.

On the other hand, it should be stressed that the majority (two-thirds) of patients who proved to be cases after hysterectomy had had no previous history of psychiatric contact.

Eysenck Personality Inventory (E.P.I.). Another measure of the patient's psychiatric status before the operation was the personality dimension of Neuroticism determined by the E.P.I.

Pre-operatively, the mean neuroticism scores for both the organic and dysfunctional groups were significantly higher than those for Eysenck's normal population, but lower than those for Eysenck's neurotic population.

Mean Neuroticism scores measured pre-operatively were significantly higher for patients who proved to be cases 18 months after the operation than for those who proved to be non-cases as determined by the P.S.E. Index of Definitions ($p < 0.001$). This suggests that the E.P.I., which is simple to administer, could be used as a predictor of psychiatric outcome.

McNair and Lorr Mood Scale. This self-administered mood scale was used in a form which measured five factors, namely anxiety, depression, tension, fatigue and vigour. The main finding of interest was that, on all five factors, pre-operative mean scores were significantly much higher for patients who proved to be cases 18 months after the operation, than for those who proved to be non-cases, as determined by the P.S.E. Index of Definitions ($p < 0.001$). This suggests that this simple adjective check list, like the E.P.I., could also be used as a predictor of post-operative psychiatric state.

Question 4: *What other factors are associated with a poor psychiatric outcome?*

Analysis is incomplete for many variables, but some potentially important factors have been analysed. For example, patients' age, social class and parity, which previous investigators have regarded as important, were found to have no significant relationship with psychiatric outcome in the present study.

More surprisingly, the duration and severity of menstrual disorder before the operation had no association with post-operative psychiatric state. This may have been because virtually all patients had menstrual disorders that were severe. Nor was there any association with other gynecological factors, such as: abdominal versus vaginal hysterectomy; removal of both ovaries; which surgeon advised and performed the operation.

CONCLUSIONS

The analysis of data is incomplete, but the evidence so far points to the following main conclusions:

1) 18 months after hysterectomy for excessive menstruation of benign origin, the majority of patients were less disturbed psychiatrically than before the operation.

Of the patients who were psychiatric cases at 18-month follow-up, the majority had shown significant psychiatric disturbance pre-operatively in terms of P.S.E. status, neuroticism measured by the E.P.I., mood disturbance measured by the Lorr and McNair scale, and (to a lesser extent) history of contact with the psychiatric services.

From these findings, we would conclude that the operation does *not* often lead to psychiatric disorder.

This conclusion is in sharp contrast with earlier reports in the literature to the effect that hysterectomy leads to a heavy toll of psychiatric morbidity. Our contrasting conclusion may be explained partly by our study being prospective. If our first contact with the patients had been after the operation (as in most previous investigations), we might have attributed any observed psychiatric morbidity to the operation itself. In a recent survey in St. Louis, Martin et al. (1977) also found high levels of psychiatric illness in patients before hysterectomy, and likewise emphasized the need to evaluate post-hysterectomy symptoms in relation to pre-operative state.

2) There was no evidence that patients with dysfunctional uterine bleeding were more disturbed psychiatrically than patients with demonstrable pathology in the uterus, either before the operation or afterwards. This finding does not support the notion that dysfunctional uterine bleeding is largely "psychosomatic," or that (as some recent writers have argued) patients with this diagnosis are having unnecessary operations.

3) The hysterectomy patients as a group were more disturbed psychiatrically than a sample of women from the general population, both before the operation and 18 months afterwards.

From this, we conclude that psychiatric disorder probably plays a role in the risk of receiving a hysterectomy. That is to say, many patients are selected for surgery because they have menorrhagia in association with some psychiatric disturbance. This conclusion agrees with Ballinger's inference from a study of women attending a gynecological out-patient clinic in Dundee—that there was "an excess of women in the early stages of psychiatric illness presenting with symptoms for which hysterectomy is a possible treatment" (Ballinger, 1977). The study by Martin et al. (1977) in St. Louis points to the same conclusion.

Whilst psychiatric disturbance may have been an important determinant of surgery, it does not follow that the operations are "unnecessary." The majority of the patients had suffered from disabling menorrhagia which was relieved by the operation, and many were better psychiatrically after the operation than they were before.

REFERENCES

Ackner, B.: Emotional aspects of hysterectomy. *Advances in Psychosomatic Medicine,* 1:248-252, 1960.

Ballinger, C. B.: Psychiatric morbidity and the menopause: Survey of a gynecological out-patient clinic. *British Journal of Psychiatry,* 131, 83-89, 1977.

Barker, M. G.: Psychiatric illness after hysterectomy. *Brit. Med. J.,* 2:91-95, 1968.

Bragg, R. L.: Risk of admission to mental hospital following hysterectomy or cholecystectomy. *Am. J. Public Health,* 55:1403-1410, 1965.

Brown, G. W. and Rutter, M.: The measurement of family activities and relationships: A methodological study. *Human Relations,* 19:241-263, 1966.

Eysenck, H. J. and Eysenck, S. B. G.: *The Eysenck Personality Inventory.* London: University of London Press, 1963.

Fairbairn, A. S. and Acheson, E. D.: The extent of organ removal in the Oxford area. *J. Chronic Dis.,* 22:111-122, 1969.

Lindemann, E.: Observations on psychiatric sequelae to surgical operations in women. *Am. J. Psychiat.,* 98:132-137, 1941.

Martin, R. L., Roberts, W. V., and Clayton, P. J.: Psychiatric illness and non-cancer hysterectomy. *Dis. Nerv. Syst.,* 38 (12):974-975; 979-980, 1977.

NcNair, D. M., and Lorr, M.: An analysis of mood in neurotics. *J. Abnorm. Soc. Psychol.,* 69 (6):620, 1964.

Meikle, S.: The psychological effects of hysterectomy. *Canad. Psychol. Review,* 18 (2): 128-141, 1977.

Oxford Regional Hospital Board: *Area Gynaecological Reports for 1960 and 1970.* Oxford, 1973.

Patterson, R. M. and Craig, J. B.: Misconceptions concerning the psychological effects of hysterectomy. *Am. J. Obs. Gyn.,* 85:104-111, 1963.

Richards, D. H.: Depression after hysterectomy. *Lancet,* 2:430-432, 1973.

Stengel, E., Zeitlyn, B. B., and Rayner, E. H.: Post-operative psychoses. *J. Ment. Sci.,* 104:389-402, 1958.

Wing, J. K., Cooper, J. E., and Sartorius, N.: *Description and Classification of Psychiatric Symptoms.* London: Cambridge University Press, 1974.

Wing, J. K., Mann, S. A., Leff, J. P., and Nixon, J. M.: The concept of a "case" in psychiatric population surveys. *Psychol. Med.,* 8:203-217, 1978.

4

Psychiatric Disorders and Treatment: A Community Survey

JEROME K. MYERS, PH.D.
and
MYRNA M. WEISSMAN, PH.D.

A first priority of the President's Commission on Mental Health, established in February, 1977, was the identification of how the mentally ill are being served, to what extent they are underserved, and who is affected by such underservice (The White House, 1977). The need for such information is great, but as Regier, Goldberg and Taube point out, data are needed in at least three areas in order to provide it: 1) the true prevalence of mental illness; 2) the treated prevalence; and 3) a known relationship between the presence of a mental disorder and the type and amount of treatment needed (Regier et al.). Although there is substantial information on the treated prevalence of psychiatric disorders by professional mental health workers, there is much less on treatment by general health practitioners or other professionals. Estimates on true prevalence based on overall level of impairment can be made, but little

---

Portions of this chapter are also presented in "Psychiatric disorders and their treatment: A community survey," by Jerome K. Myers and Myrna M. Weissman, *Med. Care,* Dec., 1979.

This work is supported by US PHS grant #1 RO1 MH25712, from the Center for Epidemiologic Studies, National Institute of Mental Health; Alcohol, Drug Abuse and Mental Health Administration (ADAMHA), Rockville, Maryland.

is known about the extent of clinical psychopathology or diagnosed psychiatric illness in the community. Still less is known about the relationship between the treatment of psychiatric disorders and true prevalence in the community.

The purpose of this paper is to determine the relationship between true and treated prevalence in a community by examining the use of mental health and other professional services for emotional problems and the relationship of this use to the individual's diagnostic status. The results are based upon the third round of interviews in a longitudinal community study in New Haven, Connecticut. The third area of needed information noted above, the adequacy of services provided, is beyond the scope of this paper.

METHOD

In 1967, a longitudinal survey of a systematic sample of 938 adults (18 years of age or older) of a community mental health center catchment area in New Haven was undertaken. The catchment area has a population of approximately 72,000 which includes a changing inner-city section of 22,000 and a more stable industrial town of 50,000. It represents a cross-section of the community's population and includes all ethnic, racial, and socioeconomic groups. An in-person interview was conducted with each respondent in the study, and among the materials collected were data on sociodemographic characteristics, use of health facilities, use of social services and other professional services, and psychiatric symptoms. In 1969 and in 1975-1976, the same population was reinterviewed.

In the past, community studies were forced to use symptom scales to define mental illness because of the lack of suitable diagnostic instruments for such large-scale surveys. Recently, however, there have been developments in technologies for improving the reliability and the validity of psychiatric diagnoses in both clinical and community settings, and there have been more precise descriptions of the psychiatric syndromes. One new diagnostic technique, a categorical approach developed by Spitzer, Endicott and Robins (SADS-RDC) (1975), was employed, therefore, in the 1975-76 study in which 515 persons were interviewed. Because there are missing data for six of the 515 persons, tables are based on 509 persons. Persons who died, moved out of the country, could not be located, or refused to participate during the study did not differ greatly from those included in terms of sociodemographic characteristics or symptom status (Weissman et al., 1978).

Diagnostic Assessment

Information for making diagnostic judgments was collected on the Schedule for Affective Disorders and Schizophrenia (SADS) (Endicott & Spitzer, 1978). The SADS is a structured interview guide with an accompanying inventory of rating scales and specific items. It records information on the subject's functioning and symptomatology. Although the name of the instrument suggests that it is specific only to affective disorders and schizophrenia, in fact it is an overall mental status inventory that contains the information necessary for making diagnostic judgments for most major psychotic, neurotic, and personality disorders. This method has been shown to reduce the portion of variance in diagnoses due to differing interviewing styles and coverage. There are several versions of the SADS, depending on the time period assessed—current, past five years, or life time. We employed the life time version which also includes an assessment of the respondent's current status.

Based on the information collected on the SADS, the respondents were classified on the Research Diagnostic Criteria (RDC), which are a set of operational definitions with specific inclusion and exclusion criteria for a variety of diagnoses (Spitzer et al., 1978). These operational definitions were developed for reducing the variance due to differing criteria between clinicians. Differing criteria have been shown to account for the largest source of errors between clinicians.

The RDC have evolved from a decade of research on diagnosis. The conditions included have the most evidence of validity in terms of clinical description, consistency over time, familial association, and response to treatment. The American Psychiatric Association *Diagnostic and Statistical Manual—Third Edition (DSM-III)* is based in part on the RDC.

Diagnoses on the RDC are made both for the current time period and for life time, except for several diagnoses which are considered life time diagnoses only, whether or not the subject is currently manifesting symptoms.

Interviewers, Training, Reliability

There were two raters with Master- and Bachelor-level education and previous experience in clinical psychiatry and interviewing. Both raters, under the guidance of a doctoral-level person and with psychiatric consultation, received three months of training on the SADS and RDC, following which interrater reliability was tested and found to be excellent (Weissman & Myers, 1978).

RESULTS

Treatment for an Emotional Problem

During the year previous to the 1975-76 interview, 8.9 percent of persons in the New Haven study were treated for emotional problems by a variety of sources, as shown in Table 1. The most common source was outpatient treatment by a mental health professional (5.5 percent) followed by a non-psychiatric physician (2.4 percent) and by other professionals (e.g., clergy, non-psychiatric social worker in a family agency, etc.) (1.8 percent). Psychiatric hospitalization was less common (1.6 percent). Since some respondents were treated in a variety of settings, the total percentage of individuals treated was only 8.9 percent.

TABLE 1

Treatment for Emotional Problems during the Past Year
(N = 509)

	Percent
Mental Health Professional (Outpatient)	5.5
Non-Psychiatric Physician	2.4
Other Professional	1.8
Psychiatric Hospitalization	1.6
Any of the Above	8.9

Treatment for an Emotional Problem and Psychiatric Disorder

The data presented thus far pertain to treatment of all respondents during the year prior to the 1975-76 interview, whether or not they met criteria for a psychiatric diagnosis. Since we would expect treatment to be related to psychiatric status, we next examined our data by current psychiatric diagnostic status. In 1975-76, 17.8 percent of the population studied had a probable or definite current psychiatric diagnosis according to the SADS-RDC. This meant that they not only qualified for a diagnosis but had had symptoms of that disorder within the last few weeks. Treatment was indeed related to diagnosis (Table 2); 31.1 percent of all persons with a current psychiatric diagnosis had been treated recently, contrasted with only 4.1 percent of respondents without a current diagnosis. (The fact that 4 percent of the population without a current diagnosis had been treated did not, of course, mean that they had not *needed* treatment. Although free of psychiatric disorder currently, they could well have qualified as psychiatrically ill at the time they were receiving help, earlier in the year.) The most common source of treatment for both groups was the mental health professional in an outpatient setting, followed by a nonpsychiatric physician, other professionals, and hospitalization.

TABLE 2

Treatment for Emotional Problems during the Past Year by Diagnosis

	Current Psychiatric Diagnosis (N = 90) Percent	No Current Psychiatric Diagnosis (N = 419) Percent
Mental Health Professional (Outpatient)	18.9	0.7
Non-Psychiatric Physician	7.8	0.7
Other Professionals	6.7	1.2
Psychiatric Hospitalization	5.6	2.6
Any of the Above	31.1	4.1

Mental health professionals include psychiatric social workers and clinical psychologists, as well as psychiatrists. Treatment by a psychiatrist alone was infrequent. Only 1.0 percent of persons without a current diagnosis and 4.4 percent with a current diagnosis saw a psychiatrist during the past year. Overall, only 1.6 percent saw a psychiatrist.

Sociodemographic Factors and Treatment for Emotional Problems

We next examined the effect of six sociodemographic factors: age, race, social class, marital status, sex, and religion on likelihood of receiving treatment for emotional problems. Analyses were conducted separately for those with and without current diagnoses. Only age and sex were associated with treatment. Among those with a current psychiatric diagnosis, younger persons (under 45) were more likely to have received treatment than older respondents (Figure 1). The same tendency appeared for persons without a diagnosis.

Sex differences were also pronounced (Figure 2). Among those with a psychiatric diagnosis, a much higher percentage of women, as contrasted with men, received treatment. Again the same trend was seen among persons without a current diagnosis.

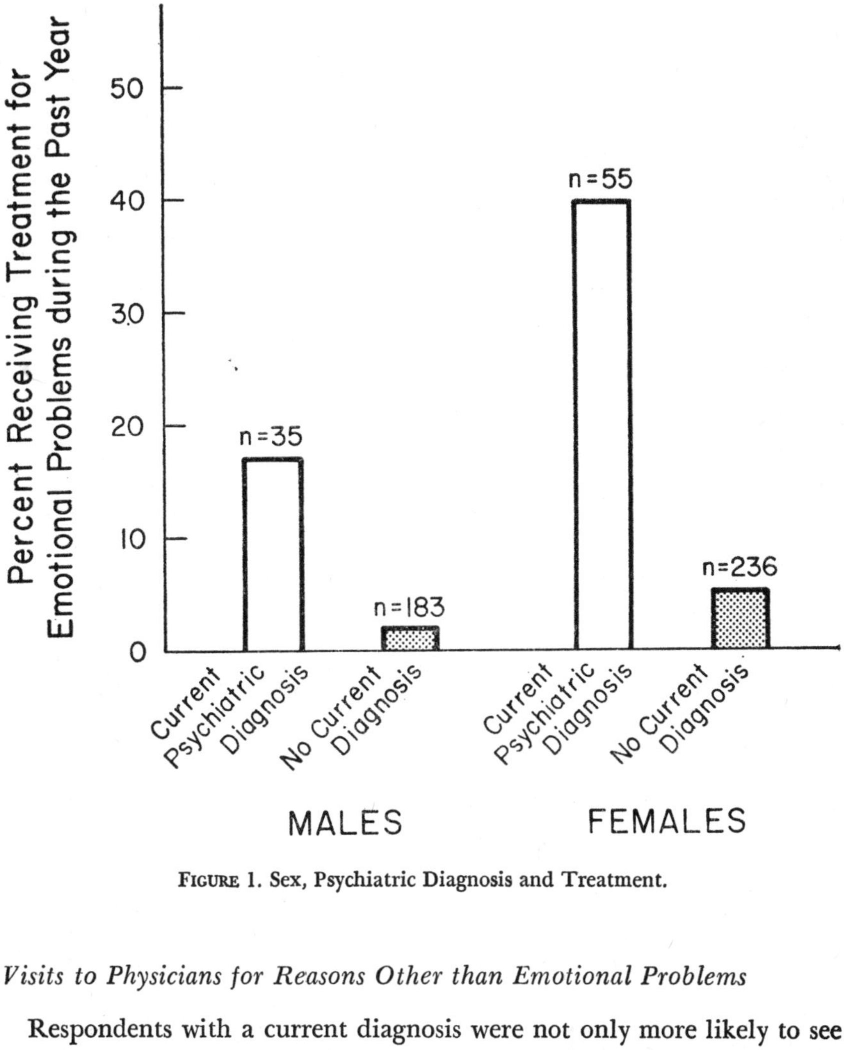

FIGURE 1. Sex, Psychiatric Diagnosis and Treatment.

Visits to Physicians for Reasons Other than Emotional Problems

Respondents with a current diagnosis were not only more likely to see professionals about emotional problems, but they also got more physician care for other purposes. As can be seen in Table 3, most subjects, with or without a diagnosis, saw a physician at least once during the year: 89 percent of all persons with a psychiatric diagnosis and 82 percent of those without a diagnosis. But those with a diagnosis were the more frequent visitors: 43 percent with a diagnosis but only 26 percent without a diagnosis had six or more visits to a physician during the year for reasons *other* than emotional problems.

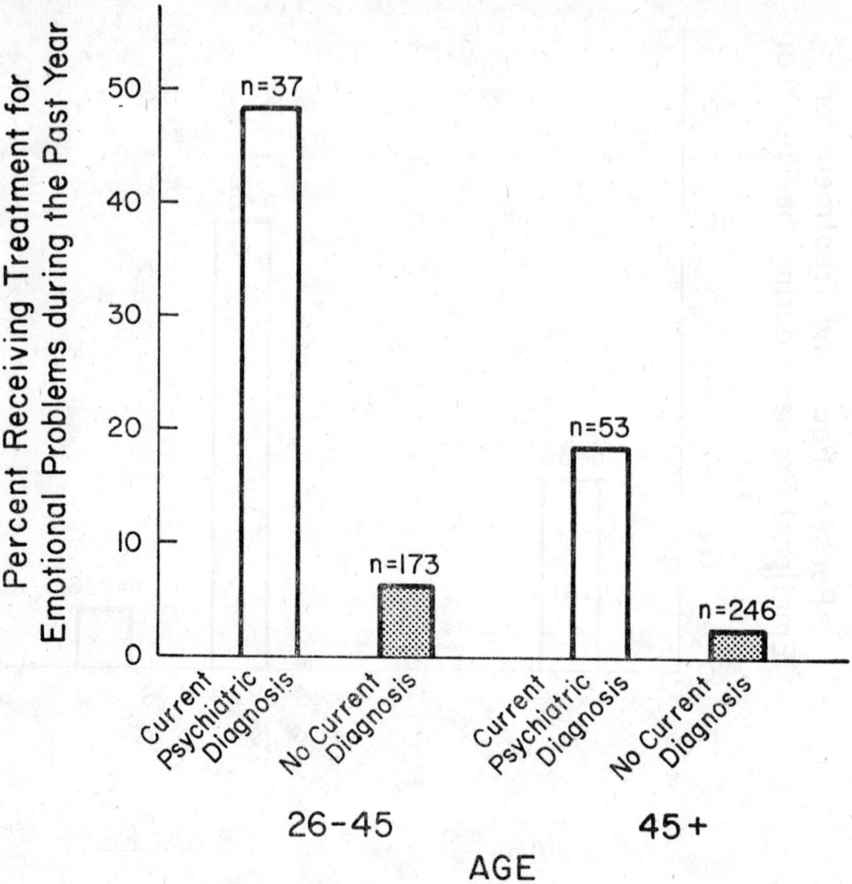

FIGURE 2. Age, Psychiatric Diagnosis and Treatment.

TABLE 3

Visits to Non-Psychiatric Physicians during the Past Year for Reasons Other than Emotional Problems

Number of Visits To A Non-Psychiatric Physician During The Past Year	No Current Psychiatric Diagnosis (N = 419) Percent	Any Current Psychiatric Diagnosis (N = 90) Percent
Any	82%	89%
Six or More	26%	43%

SUMMARY AND IMPLICATIONS

In summary, our New Haven survey found that about 9 percent of the population seeks treatment for an emotional problem during a year. Moreover, there is a relationship between past treatment and current need. Persons with a current psychiatric diagnosis, as contrasted with those without a diagnosis, have been more frequent users of the psychiatric and general medical health care system. However:

1) The overall number of persons with a current psychiatric diagnosis who received treatment for an emotional problem is low, e.g., only about one-third of persons with a current diagnosis were treated by any professional for an emotional problem during the year prior to the interview.

2) The most frequent treatment for an emotional problem was outpatient with a mental health professional usually *not* a psychiatrist. Treatment for an emotional problem by a nonpsychiatric physician or a non-mental health professional occurred with about equal frequency as with a mental health professional.

3) Substantially more women than men and a greater number of younger than older persons received treatment for their emotional problems. Men and particularly older men are grossly underserved.

4) Persons with a psychiatric diagnosis, as contrasted with those without, are more frequent users of nonpsychiatric physicians.

It has been shown that many patients presenting to medical clinics have psychiatric disorders (Locke, 1966; Locke et al., 1967; Locke & Gardner, 1969; Locke et al., 1966; Rosen et al., 1969) and that men and the elderly are less likely to come for treatment when they have psychiatric problems (Shanas, 1974; Tischler et al., 1975; Hinkle et al., 1960).

The consistency of these findings has implications for mental health care delivery. They highlight the importance of the nonpsychiatric physician and non-mental health personnel in the detection, treatment, and referral of persons with psychiatric disorders and suggest the need for further research on barriers to treatment for persons with psychiatric disorders, such as access and stigma, especially for males and the elderly.

As the United States debates the various forms of national health insurance, a question arises about the inclusion of treatment for mental disorders. Concern is raised that psychiatrically ill persons will overuse services. In fact, these data show that persons with psychiatric disorders are in the health care system but not necessarily in the mental health system. If mental health services are included, some of the heavy use of non-mental health services by persons with psychiatric disorders may be transferred to the mental health sector. This transfer, if coupled with early detection and appropriate treatment, could serve to reduce overall utilization of health care by the psychiatrically troubled.

REFERENCES

ENDICOTT, J. and SPITZER, R. L.: A diagnostic interview: The Schedule for Affective Disorders and Schizophrenia. *Arch. Gen. Psychiat.*, 35:837-844, 1978.

HINKLE, L. E., REDMONT, R., PLUMMER, N. et al.: An explanation of the relation between symptoms, disability, and serious illness in two homogeneous groups of men and women. *Women in Industry*, 50:1327-1336, 1960.

LOCKE, B. Z.: Patients, psychiatric problems and nonpsychiatric physicians in a prepaid group practice medical program. *Am. J. Psychiat.*, 123:207-210, 1966.

LOCKE, B., FINUCANE, D., and HASSLER, F.: Emotionally disturbed patients under care of private nonpsychiatric physicians. *Psychiatry Research Report*, No. 22:235-248, 1967.

LOCKE, B. and GARDNER, E.: Psychiatric disorders among the patients of general practitioners and internists. *Public Health Reports*, 84:167-173, 1969.

LOCKE, B., KRANTZ, G., and KRAMER, M.: Psychiatric need and demand in a prepaid group practice program. *Am. J. Public Health*, 56:895-904, 1966.

REGIER, D. A., GOLDBERG, I. D., and TAUBE, C. A.: The *de facto* U.S. Mental Health Services System: A public health perspective. *Arch. Gen. Psychiat.*, 35:685-693, 1978.

ROSEN, B., LOCKE, B., and GOLDBERG, I.: Identification of emotional disturbance in patients seen in general medical clinics. *J. Hosp. Com. Psychiat.*, 23:364-370, 1969.

SHANAS, E.: Health status of older people. *Am. J. Public Health*, 64:261-264, 1974.

SPITZER, R., ENDICOTT, J., ROBINS, E.: Clinical criteria for pyschiatric diagnosis and DSM-III. *Am. J. Psychiat.*, 132:1187-1192, 1975.

SPITZER, R. L., ENDICOTT, J., and ROBINS, E.: Research diagnostic criteria: Rationale and reliability. *Arch. Gen. Psychiat.*, 35:773-782, 1978.

TISCHLER, G., HENISH, J., MYERS, J., and BOSWELL, P.: Utilization of mental health services. *Arch. Gen. Psychiat.*, 32:416-418, 1975.

WEISSMAN, M. M. and MYERS, J. K.: Affective disorders in a United States community: The use of research diagnostic criteria in an epidemiologic survey. *Arch. Gen. Psychiat.*, 35:1304-1311, 1978.

WEISSMAN, M. M., MYERS, J. K., and HARDING, P. S.: Psychiatric disorders in a U.S. urban community: 1975-1976. *Am. J. Psychiat.*, 135:459-462, 1978.

THE WHITE HOUSE: Executive Order No. 11973—President's Commission on Mental Health. Office of the White House Press Secretary, February 17, 1977.

5

The Costs and Benefits of Psychiatric Care

DAVID GOLDBERG, D.M.
and
ROBERT JONES

In recent years, progressively greater use has been made of methods of economic analysis in the evaluation of alternative kinds of psychiatric services (Sharfstein & Clark, 1978). A major problem has been that those responsible for providing such services view their main task as the relief of suffering and distress, but the economic analysis may require them to measure "output" of a service in financial terms. Where cost-benefit analysis is concerned, the requirement that all the effects of a given program should be expressed in monetary terms deflects attention from those aspects of service which cannot be valued in this way, and makes the philistine assumption that utility and value march hand in hand. Faced with this dilemma, investigators have either declared that some benefits of psychiatric services are not measurable (Weisbord, Test & Stein, 1976) or proposed complex but artificial ways of assigning monetary values to the relief of distress (Rosser & Watts, 1973; Binner, Halpern & Potter, 1973).

The authors of the Manchester Study wish to thank the staff of the Economic Advisor's Office, Departments of Health and Social Security, England, in particular Norman Glass and Andrew Burchell, for their assistance and advice at all stages of the project. We wish to thank our psychiatric colleagues at both the hospitals for permission to carry out the study and for their full collaboration with the research. This research was supported by a grant from the Department of Health and Social Security, London.

The present paper will review some of the methods of economic analysis in current use and will propose a modification of the usual cost-benefit framework so that those "soft" costs and benefits which cannot be measured in hard financial terms are separately evaluated and then set against a more conventional cost-benefit analysis. This modification has been described in detail in a previous publication (Glass & Goldberg, 1977), but it is now possible to give some preliminary results from a study using the new methodology (Jones & Goldberg, 1980).

GENERAL COST STUDIES

Rashi Fein (1958) was the first worker to use national statistics relating to patients receiving institutional treatment in an attempt to measure the total economic cost of mental illness. *Direct costs* were defined as the total expenditure on mental illness by governments, private organizations, and the individuals for the care, cure or prevention of mental illness; *indirect costs* measure the loss that society incurs because some of its members are suffering from mental illness. Indirect costs can be measured in various ways. Fein used the value of human life based on expected lifetime earnings and confined himself to the institutionalized population, while Rice (1966) included time lost from work by mentally sick patients outside institutions, and also placed a value on mentally ill housewives based on the earnings of domestic servants. The more inclusive estimates of indirect costs show that they greatly exceed direct costs, and this gap becomes even wider if an allowance is made for the reduction in productivity of mentally ill patients who are in employment (Conley, Conwell & Arrill, 1967). By 1974, the total cost of mental illness in the United States was 36.8 billion dollars, of which only 17 billion dollars were direct costs (Sharfstein & Clark, 1978).

It is possible to carry out such general cost exercises for particular diseases. When this is done for schizophrenia, Gunderson and Mosher (1975) show that once more the indirect costs greatly exceed the direct costs. In 1971, the most conservative estimate of total cost of schizophrenia (12 billion dollars) represented 2 percent of the gross national product of the U.S.A., representing the output of a city the size of Chicago.

Fein was the first to ask whether increased expenditure on the direct costs might not reduce total costs of illness. An early study on three diverse hospitals by Wadsworth, Tonge, and Barber (1957) had shown that the hospital with a highest *per diem* cost of treatment actually had the lowest cost *per case,* since the patients had a shorter stay in hospital and therefore lost less in earnings.

There have been several such studies which might loosely be termed "cost-efficiency" studies in that they compare economic characteristics of various hospitals, often conveniently forgetting that the patients are not allocated to hospitals at random, so that one hospital may turn out to be more economically efficient than another because of the sort of patients it elects to treat. With this important limitation in mind, it should be recorded that Stern and Stern (1963) in the United Kingdom and Ullman and Gurel (1964) in the U.S.A. both showed that small hospitals were more cost-efficient than large ones. A study by McCaffree (1966) purported to show that the intensive treatment methods of the early 1960s were more economically efficient than those of the custodial era which preceded them; but there was no objective measure of effectiveness of treatment in the two eras, and indeed many of the crucial measures were estimates.

At this point it is appropriate to sound a note of caution. A badly designed or executed economic analysis may be worse than doing nothing. The researcher cuts his way through the complexities and uncertainties of mental illness, paying lip service to the importance of reducing suffering but declaring it incapable of measurement, and confines himself to the manipulation of what appears to be more straightforward sums of money. At times of economic recession, his may be a strident voice. It is therefore important that methods of analysis are used that are appropriate to the clinical problem, and that the researcher is explicit about the assumptions made by his analysis.

COST-EFFECTIVENESS ANALYSIS

In a cost-effectiveness analysis there is a single objective which is usually measured by a common physical unit (i.e. number of chronic schizophrenics returned to full employment, number of depressives symptom-free at one month), and we want either to achieve a fixed level of objective at minimum cost, or as much objective as we can for a fixed cost. There is, therefore, some sort of outcome which is explicitly stated for each service or method of treatment, and the analysis will compare the cost of achieving the goal by various means.

It is not easy to find examples of such analyses in psychiatry, since it is unusual to think of the effectiveness of treatments in such crude terms. However, if two alternative treatments are aimed at a particular set of symptoms, it is often reasonable to measure relative effectiveness by computing a mean change score for each treatment, and then set these against the mean cost of each treatment per patient. This design was used by

Schultz and McGlone (1977) in their comparison between treatment of the elderly by a nurse practitioner combined with a physician, and traditional treatment by a physician on his own. The authors present their results for each of three groups of patients: ambulatory, home-bound and those resident in nursing homes. For ambulatory patients, traditional treatment by the physician only is both more effective and costs less, while the reverse is true for patients confined to their homes. The patients living in nursing homes give us an opportunity for achieving as much of our objective as we can for a fixed cost, since for this group the two treatments cost the same but the nurse practitioner and physician are more effective.

May (1971a, 1971b) used a similar sort of design in his comparison of the relative costs and effectiveness of five different methods of treatment for schizophrenia. He showed that the five treatments varied between themselves both in terms of cost and effectiveness, but he was nevertheless able to draw fairly firm conclusions about the advantages of ataractic drugs in terms of low cost and high effectiveness, and the relative disadvantages of milieu therapy. It should be noted that both these studies focused on a particular group of patients for whom some measure of the effectiveness of treatment was available.

COST-BENEFIT ANALYSIS

In a cost-benefit analysis all the effects of a program are in principle quantified and expressed in monetary terms (Williams & Anderson, 1975). If the benefits (monetary value of the advantages) exceed the costs (monetary value of the disadvantages), then a cost-benefit analysis implies that the program should be carried out. If two or more programs are being compared, then a common decision rule is that the program with the most advantageous cost/benefit ratio should be selected. Cost-benefit analysis may be either focused on a particular problem or used to obtain rough priorities among major disease programs. However, it is necessary to carry out an exhaustive measurement of all costs and benefits that can be expressed in monetary terms. It is here that the major problem arises with cost-benefit analysis, since treatment programs typically concern themselves with aims that cannot easily be expressed in financial terms, such as the relief of symptoms and distress, and improvement in psychosocial adjustment.

In the discussion which follows, those effects of a service which cannot readily be expressed in financial terms will be described as "soft" costs in the case of symptoms and impairments to psychosocial adjustment and "soft" benefits in the case of positive measures of psychosocial adjustment.

Some investigators have carried out conventional cost-benefit analyses and mentioned in passing that some benefits of the service could not be expressed in financial terms. Murphy and Datel (1976) showed the superiority of community versus institutional living for 52 chronic patients who were released from institutions in Virginia. The economic factors analysed for each client took account of various costs of keeping him in the community, but offset these against savings on institutional costs and increases in his productivity. A similar procedure was followed by Sharfstein and Nafziger (1976) in their detailed account of a single patient. Ginsberg and Marks (1977) carried out a cost-benefit analysis of a single group of clients receiving a particular therapy—in this case behavioral psychotherapy for ambulant neuroses. All these investigators assume that they know what would have happened had their patients not received the treatment which is the subject of the study; thus, all of Murphy and Datel's patients would have remained in institutions, and none of Ginsberg and Marks' patients would have recovered spontaneously.

One solution to the problem of "soft" costs and benefits is to attempt to assign financial values to them. Rosser and Watts (1973) produce a set of weights for various combinations of distress and disability, which are themselves derived from current compensation payments made by British Courts. If, as a result of treatment, a patient moves from a combination of disability-distress valued at £1,000 to one valued at £700, then the output of the hospital for relief of that particular patient's subjective distress is valued at £300.

Binner, Halpern, and Potter (1973) and Potter, Binner, and Halpern (1975) have also attempted to place cash values on soft benefits of treatment at the Fort Logan Mental Health Center, Denver. For each patient, they calculate "an economic value of the patient's response to the program as a function of his impairment at time of admission and his level of response at discharge. (This) component, called the response value, estimates the economic value of the intangible benefits of treatment skills that are so often ignored in evaluation studies." In order to obtain the response value, the investigators compute a coefficient based on the degree of improvement, and multiply this by $10,000. It is unclear how the latter figure was arrived at, just as it is completely unclear whether the averaged pronouncements of British judges can really be used to calculate sums of money that can be reasonably added and subtracted from other, more real, sums of money.

Nor are the investigators always pleased with their own success at reducing everything to cash. Binner, Halpern, and Potter (1975) state that "concern stems from a desire to treat the values measured as 'real dollars' . . . . This means that a program which treats largely schizophrenics may not be able to show as favorable a rate of return on investment as one which treats primarily neurotic patients. . . . Programs serving such different populations should not be comparatively judged on the absolute rates of return involved." As Chapman (1978) points out, by equating "real dollars" with "estimated dollars" this form of analysis runs the risk of producing spurious and misleading results.

Glass and Goldberg (1977) have suggested a modification to the traditional cost-benefit framework in which investigators who wish to compare two services carry out a conventional cost-benefit analysis, but measure the soft costs and benefits as a separate exercise. The results of the economic comparison can be condensed to a single figure called the "Net Effect" of the comparison between two services, and this is then used to interpret the overall balance sheet of soft costs and benefits. If a service which produces more "soft" benefits is also cheaper, then it is said to "dominate" the other service; while if the service with more soft benefits is more expensive, health planners will at least have objective data to help them decide whether the extra quality is worth the extra price.

Some investigations have implicitly used this model. Weisbord, Test and Stein (1976) compared an experimental community care program for chronic patients with a traditional hospital based program and showed the latter program was more expensive as well as having fewer non-monetary benefits. In the remainder of the paper, an example of the Glass-Goldberg model will be given based on research at Manchester which compares services for schizophrenic patients available from psychiatric units based in general hospitals with those available from a large mental hospital.

THE MANCHESTER STUDY

The study was confined to one particular group of patients—schizophrenics—for two reasons. Firstly, Hoenig (1968) had already shown that the patient populations served by the two sorts of hospitals are rather different, and it is essential to compare like with like. For example, if service "A" treats minor disorders in those with high income, it will be economically superior to service "B" that treats unemployed patients with chronic psychoses and organic states, and that will be true however the two services are organized. Secondly, schizophrenics are a group of patients for whom the mental hospital might be thought especially suitable since the facilities for rehabilitation in mental hospitals are generally superior to those found in district general hospitals (DGH). The general cost studies described earlier had already shown that indirect costs of treatment are very high, so that a service that is successful in terms of returning its patients to gainful employment may be expected to have powerful advantages in a cost-benefit comparison. The mental hospital chosen for the study has very superior, modern rehabilitation workshops. The study was therefore set up in such a way that it should demonstrate any advantages that the mental hospital might have.

The study is to be reported in greater detail elsewhere (Jones & Goldberg, in press), and the present communication will give the results of only part of the study as an illustration of the method. The comparison to be reported is between the services of a large mental hospital and a small psychiatric unit in a district general hospital in providing services for cohorts of first admission schizophrenic patients. The patients were followed up between 10 and 12 years after that admission. The study was confined to first admissions to ensure that a patient who was held to be a graduate of a particular service had treatment from that service *ab initio;* had we included readmissions, there would inevitably have been patients who had "crossed over" from one service to another, and it seemed likely that there would have been great difficulties in matching the cohorts for chronicity.

Comparability of the Samples

Each hospital served as the only source of psychiatric treatment for its catchment area, so that entry of a patient into one hospital rather than the other was entirely determined by his street address. The mental hospital served a larger population than the DGH (450,000 vs. 256,000). The first task was, therefore, to reduce the catchment area of the mental hospital to the same size as the DGH, using census data of electoral wards and choosing areas in such a way that the adjusted area was exactly comparable to that of the DGH for distribution by age, sex and social class. Patients were selected for the study who had a hospital diagnosis of schizophrenia, provided that this diagnosis was supported by undoubted evidence of such a disorder recorded in the clinical notes. If there was any doubt about the diagnosis, the investigators erred on the side of excluding the patient from the study. Those who were now either dead or known to be living abroad were ignored, but great efforts were then made to track down and interview the remainder. It proved possible to contact 66 percent of these patients 12 years after their first illnesses, comprising a cohort of 50 patients from the DGH, and 49 from the mental hospital. The two cohorts were found to be demographically similar.

Measures

Each patient was interviewed by a research psychiatrist using the Present State Examination and various psychosocial assessments. A social worker interviewed any available relatives or key figures such as hostel wardens and landladies to obtain additional data on psychosocial adjustment and burden on the community. Information about health and social services that the patient had received over the past three years was obtained not only from the patient and his relatives but also from examination of the records of the family doctor and the hospital, and from local authority social service records. The family interview also asked whether anyone had had to forego earnings in order to look after the patient, or conversely had had to go to work expressly to support the patient in view of his illness.

For each cohort, the economic analysis is therefore based on a detailed examination of approximately 150 patient/years of service use, and the clinical and social assessments are based on cross-sectional measures approximately 12 years after first diagnosis of schizophrenia. To calculate hospital costs, hospital records were used to make a precise count of units of service consumed under various headings. Because British hospitals in general do not charge patients for services, it is often extremely difficult to obtain accurate patient-related costing data, and in this study the unit costs were specially calculated as a separate exercise by our economic advisors. In both hospitals, unit costs are "specialty costs" rather than "disease costs"—so that the price of an in-patient day, for example, represents the cost for an average psychiatric patient rather than that for a schizophrenic patient. We had no reason to suppose that these patients consumed either less or more than the average psychiatric patient in terms of resources. Where the general hospital was concerned, the task of disentangling the cost of a psychiatric in-patient day from that incurred by patients in other parts of the hospital involved many assumptions and lengthy calculations.

The unit costs of hospital services approximate to the "long-run marginal costs," excluding capital costs. The study did not attempt to measure the capital costs of the two schemes because the accounting difficulties cited earlier are compounded in the case of capital costs, although had it been possible to do so, it is likely that the comparison would have greatly favored the DGH. The estimate achieved may be too high where there is over-capacity in the supply of hospital services. However, in the conditions of the present-day psychiatric practice in the British National Health Service, over-capacity is not very prevalent. The unit costs are also "opportunity costs," in the sense that the resources that were used to provide them have other uses for society, but were in fact used to provide services for our patients.

Results

Some selected items of services with their unit costs are shown as Table 1.

It can be seen from Table 1 that the unit costs are not strikingly different in two hospitals, but that patients averaged fewer in-patient days in the DGH unit; this makes the largest contribution to the fact that hospital costs are considerably more expensive in the mental hospital.

These costs are brought together with other costs and benefits to the rest of the community for an overall comparison which is shown as Table 2. Under the heading "costs," we have the costs of health care, as well as social security payments and money spent on the patient by local authority (LA), welfare departments, and voluntary agencies. It can be seen that LA costs are considerably higher for the mental hospital patients, mainly because more children of these patients spend expensive time in LA group homes, in contrast to the DGH patients who are in hospital for shorter periods, and whose children tend to be looked

TABLE 1

Mean Annual Use and Unit Costs of Selected Items of Service by Patients in Each Cohort

	DGH Psychiatric Unit		Mental Hospital	
Some Selected Items of Service	Mean Annual Number of Items of Service	Unit Cost	Mean Annual Number of Items of Service	Unit Cost
In-patient days	27.3	£12.60	66.6	£18.20 (acute) £10.70 (chronic)
Day Care days	10.0	£ 4.30	12.2	£ 3.30
Out-patient visits	1.2	£11.90	1.6	£ 9.00
Depot Injection Clinic	3.8	£ 7.30	2.4	£ 8.80
Visits to Family Doctor	6.0	£ 2.30	8.0	£ 2.30
Visits by Community Psychiatric Nurse	2.2	£ 3.40	2.9	£ 3.40
Contact with Social Worker	1.5	£ 6.40	1.9	£ 6.40

TABLE 2

Mean Annual Costs and Benefits of Chronic Schizophrenia to the Community (Excluding Patient's Own Family)

	DGH Unit	Mental Hospital
COSTS:		
Psychiatric Hospital Costs	£446	£ 913
Other Health Costs	£ 73	£ 33
Local Authority Costs	£ 49	£ 188
Department of Employment Costs	£ 15	£ 10
Social Security Payments	£556	£ 621
Voluntary Agencies	£ 0	£ 1
Tax and National Insurance (N.I.) Lost (family numbers prevented from work)	£ 33	£ 86
BENEFITS:		
Patient's Tax and N.I.	−£261	−£ 225
Tax and N.I. gained (family members forced to work)	−£ 75	−£ 12
Employer's N.I. contributions (net)	−£119	−£ 61
Local Authority Charges for Services	−£ 15	−£ 18
COSTS LESS BENEFITS	+£705	+£1,536
NET GAIN TO DGH	£831	

after in (much cheaper) foster homes. If any one in the patient's family has to stop going to work in order to care for the patient, then this is also a cost, to be added to the other costs. However, various economic benefits accrue to the rest of the community from the two cohorts of patients: Some of the patients go to work, their tax and national insurance payments benefit the rest of the community. Sometimes members of the patient's families are forced to go to work in order to raise money to care for the patient, as the wife of a schizophrenic may go back to work because of her husband's illness.

The third major contribution to the superiority of the DGH unit is that its patients earn more and as a consequence also attract higher tax and national insurance contributions from their employers. It should be noted that the fact that more relatives have go to work to help look after the DGH patients is an interesting example of something which is a soft cost but a hard benefit.

In making an economic comparison between two services, one must also consider the relative hard costs and benefits as they affect the patient and his family, and these are shown as Table 3.

The first point to notice is that Social Security payments and payments by voluntary agencies appear once more; they are "transfer payments" in that they are at once a cost to the community yet a benefit to the patient. Although they will contribute to differences between the services when the community and the patient are considered separately, any differences between the services will be cancelled out when the two tables are brought together. Such payments merely serve to distribute the cost of illness over the whole community—they are not in themselves a cost although the higher taxes they require may have indirect effects on the economy.

The other point to notice is that the families of patients in the DGH service are economically better off than those in the mental hospital for three reasons: The patients themselves earn more, fewer members of their families have to give up work to care for them, and more members of their families specially go to work to raise funds to look after them. The comparison therefore favors the DGH service, despite the fact that more money has to be spent by these families on the patients' care because these patients are not in hospital for as long as the mental hospital patients.

It therefore emerges that the DGH service is the most economically advantageous both from the point of view of the community at large and for the patient and his family. These two effects can be brought together to produce an economic "net effect" of the two services in the treatment

TABLE 3

Mean Annual Benefits and Costs of Chronic Schizophrenia to the Patient and His Family

	DGH Unit	Mental Hospital
BENEFITS:		
Patient's Earnings	£609	£526
Family Members forced to work	£168	£ 29
Social Security	£556	£621
Voluntary Agencies	£ 0	£ 1
LESS COSTS:		
Family Members prevented from working	−£ 78	−£201
Special Expenses due to Illness	−£ 25	−£ 83
Local Authority Charges for Services	−£ 15	−£ 18
Patient's food while not in hospital	−£283	−£256
NET BENEFITS	+£932	+£619
NET ADVANTAGE OF DGH	+£313	

of chronic schizophrenia: this turns out to be £1,114 per patient per year in favor of the DGH. It should be noted that only £467 of this is accounted for by a difference in the psychiatric hospital costs.

Soft Costs and Benefits

This economic advantage of the DGH service can now be set against the non-monetary differences between the two services (Table 4). It

TABLE 4

Soft Costs and Soft Benefits of DGH versus Mental Hospital in Treatment of Chronic Schizophrenia

	Superior Service
COSTS	
In-patient days	DGH
Patients needing changes in drugs or dosage	DGH
*Sociability—number of impairments	DGH
*Employability—relatives' view of impairments	Mental Hospital
Patient adopts strange postures	DGH
BENEFITS	
*Sociability—total number of assets	DGH
*Heterosexual performance	DGH
Patient weeks employed**	DGH
Work ratings of: drive**	DGH
constructiveness**	DGH
realism**	DGH
*Rating of leisure***	DGH
*Rating of marital adjustment***	DGH

* M.R.C. Social performance Scale Ratings
** patients still in contact with service
*** patients out of contact with service

was found that more of the DGH patients were free of schizophrenic defect states at interview (35 percent vs. 24 percent), and more were not psychotic at interview (42 percent vs 20 percent, $p < .05$). When the other ratings were considered, there were 13 differences significant beyond the 5 percent level, of which 12 favored the DGH. Had these differences been produced by chance, one would have expected there to be approximately equal number of differences in each direction.

It will be noted that "in-patient days" appears as a soft cost as well as having contributed to the hard costs shown in Table 1. This reflects our view that patients would generally prefer to be at home than in the hospital. The same is true of "patient weeks employed," which appears as both a soft benefit and a hard benefit because employment confers psychological as well as financial advantages on a patient. Indeed, the sole difference in favor of the mental hospital—that relatives thought that fewer of the patients had impairments that would prevent them working—might have been because fewer of them were in employment. Otherwise, it can be seen that the social adjustment measures generally favor the DGH service.

Limitations of Cost-Benefit Comparisons

We will point out a number of limitations of the present study. The first two would apply to any cost-benefit comparisons between services, while the remainder are peculiar to the present study.

Firstly, this sort of comparison cannot say whether it is worth having a service at all; it can only say which of the two services is preferable. By the same token, there may be some third way of running the service which is better than either of the services that have been compared. Secondly, although the economic analysis may be helpful in showing us which component parts of a particular service contribute to its economic efficiency, it cannot tell us which aspects of the service are responsible for any "soft" advantages that it may have.

Some of the limitations of the present study have already been mentioned. One is that our hospital costs were estimated for all psychiatric patients, not those diagnosed schizophrenic. It is unlikely that disease costings rather than specialty costing would have made any difference to the comparison between services. Another is that we did not include capital costs. Had it been possible to measure capital costs, these could only have increased the economic advantages of the DGH cohort. It will be noted that we have avoided measuring the indirect costs of illness since we have preferred to confine ourselves to directly observable sums of money. However, once more it is probable that inclusion of indirect costs would have magnified the differences between the services, since it follows that a cohort with more of its members working will have fewer of its members losing earnings.

The most unfortunate limitation of the present study is that we were unable to trace 33 percent of the patients in the original cohorts. After an interval of 12 years, many patients had moved without leaving any trace, and we could not find them despite assistance from several official agencies. This high attrition rate is due to the length of time involved:

in our related study of cohorts who had been ill for between 3 and 4 years, we were able to trace 89.1 percent of the patients who were not known to have died or emigrated.

CONCLUSION

In his thoughtful review of cost-benefit analyses in the assessment of rehabilitation schemes, Noble (1977) ends by giving two reasons why economists should not undertake any further studies: "First, they are likely to mesmerise themselves into believing their results, and, second, there is grave risk that policymakers might believe the believers and set priorities based on misleading evidence."

We concede that if two services are to be compared, a tabulation of economic costs may leave a deeper impression on the mind than mere rhetoric, but we hope that the data presented here will induce thought rather than trance. The modified method of analysis illustrated here does not confuse value with price, but it does allow us to see what value costs. The results of the present analysis are decisive.

We need not ask ourselves whether society should pay a higher price for a better service, since the cheaper service is, if anything, superior in non-monetary terms and may therefore be said to "dominate" the mental hospital. This result is all the more striking in view of the fact that the patients chosen for study were those who might have been expected to benefit from the large institution's more extensive rehabilitation facilities.

It is not clear to what extent the differences observed in this study are due to the fact that patients tended to have shorter admissions to the DGH unit, or whether they might be related to the rather different use that each hospital made of its rehabilitation facilities. Further research might select units for comparison in such a way that such possibilities might be investigated.

The same study also compared a psychiatric unit at a teaching DGH with the mental hospital for cohorts of schizophrenics who had been ill for 3-4 years (Jones and Goldberg, 1980). Despite the fact that unit costs were very much greater in the teaching DGH because of the larger numbers of professional staff, the overall economic effects once more favored the DGH. This part of the study therefore confirmed Fein's view that one might cost society less by spending more. The results were also in accord with those of Jones, Sidebotham, Wadsworth et al. (1961), only this time the finding was based on demographically similar cohorts of patients with the same disease.

Finally, this study provides information about some of the intangible economic effects of schizophrenia in that it has measured the effects of the illness on other members of the patient's family. The present results were not presented to encourage policymakers to set priorities on the evidence of a single study, but to encourage others to repeat the study, and in hopes that the methodology will be useful for application in other settings.

REFERENCES

BINNER, P., HALPERN, J., and POTTER, A.: Patients, programs and results in a comprehensive mental health center. *J. Cons. Clin. Psychol.,* 41:148-156, 1973.

BINNER, P., HALPERN, J., and POTTER, A.: Workload levels, program costs and program benefits—an output value analysis, 17th Annual Meeting of the Association of Mental Health Administrators 1975 (unpublished).

CHAPMAN, J.: Techniques of economic analysis in psychiatric practice, *Brit. J. Med. Psychol.,* 52:91, 1979.

CONLEY, R., CONWELL, M., and ARRILL, M.: An approach to measuring the cost of mental illness. *Am. J. Psychiat.,* 124:775-762, 1967.

FEIN, R.: *Economics of Mental Health.* New York: Basic Books, 1958.

GINSBERG, G. and MARKS, I.: Costs and benefits of behavioral psychotherapy. *Psychol. Med.,* 7:685-700, 1977.

GLASS, N. and GOLDBERG, D.: Cost-benefit analysis and the evaluation of psychiatric services. *Psychol. Med.,* 7:701-707, 1977.

GUNDERSON, J. and MOSHER, L.: The cost of schizophrenia. *Am. J. Psychiat.,* 132:901-906, 1975.

HOENIG, J.: The desegregation of the psychiatric patient. *Proc. RSM,* 61:115-120, 1968.

JONES, R. and GOLDBERG, D. (1980): The effects of two different services on the treatment of schizophrenia: A cost-benefit approach. *Psychological Medicine.*

JONES, K., SIDEBOTHAM, R., WADSWORTH, W., TONGE, W., and PRICE, H.: Cost and efficiency in mental hospitals. *The Hospital,* 57:23-25, 1961.

MAY, P.: Cost efficiency of treatments for the schizophrenic patient. *Am. J. Psychiat.,* 127:1382-1385, 1971a.

MAY, P.: Cost efficiency of mental health care. *Am. J. Pub. Health,* 61:127-129, 1971b.

MCCAFFREE, K.: The cost of mental health care under changing treatment methods. *Am. J. Pub. Health,* 56:1013-1025, 1966.

MURPHY, J. and DATEL, W.: A cost-benefit analysis of community versus institutional living. *Hosp. and Comm. Psychiat.,* 27:165-170, 1976.

NOBLE, J. H.: The limits of cost-benefit analysis as a guide to priority setting in rehabilitation. *Evaluation Quarterly,* 1:347-380, 1977.

POTTER, A., BINNER, P., and HALPERN, J.: Readmission discount factors in program evaluation. *Am. J. Comm. Psychol.,* 3:305-314, 1975.

RICE, D. P.: *Estimating the Cost of Mental Illness.* Washington: Government Printing Office, PHS Publication No. 947-6, Health Economics Services 6, 1966.

ROSSER, R. and WATTS, V.: The development of a classification of morbidity and its use to measure the output of a hospital, SSRC Conference, 1973. Quoted in A. Williams and R. Anderson, *Efficiency in the Social Services.* Oxford: Blackwell, 1975.

SCHULTZ, P. and MCGLONE, T.: Primary health care provided to the elderly by a nurse practitioner. *J. Am. Geriat. Soc.,* 25:443-446, 1977.

SHARFSTEIN, S. and CLARK, H.: Economics and the chronic mental patient. *Schizophrenia Bulletin,* 4:399-414, 1978.

SHARFSTEIN, S. and NAFZIGER, J. C.: Community care: Costs and benefits for a chronic patient. *Hosp. Comm. Psychiat.*, 27:170-173, 1976.

STERN, B. and STERN, E.: Efficiency of mental hospitals. *Brit. J. Prev. Soc. Med.*, 17:111-120, 1963.

ULLMAN, L. and GUREL, L.: Size, staffing and psychiatric hospital effectiveness. *Arch. Gen. Psychiat.*, 11:360-366, 1964.

WADSWORTH, W., TONGE, W., and BARBER, L.: The cost and efficiency of mental hospitals. *Lancet*, 2:533-534, 1957.

WEISBORD, B., TEST, M., and STEIN, L.: An alternative to the mental hospital: Benefits and costs. Unpublished paper to American Psychiatric Association, Miami, Florida, 1976: quoted in Sharfstein and Clark (1978).

WILLIAMS, A. and ANDERSON, R.: *Efficiency in the Social Services*. Oxford: Blackwell, 1975.

III

THE PSYCHIATRICALLY ILL AS PARENTS

Introduction by Myrna M. Weissman

The three papers in this section dealing with the psychiatrically ill parent are a tribute to how far psychiatry has progressed in its research questions and its methodology in the past decade. Not too long ago, the psychiatric study of parents was synonomous with the study of the alleged overprotective, unloving, or cold mother and the impact of her negative attributes on the etiology of her offspring's psychiatric illness.

The study of parents now has expanded to include not only mothers and fathers but the entire family, siblings and other first-degree relatives. Interest in the family is no longer limited to psychodynamic theorists and therapists, but extends to geneticists, epidemiologists, and social psychiatrists. Questions are raised not only about the environmental effects of all types of psychiatrically disturbed parents on their children but about possible genetic and/or environmental transmission of specific psychiatric disorders examined singly. These papers, in different ways, examine the latter question.

Fischer and Gottesman explore a unique data set made available because of the systematic record keeping of the Scandinavians. In a preliminary analysis, where both parents are hospitalized with serious psychiatric disorders, 158 couples are examined to determine the psychiatric disorders of their 450 offspring. The investigators find an alarming rate of psychiatric illness in these children. Nearly a third of the children of these dually-ill parents have been hospitalized for psychiatric disorders. Over half of the couples have had at least one psychiatrically ill child and, perhaps even more important, psychiatric disorders seem to breed true. While this study design cannot sort out genetic from environmental factors, the alarming rates of illness in the offspring have implications for the counseling of seriously ill couples who are or may wish to become parents.

The paper by Reich et al. presents a mathematical model for examining genetic and environmental transmission of psychiatric illness in families. While it is well recognized that psychiatric disorders, as well as poverty, run in families, quantitative mathematical models using path analysis to decipher genetic and nongenetic family factors have only recently been developed. While these techniques are complicated by the rapid changes in family structures that are now taking place, they are most powerful.

Reich and his associates present a model for the analysis of family data, when a sex effect is present. Data from a family study of alcoholics are described. The main conclusion is that both genetic and nongenetic factors are important in the transmission of alcoholism and that the hereditability of alcoholism is greater in the case of men than women.

The review by Erlenmeyer-Kimling and her associates examines recent changing trends in marriage and fertility rates of schizophrenics. This review demonstrates that, in contrast to earlier studies, more schizophrenics are now likely to marry and have children. The fertility rates of schizophrenics are now about the same as those of nonschizophrenics. Moreover, a substantial number of children are born after the schizophrenic's first admission to the hospital, and many are unplanned. These findings must be considered in light of the recent prohibition on abortion payments by Medicaid in the United States. The findings also raise questions about the effects of major tranquilizers on the first trimester of pregnancy and, most important, about the impact on a child who is unplanned and then cared for by a chronically ill parent. Alternately, what is the impact on the chronically ill parent of having to meet the needs of a child, especially a child who has a greater than chance probability of also becoming ill?

Despite the difference in approach and in the specific psychiatric illnesses studied, these three papers reach somewhat similar conclusions. The risk of a similar psychiatric illness in the child of a seriously psychiatrically ill parent is increased. The child's risk increases even further if both parents are ill. Recent trends suggest that more seriously psychiatrically ill patients are living in the community, marrying, and having children. None of these studies can definitely sort out genetic from non-genetic factors. They do suggest that both factors will be important and that the proportion of variance explained by genetic and nongenetic factors will probably differ by the type of psychiatric disorder studied, by the sex of the psychiatrically ill parent, and by the sex of the offspring. These papers underscore the need for further inquiry into the genetic and nongenetic causes of specific psychiatric disorders and the need for a range of services for the families of the psychiatrically ill, as well as for the psychiatrically ill themselves when they are living in the community.

6

A Study of Offspring of Parents Both Hospitalized for Psychiatric Disorders

MARGIT FISCHER, M.D.
and
IRVING I. GOTTESMAN, PH.D.

The present study deals with the fate of approximately 450 persons both of whose parents have been hospitalized for a psychiatric disorder.

Nature has experimented with human genes associated with mental disorders in ways forbidden to an ethical science of psychopathology, providing us with material which may fill in gaps in our knowledge about the etiology of some of the psychiatric disorders. Following a line of interest in the interaction of genes and environment, the first author started the data collection some eight years back, and was then joined by the second author some years ago.

Our project deals with offspring both of whose parents were hospitalized for psychotic disorders, neuroses, or personality disorders. We excluded parent patients with traumatic and infectious brain disorders and organic psychoses, but otherwise the parental mating types are unrestricted. The material deals with the total sample of offspring, whether born before or after the hospitalization of either parent. It is a catamnestic study, as the offspring are currently adults, with the majority being over the age of 35.

This project was supported by grants from the Danish Medical Research Foundation and Scottish Rite Schizophrenic Research Program.

AIMS

Our main interest is in the two major functional psychoses: schizophrenia and affective psychosis. One question which might be elucidated by this study is the possible genetic relationship between schizophrenia and other so-called schizophrenia-spectrum-disorders. Similarly, it could be of interest to examine the possible relationship between affective psychoses and the more ill-defined reactive depressions. From previous studies we know that the risk figure for schizophrenia in the offspring of one schizophrenic parent is 15 percent. From previous dual mating studies (Kahn, 1923; Schulz, 1940; Elsässer, 1952; Lewis, 1957; Rosenthal, 1966; Erlenmeyer-Kimling, 1968, 1975; Moshalenko, 1972; Kringlen, 1978), we know that the age-corrected risk figure for schizophrenia in the offspring both of whose parents are schizophrenics is around 45 percent. For affective psychoses, the incidence of the same disorder in the offspring of parents where one has an affective psychosis is around 20 percent, and around 50 percent if both the parents have an affective psychosis. Now, if we have a group of parents where one is schizophrenic and the other has a "schizophrenia-spectrum-disorder," we can examine whether this spectrum disorder genetically has similarities to schizophrenia. If so, we would expect a risk figure somewhere between 15 percent and 45 percent.

From the genetic aspect there are several other interesting questions. One of them is the problem of the schizo-affective psychosis and the possible relationship between manic-depressive psychosis and schizophrenia. There is another related question: What characteristics identify a child who is unrelated to a schizophrenic as being at a very high risk of developing the disorder?

By selecting those families where at least two of the offspring have developed a psychosis, we might be able to determine the most "dangerous" combinations of genes and environment.

A considerable proportion of the offspring have developed into completely normal and well-functioning people. By focusing on this group it might be possible to find common characteristics and possible preventive factors.

The material also lends itself to studies of other issues. One could select families with several suicides—in one family six out of eight children have committed suicide—and scrutinize the development of norms, values, and general behavior patterns. Yet another angle would be to study the relationship between crime and madness. Whether it holds true for the whole material, we do not know at the moment, but there seems to be a subgroup, at least, with a heavy load of criminal offenses. Such a study might elucidate the society's tolerance towards abnormal behavior and concepts of crime and madness, and it might say something about family patterns or genes or both.

METHODS AND MATERIAL

Sampling

Since 1938 a register of mental illness, retardation, and neuropsychiatric diseases has been maintained at the Institute of Human Genetics of the University of Copenhagen for all of Denmark. Some cases were registered as early as 1920 in an unsystematic way and charts of cases appearing after 1938 who had had earlier admissions incorporate the earlier information. In 1953 a special system for the registration of psychiatric admissions and discharges together with information on family history was established on a national basis. This system provides the data for official statistical reports and research projects. Since 1966 the resultant register has been under the care and control of the Institute of Psychiatric Demography in Risskov (Dupont et al., 1974). Since 1969 every Danish citizen or resident has been assigned a CPR number (Civil Personal Registration number) and that number now identifies all patients in the Psychiatric Register and in the National Register.

All patients in the Psychiatric Register, approximately 150,000 cases, form the starting pool for our sample. The register consists of three files, one for last names, one for birth dates, and an "S-chart." The latter contains name, birth date, birth place, address, marital status, hospital and date of admission, preliminary diagnosis, and frequently a short summary, all on the front side of the chart. On the reverse there is information about the spouse and the biological relatives, including whether they have been admitted to a psychiatric hospital. We collected copies of all charts where the spouse had been hospitalized for a psychiatric disorder and formed our own dual mating register. From this sample we excluded cases with organic psychoses and cases who had been hospitalized only to obtain an abortion on psychiatric grounds but who had never been treated as psychiatric in-patients before or since. The sample then consisted of 198 couples where both had been treated as in-patients. One hundred and fifty-eight couples had one or more children who survived at least until age 15. We have identified approximately 450 offspring. This is a preliminary report and the tables that follow deal with 140 couples, as some of the data in the remaining 18 families have not yet been analysed.

Collection of Information

Through the National Register System (Folkeregistret) we were able to trace the patients through their last known address and determine their current address as well as all children living with them at any point of time and the latter's date of birth and full names. This procedure was time consuming but effective. After having established the name and CPR numbers of the offspring, we also traced them to their last address. In case of death we got a copy of the death certificates.

Each offspring was checked against the Psychiatric Register and all case notes of psychiatric hospitalizations reviewed. All non-hospitalized offspring were visited by a psychiatric social worker and information about upbringing, somatic and psychiatric disorders, work, marriages, etc. was collected. Furthermore, both the parents and the offspring were checked against the National Criminal Register. Only some of this material has been analysed so far.

The present report deals with the parents and the hospitalized offspring. All case notes have been examined and independent diagnoses made. We have used ICD diagnoses, applying the rules for diagnosis given in the Glossary accompanying the 8th edition (World Health Organization, 1974), with the exception of "reactive depression" which in this study has been defined as a non-psychotic depression, perhaps closest to "neurotic depression" in the ICD.

We have not been completely blind as to who were parents and offspring and sometimes not to the relationship. Three people have made diagnoses and two (Dr. Alice Bernsen and M.F.) have both diagnosed most cases. The agreement between each pair of diagnosticians was around 80 percent. In another 10 percent the disagreement was of minor importance, most involving cases where both diagnosticians were in doubt, but where one decided, for example, on personality disorder as first choice and reactive depression as second choice, while the other chose the same categories but put them the other way around.

In 10 percent there was a major disagreement, one diagnostician, for example, calling the case neurotic and the other psychotic, or one calling it schizo-affective psychosis and the other bipolar manic-depressive.

RESULTS

Table 1 shows the number of couples distributed by diagnosis of both parents. There is a total of 158 couples or 316 probands. Eighty, or approximately half, of the couples have at least one psychotic member.

Table 2 shows the number of offspring, and in parentheses the number

TABLE 1
Number of Couples. Distribution by Diagnosis

Diagnosis of One Parent	Diagnosis of Other Parent								
	Schizophrenia	Bipolar Manic-Depression	Unipolar Depression	Reactive Depression	Senile Dementia	Personality Disorder + Neurosis	Alcohol/ Drug Abuse	All Other Diagnosis Including Undiag-nosed	Total
Schizophrenia	6								6
Bipolar manic-depression	8	3							11
Unipolar depression	3	5	1						9
Reactive depression	9	5	4	4					22
Senile dementia	3	—	2	1	2				8
Personality disorder + neurosis	13	7	5	10	2	23			60
Alcohol/drug abuse	1	—	—	1	1	2			5
All other diagnoses including undiagnosed	2	3	—	5	—	8		19	37
Total	45	23	12	21	5	33		19	158

of hospitalized offspring, distributed by diagnosis of parents. There is a total of 452 offspring of whom 121 or 27 percent have been hospitalized.

Table 3 shows the number of couples where at least one of the parents is schizophrenic. There are 45 such couples with a total of 111 children. Almost two-thirds of the non-hospitalized children are over 35 years but obviously some age correction is needed. For this presentation we have used a method less crude than Weinberg's but not as accurate as Strömgren-Slater's. We have reduced the non-hospitalized offspring in the following way: Under 16 = 0, 16-25 = ¼, 26-35 is counted one-half and those who are 36-44 as ¾, and 1 for all over 45 years old. There is a problem with age correction in a study like this where the risk period varies from one diagnostic category to another. It appears from the table that 27/111—about ¼ of all the children—have been hospitalized for a mental disorder, or 30 percent if age-corrected.

Table 4 shows the relationship between diagnosis of the parents and diagnosis of the offspring. There are two points of interest in this table. First—though the number is small—it confirms previous findings that the risk of schizophrenia in the offspring of two schizophrenics is around 35-40 percent and the risk for a psychosis in the offspring of schizophrenia plus affective psychosis (counting bipolar and unipolar together) is also 35-40 percent. When the offspring of two schizophrenics develop a psychosis, it is schizophrenia, while the mating schizophrenia plus affective psychosis produces half schizophrenic and half affective psychosis. So, in fact, the risk figure is 17 percent for schizophrenia and 17 percent for affective psychosis, which is not significantly different from the expected figures where one parent is respectively schizophrenic or manic-depressive. Thus psychosis is shown to breed true to type here, but see Table 6 for some exceptions.

Table 5 presents couples where at least one of the parents has a bipolar manic-depressive psychosis. There are 27 such couples with a total of 87 offspring (age-corrected: 73.5), of whom 23 have been hospitalized.

Table 6 shows the distribution of offspring in relation to diagnosis of the parents where one parent has a bipolar manic-depressive psychosis. It appears that the mating of bipolar manic-depressive psychosis with a unipolar depressive psychosis gives an age-corrected risk figure for psychosis in the offspring of 32 percent. Of the seven psychotic children in this group, three are bipolar manic-depressive, two unipolar depressive and two schizophrenic. Furthermore, there are two with non-psychotic disorders. Another interesting figure appears for the mating of bipolar manic-depressive with reactive depression. The risk figure for the offspring

TABLE 2

Number of Offspring, Total and (in Parentheses) Hospitalized. Distribution by Diagnosis of Parents

Diagnosis of one Parent	Diagnosis of Other Parent								
	Schizophrenia	Bipolar Manic-Depression	Unipolar Depression	Reactive Depression	Senile Dementia	Personality Disorder + Neurosis	Alcohol/ Drug Abuse	All Other Diagnosis	Total
Schizophrenia	14(3)								14 (3)
Bipolar manic-depression	21(6)	6 (1)							27 (7)
Unipolar depression	5	26 (9)	1 (—)						32 (12)
Reactive depression	27(5)	22 (7)	11 (6)	13 (3)					73 (21)
Senile dementia	11(3)		7 (4)	1 (—)	4 (2)				23 (9)
Personality disorder + neurosis	44(7)	22 (4)	19 (3)	29 (6)	4 (—)	73 (29)			191 (49)
Alcohol/drug abuse	—		—	1 (—)	1 (1)	2 (—)	2 (—)		6 (1)
All other diagnoses including unanalyzed	3(—)	2 (—)	—	15 (—)	—	20 (3)	—	46 (16)	86 (19)
Total	115(27)	78 (21)	38 (13)	69 (9)	9 (3)	95 (32)	2 (—)	46 (16)	452 (121) 27%

TABLE 3

Offspring of Parents Both Hospitalized for Mental Disorder. Distribution by Diagnosis of Parents and Number of Offspring. One Parent Schizophrenic

Main Diagnosis of Other Parent	No. of Couples	Non-Hospitalized Offspring 16-25	26-35	36-45	45	Hospitalized Offspring	Total N	Age Corrected*
Schizophrenia	4	3	3	1	—	2	9	5
Schizo-affective	2	—	—	—	2	1	3	3
Bipolar manic-depression	8	3	1	4	7	6	21	17¼
Unipolar depression	3	—	1	—	1	3	5	4½
Reactive depression	9	—	4	2	16	5	27	23¾
Senile dementia	3	1	—	—	7	3	11	10¼
Personality disorder + neuroses	13	6	5	8	5	7	31	22
Alcohol or drug abuse	2	1	2	—	—	—	3	1¼
All other diagnoses	1	—	—	—	1	—	1	1
Total	45	14	16	15	39	27	111	88

* Age correction for non-hospitalized:
16-25 = ¼
26-35 = ½
36-45 = ¾
> 45 1

TABLE 4

Distribution by Diagnosis of Parents and Offspring.
One Parent Schizophrenic

Main Diagnosis of Other Parent	Total No. of Off-spring Age Corrected	Diagnosis of Hospitalized Offspring: Schizo-phrenia	Schizo-Affective	Bipolar Manic-Depression	Unipolar Depression	Reactive Depression	Personality Disorder + Neurosis	Alcohol/ Drug Abuse	All Other Diagnoses (+Suicide)	% Psychotic	% Non-Psychotic
Schizophrenia	5	2	—	—	—	—	—	—	—	40	—
Schizo-affective	3	1	—	—	—	—	—	—	—	33	—
Bipolar manic-depression	17¼	2	1	2	—	—	—	—	1	30	6
Unipolar depression	4½	1	—	2	—	—	—	—	—	66	—
Reactive depression	23¾	—	—	—	—	1	4	—	—	—	21
Senile dementia	10¼	1	—	—	—	—	1	—	1	9	18
Personality disorder + neurosis	22	3	—	—	—	—	2	—	2	13	18
Alcohol or drug abuse	1¼									—	—
All other diagnoses	1									—	—
Total	88	10	1	4	—	1	7	—	4		

TABLE 5

Distribution by Age and Diagnosis of Parents. Number of Offspring. One Parent Bipolar Manic-Depressive

Main Diagnosis of Other Parent	No. of Couples	Non-Hospitalized Offspring 16-25	26-35	36-45	> 45	Hospitalized Offspring	Total N	Age Corrected
Bipolar manic-depression	1	—	1	1	—	—	2	1¼
Unipolar depression	5	—	6	6	5	9	26	21½
Schizophrenia	8	3	1	4	7	6	21	17¼
Schizo-affective	1	—	—	—	2	—	2	2
Reactive depression	4	—	2	—	4	7	13	12
Senile dementia	—	—	—	—	—	—	—	—
Personality disorder + neurosis	7	—	2	10	6	4	22	18½
Alcohol or drug abuse	1	—	—	—	—	1	1	1
Total	27	3	12	21	24	23	87	73½

is here 25 percent for developing a psychosis and 33 percent for developing a non-psychotic mental disorder.

Table 7 presents those couples where one parent has a schizo-affective psychosis. There are only six such couples with an age-corrected number of offspring of 18½. It is interesting to see here that the mating schizo-affective plus reactive depression gives an age-corrected risk figure in the offspring of 45 percent for developing a psychotic disorder and 25 percent for developing a non-psychotic disorder. It appears that the hospitalized offspring are scattered among the diagnostic groups.

Table 8 shows the number of couples and number of offspring where at least one parent has a personality disorder or a neurosis. There are 63 such couples with a total of 147 children of whom 48 have been hospitalized.

Table 9 shows the distribution of hospitalized offspring of the 63 couples where at least one of the parents has a personality disorder or a neurosis. If we look at the mating of personality disorder plus reactive depression, it appears that the age-corrected risk figure is 44 percent for developing a non-psychotic disorder, usually personality disorder or neurosis. None of these offspring has developed a psychosis. The following line shows that the risk figures in the offspring also are fairly high for the mating of personality disorder plus personality disorder. Thirty-three percent have developed a non-psychotic disorder and 5 percent have developed a single psychosis, schizophrenia.

Discussion of Relationship Between Diagnosis of Parents and Diagnosis of Offspring

The mating of schizophrenia plus reactive depression or schizophrenia plus personality disorder produces similar risk figures for non-psychotic disorder in the offspring of 21 percent and 18 percent respectively. However, only one of these two matings—schizophrenia plus personality disorder—produces any psychotic offspring, of whom there are 13 percent, all schizophrenic. This figure is not higher than one would expect if one parent was schizophrenic and the other was well (see Table 4). This suggests that reactive depression, senile dementia, and personality disorder add nothing to the risk of schizophrenia in the offspring.

Another finding is that for the offspring of one bipolar affective parent the risk of developing a psychotic disorder is almost the same whether the other parent is bipolar manic-depressive or a reactive depression, which might suggest that what here is called reactive depression is a heterogeneous disorder, some cases belonging to the affective psychoses and others to the neurotic disorders. Another possibility is that what we call

Table 6

Offspring of Parents Both Hospitalized for Mental Disorder. Distribution by Diagnosis of Parents and Offspring. One Parent Bipolar Manic-Depressive

Main Diagnosis of Other Parent	Total No. of Off-spring Age Corrected	Diagnosis of Hospitalized Offspring									
		Bipolar Manic-Depression	Unipolar Depression	Schizo-phrenia	Schizo-Affective	Reactive Depression	Personality Disorder + Neurosis	Alcohol/Drug Abuse	All Other Diagnoses	% Psychotic	% Non-Psychotic
Bipolar manic-depression	1¼	—	—	—	—	—	—	—	—	—	—
Unipolar depression	21½	3	2	2	—	1	1	—	—	32	9
Schizophrenia	17¼	2	—	2	1	—	—	—	1	29	6
Schizo-affective	2	—	—	—	—	—	—	—	—	—	—
Reactive depression	12	2	—	1	—	3	1	—	—	25	33
Personality disorder + neurosis	18½	—	—	1	—	—	2	—	—	5	10
Alcohol or drug abuse	1	—	—	1	—	—	—	—	—	100	—
Total	73½	7	2	7	1	4	4	—	1		

TABLE 7

Distribution by Diagnosis of Parents and Offspring.
One Parent Schizo-Affective

Main Diagnosis of Other Parent	No. of Couples	Total No. of Offspring Age Corrected	Diagnosis of Hospitalized Offspring: Schizophrenia	Schizo-Affective	Bipolar Manic-Depression	Unipolar Depression	Reactive Depression	All Other Diagnoses + Suicide	% Psychotic	% Non-Psychotic
Schizophrenia	2	3	1	—	—	—	—	—	33	—
Reactive depression	4	15½	1	3	1	2	2	2	45	25
Total	6	18½	2	3	1	2	2	2		

TABLE 8

Distribution by Age and Diagnosis of Parents. Number of Offspring. One Parent Personality Disorder or Neurosis

Main Diagnosis of Other Parent	No. of Couples	Non-Hospitalized Offspring 16-25	26-35	36-45	> 45	No. of Hospitalized Offspring	Total N	Age Corrected
Schizophrenia	13	6	5	8	5	7	31	22
Bipolar manic-depression	7	—	2	10	6	4	22	18½
Unipolar depression	5	—	6	—	3	3	12	9
Reactive depression	10	—	1	4	13	13	31	29½
Personality disorder + neurosis	23	5	16	12	13	20	66	51¼
All other diagnoses	5	5	1	—	5	1	12	7¾
Total	63	16	31	34	45	48	174	138

TABLE 9

Distribution by Diagnosis of Parents and Offspring.
One Parent Personality Disorder or Neurosis

Main Diagnosis of Other Parent	Total No. of Offspring Age Corrected	Diagnosis of Hospitalized Offspring: Schizophrenia	Bipolar Manic-Depression	Unipolar Depression	Reactive Depression	Personality Disorder + Neurosis	Suicide	All Other Diagnosis	% Psychotic	% Non-Psychotic
Schizophrenia	22	3	—	—	—	2	1	1	13	18
Bipolar manic-depression	18½	1	—	—	—	2	—	1	5	16
Unipolar depression	9	—	—	1	—	1	—	1	11	22
Reactive depression	29½	—	—	—	2	9	1	1	—	44
Personality disorder + neurosis	51¼	3	—	—	2	11	—	4	5	33
All other diagnoses	7¾	1	—	—	—	—	—	—	13	—
Total	138	8	—	1	4	25	2	8		

reactive depression has some genes in common with the affective psychoses. Another intriguing fact is the number of schizophrenic offspring in the matings where one of the parents is a bipolar manic-depressive. From a genetic point of view, it is understandable that some of the offspring of bipolar manic-depressive plus schizophrenia are schizophrenic, but the schizophrenics also appear in matings in which neither parent was schizophrenic.

Another interesting finding is the high risk figure for non-psychotic disorders in the offspring of matings between a personality disorder and reactive depression or personality disorder. The figures here are just as high as between two psychotic parents. It might be added that these risk figures include only hospitalized offspring. The subsequent analysis including non-hospitalized offspring will presumably give even higher figures.

REFERENCES

DUPONT, A., VIDEBECH, T., and WEEKE, A.: A cumulative national psychiatric register. *Acta Psychiat. Scand.*, 50:161-173, 1974.

ELSÄSSER, G.: *Die Nachkommen geisteskranker Elternpaare.* Stuttgart: Georg Thieme, 1952.

ERLENMEYER-KIMLING, L.: Studies of the offspring of two schizophrenic parents. In: D. Rosenthal and S. Kety (Eds.), *The Transmission of Schizophrenia.* Oxford: Pergamon, 1968.

ERLENMEYER-KIMLING, L.: A prospective study of children at risk for schizophrenia. In: R. Wirt, G. Winshur, and M. Roff (Eds.), *Life History Research in Psychopathology 4.* Minneapolis: University of Minnesota Press, 1975.

KAHN, E.: *Studien über Vererbung und Entstehung geistiger Störungen.* Monogr. Gesamtgeb. Neurol. Psychiat., 36, 1923.

KRINGLEN, E.: Adults offspring of two psychotic parents, with special reference to schizophrenia. In: L. C. Wynne, R. L. Cromwell, and S. Matthysse (Eds.), *The Nature of Schizophrenia.* New York: John Wiley & Sons, 1978.

LEWIS, A. J.: The offspring of parents both mentally ill. *Acta genet.* (*Basel*), 7:349-365, 1957.

MOSHALENKO, V. D.: A comparative study of families with one or two schizophrenic parents. *Zhurnal Neuropatologii, Psikiatrii imeni S.S. Korsakova,* 72:86-92, 1972. (Cited in: I. Gottesman and J. Shields: A critical review of recent adoption, twin and family studies of schizophrenia, *Schizophrenia Bulletin,* 360, 1976).

ROSENTHAL, D.: The offspring of schizophrenic couples. *J. Psychiat. Res.*, 4:169-188, 1966.

SCHULZ, B.: Kinder schizophrener Elternpaare. *Z. ges. Neurol. Psychiat.*, 168:1-3, 1940.

WORLD HEALTH ORGANIZATION: *Glossary of Mental Disorders and Guide to Their Classification* (for use in conjunction with the *International Classification of Diseases,* 8th revision). Geneva, 1974.

7

The Contribution of Affected Parents to the Pool of Affected Individuals: Path Analysis of the Segregation Distribution for Alcoholism

THEODORE REICH, M.D., JOHN RICE, PH.D.,
C. ROBERT CLONINGER, M. D.
and
COLLINS LEWIS, M.D.

All of the major psychiatric illnesses tend to aggregate in families. The magnitude of this effect is usually large and it is thought to be the consequence of genetic transmission, contagion, or both. The family members at the highest risk for an illness are the immediate relatives of an affected individual. This is not surprising since the more closely related individuals are, the more they share genetic, cultural, and environmental events. The study of multi-generational pedigrees indicates that psychiatric illnesses are transmitted from parents to offspring. Thus, one consequence of psychiatric disorder is elevating the risk of that same disorder in one's children and grandchildren.

The study of the transmission of illness from parent to child has been undertaken chiefly by medical geneticists. They have attempted to infer from patterns of familial transmission which of a variety of genetic hypotheses seems most likely. Attempts have been made to determine whether psychiatric disorders are associated with a single gene or a poly-

Supported in part by USPHS grants AA-03539, MH-31302, and MH-25430, and Research Scientist Development Award MH-00048 (CRC).

genic system and the environmental contribution of the parent has usually been treated as "error" or "noise" in the system. New methods are being developed which allow more complex hypotheses to be tested. The contribution of environmental, as well as genetic transmission can now be studied, as well as the effects of various types of assortative mating. These new developments still go by the name of "genetics" but might more aptly be termed "intergenerational transmission" since they are no longer limited to exclusively genetic hypotheses. This chapter will sketch some new developments in the testing of genetic and non-genetic modes of transmission, and will apply these methods to a study of the contribution of parents' alcoholism to the incidence of alcoholism in their children.

The common mental disorders share many characteristics which make the analysis of family data difficult. Age of onset and sex specific incidences are often variable. The severity of illness may vary so much that it may be difficult to decide whether affected members of the same family actually have the same illness. Many cases have no affected family members, and the distribution of illness does not yield Mendelian segregation rations. Assortative mating is common and further complicates attempts to unravel possible genetic factors.

Studies of monozygotic and dizygotic twins and their offspring, of half siblings reared apart and together, and of parents and offspring separated by adoption have indicated that genetic factors must play some role in the familial aggregation of almost all psychiatric disorders (Slater & Cowie, 1974). Comparing the familial distribution of illnesses in intact nuclear and extended families with that in families in which children have been separated from parents by adoption suggests, however, that non-genetic or "cultural" factors are also significant. Thus, both genetic and environmental variables must be included at the outset in any attempt to understand the patterns of familial aggregation.

In order to integrate existing observations and to suggest new research designs which might shed light on the mode of transmission of these disorders, a number of quantitative mathematical models have been developed. In constructing these models, assumptions are made explicit so that competing hypotheses can be statistically compared. The power of different designs to resolve ambiguities can be measured, and results from studies of different types can be integrated. Experimental design is further improved by rational choices of sample size. At least in part as a consequence of mathematical modeling, old problems have been restated in a new and solvable way and new problems have been discovered.

An important feature of mathematical modeling is that an analysis of the distribution of a disorder in a population in one generation can be the basis for predicting its distribution in subsequent generations. While these dynamic multigenerational predictions have not yet been verified against experience for human beings, their development has led to a clear specification of the possible consequences of current and past mating patterns for the health of the population. We can now state with some precision the effects that rapid changes in family structure would have on the incidence of the familial disorders in future generations. These predictions require certain assumptions about etiology. If the relevant factors, for example, are almost purely genetic, then the rates of psychiatric illness will drop if the reproductive fitness of affected individuals is low. By contrast, if the disorder is largely the consequence of environmental stress, then changes in family structure may result in an increased population prevalence (Cavalli-Sforza & Feldman, 1973; Feldman & Cavalli-Sforza, 1975).

One difficulty in developing appropriate models for the transmission of common disorders is the "heterogeneity" problem. It is possible that the common familial diseases are actually composed of several different etiologically distinct diseases which we treat in a unitary fashion because our classification scheme is inadequate. Ignoring these heterogeneities may well obscure the very mechanisms we wish to discover. Two approaches to this difficult problem have been recently described. First, Elston and Yelverton (1975) have suggested that large extended pedigrees be collected and studied individually. The assumption is made that all affected members of a large pedigree (50 or more members) have the same disorder. If hypotheses about the transmission of the disorder are then supported, this increases our confidence that the assumption about homogeneity of the disorder was correct. However, if two large families are studied, and the transmission hypothesis is not supported in *both,* we conclude that there are at least two separate disorders. By the repeated study of many extended pedigrees, it may be possible to devise a classification scheme based on the mode of transmission of the subforms of a disorder.

Reich et al. (1979) have suggested that subclassifications of a disorder can be tested to learn whether they are transmitted together or independently. If they are transmitted independently, this suggests that they are actually independent disorders mistakenly lumped because of phenotypic resemblances. In this approach, phenotypic subclassifications based on severity or morphology seem to offer the best opportunity for the discovery of independently transmitted subforms.

In past analyses of family data, relatives of different probands have been combined into a single group (e.g., all brothers, or all fathers, or even all first degree relatives). The average incidence of the disorder in the *grouped* relatives or its mean deviation from the population mean is then presented. Current approaches emphasize the importance of testing each proband and his family as a separate replication of the hypothesis. Family size is thereby taken into account. This method is known as segregation analysis. For some time the method of choice for testing single gene hypotheses, it has recently been extended to more complex modes of transmission (Reich et al., 1979).

Morton (1974) and Rao and Morton (1974) have used path analysis to define a system of correlations which can be used to measure genetic and non-genetic factors in families with varying structures. They have introduced assortative mating based on social homogamy and indices for environmental factors, greatly improving the power to detect both genetic and non-genetic effects. The genetic effects included are both those assuming a single major locus and polygenic inheritance.

Another method which attempts to determine non-genetic as well as genetic components of transmission is given by Chakraborty and Schull (1978). These authors have studied the properties of "family sets," a set consisting of a proband, a sibling, a cousin, and a comparable unrelated individual of the proband's generation. A sample of family sets is drawn from a general population. A regression analysis is used to measure the components of variance. The approach is based on the fact that each family set consists of individuals who share one half, one eighth, and no genes in common. In addition, cousins and unrelated individuals do not share an environment of rearing, so that environmental and genetic effects can be separated.

Cloninger et al. (1979) have proposed a model which includes both polygenic and non-genetic transmissible factors. This model includes assortative mating between persons with the same disorder and also takes into account family structure, so that intact families and families in which parents of children are separated by adoption can be included in the same analysis, making it possible to study the relative importance of genetic and non-genetic transmission. The correlations between individuals reared under a wide spectrum of types of family structure when no sex effect is present are also given.

An alternative approach (Rice et al., 1978) uses observations on multiple classes of relatives in intact families. This model includes transmissible factors which are genetic and non-genetic operating together. No attempt is made to distinguish genetic from non-genetic factors, but they are treated together as events which can influence the transmission of a phenotype from parents to offspring. Direct phenotypic assortative mating is included, and the relationship of assortative mating to changes in the variance of the trait in the population in each succeeding generation is described. Although this model does not permit the separation of genetic and non-genetic transmissible effects, many hypotheses about the transmission of the disorder can be tested.

In this chapter, data from a controlled family study of alcoholism will be analyzed using path analysis of the segregation distribution. In addition to the usual data for first degree relatives, information from grandparents and spouses will be included. The grandfathers provide a second degree relative and the spouses provide a non-genetically linked associate. In addition, the sex of the family member will be considered since it is well known that there are important social differences in drinking patterns of males and females. Our method allows testing of a series of hypotheses and within the confines of the model the most parsimonious acceptable formulation is given. These results are then compared with the results of an adoption study so that the transmissibility of alcoholism can be factored into a genetic and non-genetic part.

THE THEORETICAL MODELS

The Multifactorial Model

The multifactorial model for the inheritance of semi-continuous traits has been described by Falconer (1965, 1967), Reich et al. (1972, 1975) and Curnow and Smith (1975). In this model it is assumed that the manifestation of a qualitative trait is governed by a normally distributed variable X, termed the liability scale. Affectational status is determined by whether the individual passes one or more threshold values of X. In the case of one threshold, an individual is "affected" if his score on X is greater than the threshold value, and "unaffected" otherwise. Multiple thresholds may be used if individuals can be graded by severity of illness (Reich et al., 1972). Estimates of population prevalences yield direct estimates of the threshold values.

If pairs of individuals are sampled at random from a population, then the maximum likelihood estimate of their correlation in liability is given by the tetrachoric correlation coefficient (Kendall & Stuart, 1973) which is determined by the 2 x 2 table of observed phenotypes. In human genetics, however, pairs are often sampled using the proband method of selecting pairs through affected individuals. Under either sampling scheme, the maximum likelihood estimate of the correlation is that correlation in a bivariate normal distribution which yields the observed proportions. This may be ascertained either by numerical integration or by using the approximation described by Reich et al. (1972).

Segregation analysis (Elandt-Johnson, 1971) is needed in the analysis of family study data since the unit of sampling is the family and the observations within the family are not statistically independent. In addition, when families are sampled using the proband method, ascertainment bias must be taken into account, because a family with several affected individuals in it has a greater chance of falling into the sample. The procedure for the estimation of the underlying correlations from family data is described by Reich et al. (1979) and Rice et al. (1979).

For a trait in which rates for men and women differ, separate liability distributions X_M and X_F are assumed for males and females, and hence the population prevalences K_{PM} and K_{PF} may differ, where P = Population, M = Male, F = Female. In addition, the correlations between relatives may be sex-dependent. The multifactorial model with sex effects contains ten parameters which must be estimated: (a) the four parent offspring correlations r_{POMM}, r_{POMF}, r_{POFM}, and r_{POFF}; (b) the three sibling correlations r_{OOMM}, r_{OOMF} and r_{OOFF}, where the first two subscripts refer to the relationship (i.e., r_{PO} = parent-offspring, r_{OO} = offspring-offspring) and the second two subscripts refer to their respective sex; (c) the two population prevalences K_{PM} and K_{PF}; and (d) the correlation m between mates. The sex effect model for a quantitative trait has been described by Rice et al. (1980).

Path Analytic Models of Multifactorial Inheritance

Path analysis is a technique introduced by Wright (1918) to evaluate an *a priori* causal relationship between a set of variables which explains the observed correlations among them. Rice et al. (1978) and Cloninger et al. (1979) have described two path models of family resemblance which allow for direct parent-to-offspring transmission of environmental factors (cultural inheritance), polygenic inheritance, phenotypic assortative mating, correlated environments of rearing, and variable family structure.

The TAU model (Rice et al., 1978) is appropriate when data are obtained from individuals reared in intact nuclear families (or more generally, in any rearing environment in which both natural parents can transmit cultural as well as genetic factors). This model assumes that the underlying liability scales may be partitioned as

$$X_M = t_M T_M + e_M E_M, \quad (1)$$

$$X_F = t_F T_F + e_F E_F. \quad (2)$$

where T_M and T_F denote all factors (both genetic and cultural) which are transmissible from the mother and father, respectively, to an offspring of either sex. The variables E_M and E_F denote all other factors with a covariance equal to zero ($COV(T_M, E_M) = COV(T_F, E_F) = 0$). The parameters t_M, e_M, t_F and e_F are path coefficients (standardized partial regression coefficients) and measure the contribution of the corresponding variable to the determination of the overall liability value.

Transmissions from parent to offspring are governed by the equations

$$T_{OM} = \tau_{MM} T_M + \tau_{FM} T_F + r_M R_M, \quad (3)$$

$$T_{OF} = \tau_{MF} T_M + \tau_{FF} T_F + r_F R_F, \quad (4)$$

where OM and OF denote male and female offspring, respectively, and R_M and R_F are uncorrelated residuals. The path coefficients τ_{MM}, τ_{FM}, τ_{MF} and τ_{MM} measure the contribution of a parent to an offspring when the first subscript denotes the sex of the parent and the second denotes the sex of the child. Direct phenotypic assortative mating is described by the path equation

$$X_M = m X_F + u U, \quad (5)$$

where m is the correlation between the liabilities of mates, and U is the uncorrelated residue. Other types of assortative mating based on secondary homogamy or a combination of primary and secondary homogamy also have been formulated by Rao et al. (1979).

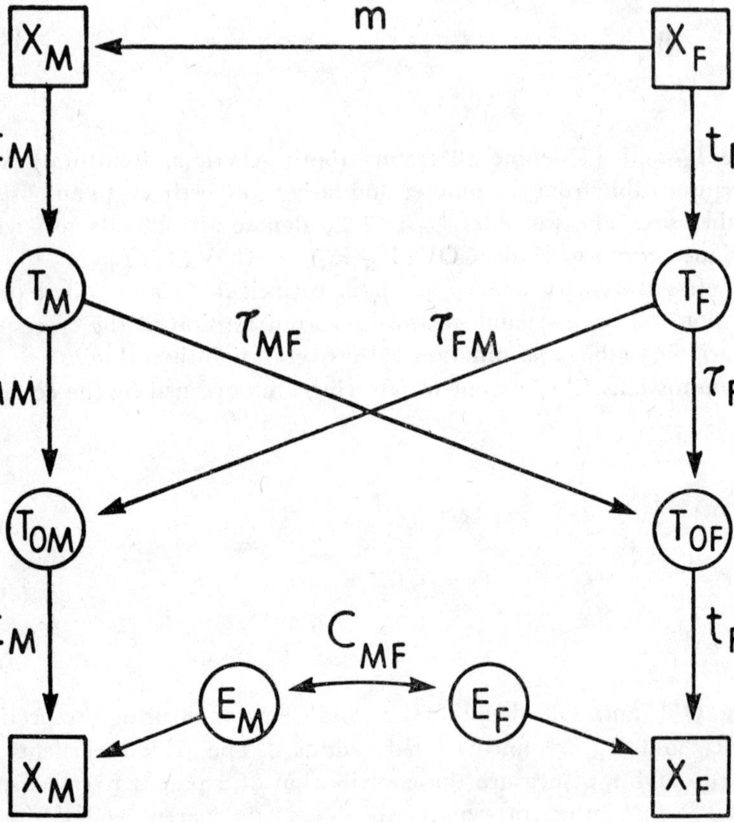

Fig 1. Path diagram of the transmission of complex (genetic and non-genetic) factors from parents to offspring when a sex-dimorphism is present.

The above equations may be conveniently represented by the path diagram in Figure 1 which depicts the relationship between a son, a daughter and their parents. In addition to the above parameters, the model allows for correlations c_{MM}, c_{MF}, and c_{FF} between the environments of siblings reared together which cannot be explained by transmission from parents (e.g., effects of attending the same school).

TABLE 1

Variables and Parameters of the TAU Model

Variable/Parameter	Description
X_i	Liability distribution of individuals of sex i (i = M or F)
T_i	Factors transmissible from a parent of sex i to an offspring
E_i	Non-transmissible factors for individuals of sex i
t_i	Extent to which transmissible factors influence X_i (t_i^2 is proportion of thc variance of X_i which is transmissible)
e_i	Extent to which non-transmissible factors influence X_i
K_{pi}	Population prevalence of the phenotype for sex i
τ_{ij}	Extent to which the transmissible factors of a parent of sex i influence the transmissible factors of an offspring of sex j
C_{ij}	Extent to which the non-transmissible environments of siblings of sexes i and j are correlated
m	Extent to which the liability of mates are correlated

Using the rules of path analysis (Li, 1975), the correlation in liability may be expressed in terms of the parameters of the TAU model:

$$r_{POMM} = \tau_{MM} t_M^2 + m \tau_{FM} t_M t_F \quad (6)$$

$$r_{POMF} = \tau_{MF} t_M t_F + m \tau_{FF} t_F^2 \quad (7)$$

$$r_{POFM} = \tau_{FM} t_M t_F + m \tau_{MM} t_M^2 \quad (8)$$

$$r_{POFF} = \tau_{FF} t_F^2 + m \tau_{MF} t_M t_F \quad (9)$$

$$r_{OOMM} = \{\tau_{MM}^2 + \tau_{FM}^2 + 2m \tau_{MM} \tau_{FM} t_M t_F\} t_M^2 + c_{MM} e_M^2 \quad (10)$$

$$r_{OOMF} = r_{OOFM} = \{\tau_{MM} \tau_{MF} + \tau_{FM} \tau_{MM} + m (\tau_{MM} \tau_{FF} + \tau_{FM} \tau_{MF}) t_M t_F\} t_M t_F + c_{MF} e_M e_F \quad (11)$$

$$r_{OOFF} = \{\tau_{MF}^2 + \tau_{FF}^2 + 2m \tau_{MF} \tau_{FF} t_M t_F\} t_F^2 + c_{FF} e_F^2 \quad (12)$$

The families collected in our study allow the estimation of the correlations given by equations (6) - (12), as well as m, although these 8 observations are not sufficient to simultaneously estimate all of the underlying path parameters. However, the hypotheses that $\tau_{MM} = \tau_{MF}$

$= \tau_{FM} = \tau_{FF} = \tau$ may be tested. This model is termed the *Environmental Model.* It states that parents of both sexes transmit culture and genetic effects equally to offspring of both sexes, and that observed differences between males and females are due entirely to non-transmissible factors—i.e., to cultural or situational differences that are *not* specific to having one set of parents rather than another. An additional correlation which we use is the correlation between a grandfather and grandson (we have insufficient data to use grandmothers and granddaughters). The grandfather-grandson correlation is given by:

$$r_{GOMM} = \tau^2 (t_M{}^2 + m\, t_M t_F)(1 + m\, t_M t_F). \qquad (13)$$

The TAU model can not be used to estimate the relative contributions of genes and transmitted environmental factors. However, by also using the adoption data of Goodwin et al. (1973), we are able to apply the BETA model of Cloninger et al. (1979) to obtain an estimate of h^2, the (narrow) heritability, which is that proportion of the variance due to additive genetic effects, and b^2, which is that proportion of the variance due to cultural transmission.

Under the condition that $\tau = \frac{1}{2}$ and the parameter β described by Cloninger et al. (1979) is also $\frac{1}{2}$, data for families in which parents do not live with their children, and so cannot transmit non-genetic factors, can also be incorporated into the TAU model. The path diagram relevant to incorporating the correlation r_{poad} between biological parents and their adopted-away child is given in Figure 2 when X_M and X_F are partitioned as

$$X_M = h_M A_M + b_M B_M + e_M E_M, \qquad (14)$$

$$X_F = h_F A_F + b_F B_F + e_F E_F. \qquad (15)$$

Here A_M and A_F denote the effects of genetic factor and B_M and B_F the effects of cultural factors for males and females, respectively. The parameter $h_M{}^2$ and $h_F{}^2$ denote the male and female heritabilities, respectively, and $b_M{}^2$ and $b_F{}^2$ the proportion of the variance explained by cultural factors.

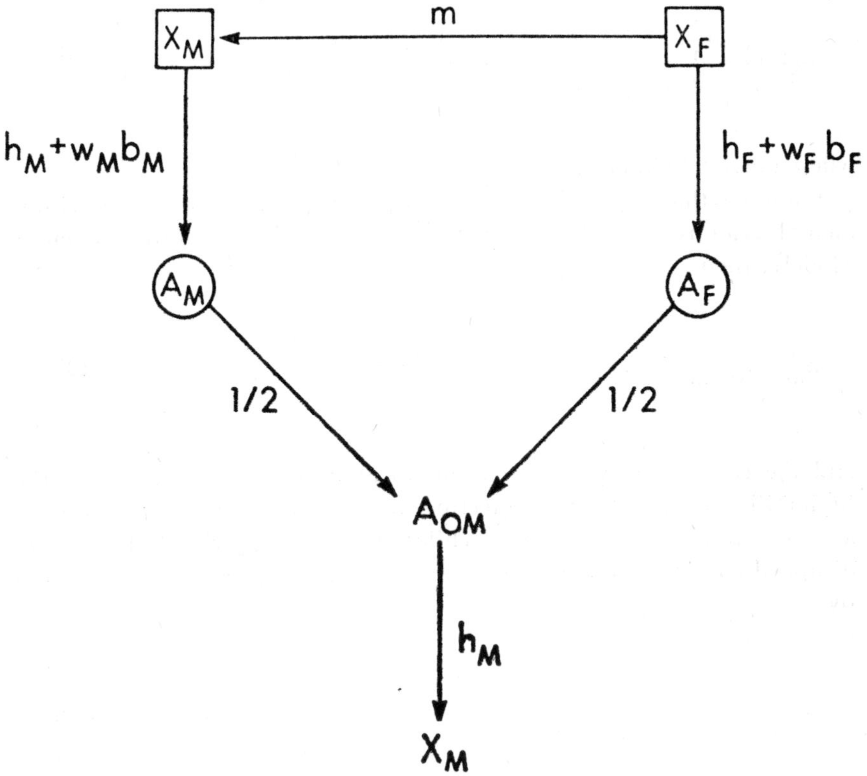

FIG 2. Path diagram of the transmission of genetic factors from parents to a son who has been given up for adoption.

The relationship between the two parameter sets is given by

$$t_M{}^2 = h_M{}^2 + 2w_M\, h_M\, b_M + b_M{}^2 \quad (16)$$

$$t_F{}^2 = h_F{}^2 + 2w_F\, h_F\, b_F + b_F{}^2, \quad (17)$$

where w_M and w_F are the within person correlations between genetic and cultural factors for males and females, respectively. As in Cloninger et al. (1979), these parameters can be found by solving the equations

$$w_i^2 + \left\{\frac{m(h_i^2 + b_i^2) - 1}{m\, h_i\, b_i}\right\} w_i + 1 = 0 \tag{18}$$

where i denotes either M or F.

Assuming that X_M and X_F differ only for non-transmissible environmental reasons (i.e. the disorder is described by the Environmental Model), then

$$b_M = b_F\, h_M / h_F, \tag{19}$$

and the correlation r_{poad} is sufficient to allow for the estimation of the heritability of the trait. Neglecting the possibly smaller variance of adopted children versus natural children (because obviously ill or handicapped children are excluded from the adoption process), r_{poad} is given by

$$r_{poad} = ½\, h_m \{(h_M + w_M b_M) + m(h_F + w_F b_F)\}. \tag{20}$$

Parameter Estimation and Hypothesis Testing

The FORTRAN programs XQSEG and XQTAU, described by Rice et al. (1980), were used to estimate the multifactorial correlations and the parameters of the TAU model, respectively. The general purpose maximum likelihood package MAXLIK (Kaplan & Elston, 1972) was used to search the parameter space and to provide standard errors.

The program provides maximum likelihood estimates of population prevalences using the segregation distribution of nuclear families together with data which estimate K_{PM}, K_{PF} and m. The program XQTAU uses the parameters of the TAU model to calculate the correlations given by equations (6) - (13), and then calculates the likelihood from these correlations as in XQSEG. For either program, MAXLIK is used to find the parameters which maximize the likelihood L of the data.

Linear constraints can be placed on tests of the hypotheses by using the likelihood ratio test (Kendall & Stewart, 1973). This test is done by first obtaining the likelihood L_1 without any constraints, and then obtaining the likelihood L_0 by imposing linear constraints on the parameters of the model. The asymptotic distribution of

$$-2 \ln\left(\frac{L_0}{L_1}\right) = -2 (\ln L_0 - \ln L_1) \tag{21}$$

is known to be a chi-squared distribution with λ degrees of freedom when λ linear constraints are imposed. Here, the likelihood ratio test is the uniformly most powerful test between the two hypotheses.

A FAMILY STUDY OF ALCOHOLISM

A random sample of white male and female subjects was chosen from three psychiatric inpatient units of the Department of Psychiatry of Washington University. Additional subjects were obtained from a county parole office. Each subject was interviewed with a structured interview of known reliability and received a psychiatric diagnosis using criteria developed by Feighner et al. (1972). Patients who received a diagnosis of "definite" or "probable" alcoholism became probands in the study. Seventy-four probands were chosen from the inpatient population and 57 from the parole office sample. Thirty-two "control probands" who were medically or surgically ill inpatients and who had no psychiatric illness after interview were also chosen. The controls were selected so that their age distribution matched that of the alcoholic probands.

All current or last spouses and all first-degree relatives were contacted for interview. Personal interviews have been completed with approximately 70 percent of the living relatives who resided within a 100-mile radius of St. Louis. Each proband and relative was given a structured psychiatric interview, a battery of psychological personality tests, and a schedule to measure relevant rearing experiences. A family history was obtained from each subject. These family histories plus hospital and other records allowed us to assign a diagnosis to subjects who could not be interviewed. Diagnoses were made by two psychiatrists and differences resolved by consensus. Probands who had been adopted were excluded from the sample. In this report data are presented for families of 130 alcoholic and 32 control probands. Included were sibs, parents, spouses, and grandfathers of control and alcoholic probands. The study is still in progress and this is a preliminary report.

Population prevalences of current or past alcoholism were estimated from the first-degree relatives and spouses of control probands. Since the alcoholics and control probands had similar age distributions, there was

TABLE 2 (a)

Prevalence (in percent) of Alcoholism in Relatives of Probands
(Total number of observations are in parentheses)

Probands	Relatives					
	Fathers	Mothers	Brothers	Sisters	Grandfathers	Spouses
Male Alc. (103)	47 (102)	20 (102)	62 (109)	12 (100)	16 (196)	18 (38)
Female Alc. (27)	48 (27)	15 (27)	56 (25)	21 (34)	4 (50)	39 (23)
Total Alc. (130)	47 (129)	19 (129)	61 (134)	14 (134)	11 (246)	26 (61)

TABLE 2 (b)

Prevalence (in percent) of Alcoholism in the Relatives of
Male and Female Control Probands
(Total number of observations are in parentheses)

Probands	Relatives		
	Male (1st degree)	Female (1st degree)	Grandfathers
Male & Famale Controls (32)	20 (132)	4 (123)	5 (64)

TABLE 2 (c)

Prevalence (in percent) of Alcoholism in Siblings of Alcoholics
Subdivided by the Presence of Alcoholism in Parents
(Total number of observations are in parentheses)

$\chi^2_2 = 6.63 \quad 0.05 > p > 0.025$

	0 Parents Aff.		1 or 2 Parents Aff.	
	Brothers	Sisters	Brothers	Sisters
Male & Female Alc. Probands (130)	52 (52)	8 (62)	67 (82)	19 (72)

no need to age adjust these data. For this analysis, sibships were truncated by dropping the uninterviewed and/or the youngest sibs if more than five were interviewed. Reducing the sample in this fashion permitted the use of a minicomputer. In order to test hypotheses about the mode of transmission of alcoholism, the hypotheses were first ordered from the most general to the most particular. Using a general purpose maximum likelihood optimization routine, MAXLIX (Kaplan & Elston, 1972), the most general formulation of the multifactorial model was fitted to the data. A series of increasingly restrictive assumptions were then added one at a time and each new model was fitted to the data. Every new model was compared to the prior one using a likelihood ratio chi-squared statistic. If the new restriction did not result in a statistically significant reduction in the chi-square, it was accepted. By repeated applications of this test, the most parsimonious model was chosen.

RESULTS

The lifetime prevalences of alcoholism in the first-degree relatives, spouses, and grandfathers of alcoholic and control probands are displayed in Table 2 (a) and 2 (b). While prevalences are higher than those reported a decade ago by Winokur et al. (1970), the pattern is unchanged: Male relatives are at greater risk than female relatives, and incidences are very similar in relatives of male and female probands. Rates in relatives of alcoholics are higher than rates in relatives of control subjects.

Before concluding that elevated rates in relatives of alcoholic probands as compared with controls mean that alcoholism is familial, we must consider the possibility that the difference is due to ascertainment bias. If ascertainment bias were the sole explanation, the risks to sibs of an alcoholic would be independent of the presence or absence of the disorder in a parent. In Table 2 (c), the prevalence of alcoholism in siblings when parents are unaffected is compared with the prevalence when one or more parents are alcoholic ($\chi^2_2 = 6.63$, $.05 > p > .025$). Having an affected parent *does* increase the prevalence in sibs, and thus the clustering of alcoholism in the families of alcoholics shows that some form of family transmission occurs.

TABLE 3

Correlations Between Relatives Obtained by Fitting An Unrestricted General Multifactorial Model to the Entire Data Set.
Log Likelihood = —505.72

$r_{poMM} = 0.50 \pm 0.09$	$r_{ooMM} = 0.60 \pm 0.08$
$r_{poMF} = 0.38 \pm 0.10$	$r_{ooMF} = r_{ooFM} = 0.41 \pm 0.10$
$r_{poFM} = 0.46 \pm 0.12$	$r_{ooFF} = 0.48 \pm 0.13$
$r_{poFF} = 0.31 \pm 0.13$	$m = 0.52 \pm 0.08$
$K_M = 0.20 \pm 0.03$	$r_{goMM} = 0.32 \pm 0.12$
$K_F = 0.056 \pm 0.01$	

The most general formulation of the multifactorial model assumes only that the liability of a family of size p is distributed as a p-variate normal. Fitting this model to all the data yields a parameter set which is displayed in Table 3. The value of the log likelihood function is —505.72. It should be noted that the likelihood function does not offer a test of the goodness of fit of the model to the data. Rather, it will be used to test the hypotheses displayed in Table 4.

TABLE 4

Hypothesis Testing Using the General Path Analytic Model and Segregation Analysis
(Parameters which are fixed are noted by an asterisk)

Hypothesis	m	t_M	t_F	Tau	C_{MM}	C_{MF}	C_{FF}	K_{PM}	K_{PF}	Log Likelihood
1) $\tau_{MM} = \tau_{FF} = \tau_{MF} = \tau_{FM}$	.52	.81	.59	.56	.21	.07	.45	.20	.06	–505.77
2) $\tau = 0.5$	.53	.87	.63	.50*	.33	.16	.61	.20	.05	–505.86
3) $C_{MM} = C_{FF} = C_{MF}$	.53	.86	.63	.50*	.32	32*	.32*	.20	.05	–506.70
4) $t_M = t_F$	.53	.78	.78*	.50*	.33	.33*	.33*	.21	.05	–508.50
5) $C_{MM} = C_{FF} = C_{MF} = 0$	.51	.88	.65	.50*	0*	0*	0*	.21	.06	–509.15

The general model described in Table 3 was first constrained by setting all of the tau values equal to each other and fitting a new model, Table 4, 1). The log likelihood of the constrained model differs only trivially from that of the general model and cannot be rejected ($\chi^2_2 = 1.0$, $.50 > p > .25$). The hypothesis that all the values of tau are equal is acceptable and we may conclude that the transmissible factors of parents influence the transmissible factors of their offspring to the same extent regardless of the sex of the parent or offspring.

Next, the hypothesis that every tau equals 0.5 is compared with the less restrictive formulation that they are only equal to each other. The results are displayed in Table 4, 1) and 2). The value of tau cannot be distinguished from 0.5 ($\chi^2_1 = 0.18$, $.75 > p > .50$). In the remaining analyses tau is fixed as 0.5. Because parents and offspring share exactly one-half of their genes, the value of tau for a purely polygenic trait would be 0.5. If non-genetic as well as genetic transmission occurred, then the value might deviate from 0.5. Unfortunately, cultural transmission can mimic polygenic transmission and tau may equal 0.5 even if non-genetic factors are present.

The hypothesis that the effect of the siblings' common environment does not vary with sex is tested in Table 4, 3). This hypothesis is acceptable ($\chi^2_1 = 1.68$, $.5 > p > .25$) and these parameters are henceforth set equal to each other.

The hypothesis that there is no environmental effect common to siblings is tested by setting the common environmental parameters equal to 0 in Table 4, 5). However, when we compare the log-likelihood function to results when that assumption was *not* made in 4, 3), we find a significant difference, and this hypothesis is rejected ($\chi^2_1 = 4.90$, $0.05 > p > 0.025$). Therefore, we assume there *is* a non-transmissible environmental effect common to siblings of both sexes.

Earlier studies of sex differences in alcoholism rates by Reich et al. (1975) and Cloninger et al. (1978) concluded that non-familial environmental factors could entirely explain these differences. No evidence was found for any sex-linked genetic or non-genetic transmissible factor. This hypothesis is tested in Table 4, 4). When t_M is set equal to t_F, there is a marginally significant decrease in the log likelihood ($\chi^2_1 = 3.6$, $0.1 > p > 0.05$), as compared with Table 4, 3). Thus we conclude that t_M and t_F are probably unequal. The fact that the t_F is lower than t_M in Table 4, 3) suggests that women may be more sensitive to environmental factors than men are.

In summary, we conclude that Model 3) is the most parsimonious formulation of the multifactorial model which fits the family distributions.

Up to this point, genetic and non-genetic transmissible factors have been treated as a single element and provide the parameters $t_M^2 = 0.74$ and $t_F^2 = 0.40$. This is the measure we sought: that is, the proportion of total phenotypic variance which can be explained by transmissible factors in males and females. Since t^2 is higher in males, we conclude that non-familial environmental factors have more impact on alcoholism in females.

Partitioning the transmissible factors into those that are genetic and those that are environmental requires observations of relatives who are reared apart. If an estimate of the correlation in liability to develop alcoholism of parents and offspring who have been separated at birth were available, then an estimate of the degree of genetic determination (h^2), the degree of cultural determination (b^2), and the interaction between them (w) could be made. Using the path model described in Figure 2 and equations (16) through (20), and using parameter values in Table 4, 3), the relative proportions of genetic and non-genetic transmissible variance were calculated for a wide variety of correlations between separated fathers and sons (r_{poad}). These proportions are displayed in Figure 3. Where the correlation on the curve is .00, i.e., when an adopted-away offspring is at no greater risk than a randomly sampled

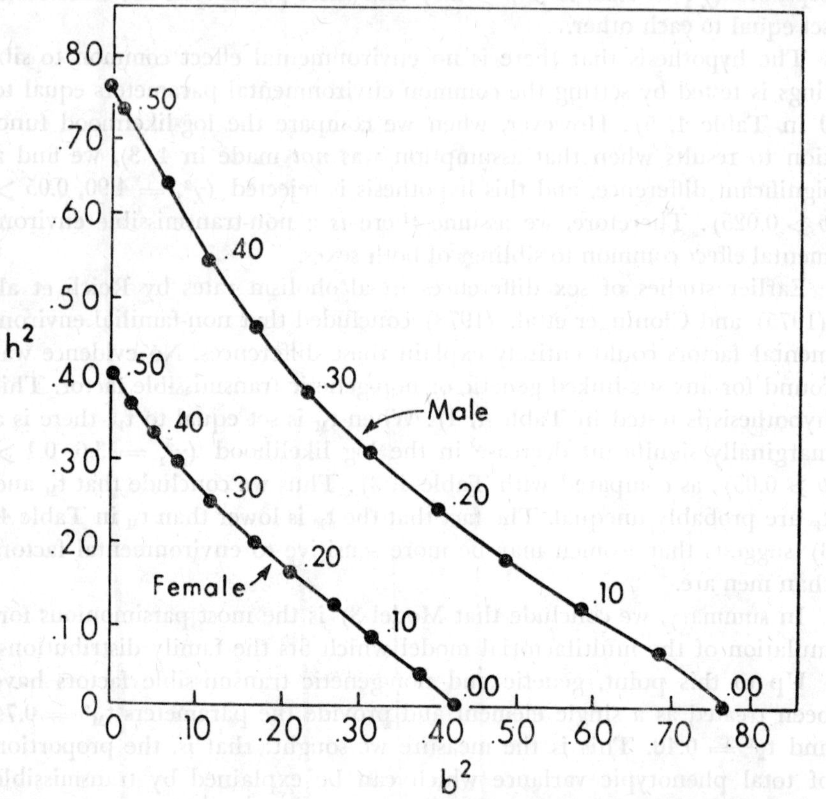

FIG 3. The proportion of the total variance due to genetic (h^2) and cultural (b^2) factors as function of the correlation in liability to develop alcoholism between alcoholic fathers and sons who have been adopted-away ($t^2_M = 0.74$, $t^2_F = 0.40$).

individual, transmission is entirely non-genetic (note b^2 is at its maximum and h^2 is 0). Where the correlation approaches .5, transmission is entirely due to genetic factors (h^2 approaches its maximum and b^2 is 0).

Goodwin et al. (1973) reported the lifetime prevalence of alcoholism as 18 percent in the adopted-away sons of Danish alcoholic fathers and contrasts this with an incidence of 5 percent in control adoption families. The correlation between the biological fathers and their adopted-away sons (r_{poad}) is 0.383 ± 0.11. Using this figure and those in Table 4, 3), the heritability of alcoholism is $h_M{}^2 = 0.51$ in males, and $h_F{}^2 = 0.29$ in females. The amount of variance explained by transmissible non-genetic factors is $b_M{}^2 = 0.13$ and $b_F{}^2 = 0.08$. The within person genic-cultural correlations are $w_M = 0.20$ and $w_F = 0.07$. The amount of phenotypic variance explained by within person genic-culture (2wbh) is 0.10 in males and 0.03 for females. Since Goodwin's study used different criteria for diagnosis and was done in Denmark, the comparability of the Danish and St. Louis data sets is uncertain. If we could assume his results would apply to adoptees from the same population that our sample comes from, we would conclude that both genetic and non-genetic factors are important in the transmission of alcoholism and that the importance of both types of transmissible factors is less for women.

EXTENSIONS OF THE MODEL

At present we are extending the path model presented here so that a wider range of hypotheses may be tested when a larger data set becomes available. In particular, we will see whether the contribution of parents who are separated from their families by divorce varies with the age of their offspring at the time of their separation. Since many of the families in which alcoholism occurs have been broken by divorce, an adequate sample should be available. In addition we plan to assess the influence of grandparents who have participated in child rearing.

We have assumed in this paper that the correlation between spouses (assortative mating) resulted from mutual selection of mates with similar liability distributions. The possibility that such an association is entirely due to non-familial random factors was tested and rejected. There are, however, many other reasonable formulations of assortative mating such as social homogamy or cultural association. Path models which involve the study of in-laws are being developed to allow us to separate assortative mating due to selection of similar mates from contagion after marriage.

Psychopathology such as alcoholism frequently leads to divorce, the children often being brought up by one parent with or without a step-parent. Since alcoholism frequently recurs in the second generation, disrupted family structure due to parental alcoholism may also become familial. In addition, divorce may be familial among non-alcoholics. If alcoholism should play a large role in explaining divorce risks, then a different equilibrium state would be reached after several generations of assortative mating and many of the parameters of the model would be different. We are exploring the impact systematic changes in family structure would have on the future familial distribution of complex genetic and non-genetic phenotypes such as alcoholism.

In this analysis individuals were diagnosed either as alcoholic or non-alcoholic. A great deal more could be learned if a quantitative scale for alcoholism correlated closely with the underlying liability distribution were available. Parameter estimates could then be made with greater precision, and more hypotheses could be tested. We are developing such a quantitative index and we shall extend our computer programs to include quantitative as well as diagnostic values.

DISCUSSION

Many different models have been developed to describe the familial distribution of common familial disorders. If more than one model is found to fit, then a search needs to be made for divergent predictions which can serve as critical experiments to distinguish between models. By application of these models to numerous data sets, enough evidence may be collected to support one mechanism in an unambiguous fashion. In comparing results across data sets, however, extreme caution must be used because the conclusions reached are local. That is, they are based on a particular data set at a particular time. Failures to replicate may therefore be the result of real differences between the two populations, rather than a disproof of the model.

Once a model has been selected, and its parameter estimates established, the next step is to attempt to measure non-genetic transmission, non-familial environmental effects, and genetic liability. Once these risk factors are specified, it will be possible to predict which individuals are more or less likely to transmit the disorder. In addition, the circumstances which may retard or accentuate transmission will be known. Our ability to accurately assess the risk for offspring's developing the disorder could then be greatly improved, with separate estimates for alternative environments.

Validating a hypothetical structure requires more than the illustration that the structure is a good description of the data. The hypothetical structure allows making predictions about the future composition of the population given prior observations, predictions which can be checked. If they are correct, the plausibility of the model is strengthened. For example, the conclusion suggested by the analysis of the familial distribution of alcoholism is that the observed sexual dimorphism is entirely explained by non-familial environmental factors such as adequate exposure to heavy drinking. The model predicts that women who drink as often and as heavily as men are equally likely to become alcoholic. According to this hypothesis, if sexual norms for permissible drinking behavior continue to converge, we should find male-female alcoholism rates also converging.

The methods outlined here allow the discovery and measurement of familial and non-familial environmental factors which influence the risk of alcoholism. Determining these factors may make experimental interference with disease transmission possible, and the success of that interference can be verified using traditional epidemiological techniques. Reducing the incidence of a disorder such as alcoholism in susceptible individuals in a controlled fashion would provide very strong support for the model which predicted this outcome.

SUMMARY AND CONCLUSIONS

A model for the transmission of a complex phenotype which includes both genetic and non-genetic transmissible elements is described. Segregation analysis and path analysis are used to estimate the parameters of the model and to test hypotheses. A family study of alcoholism is included as an example. Genetic and non-genetic transmissible factors are initially treated as a single element and the proportion of phenotypic variance attributable to transmissible factors is found to be 0.74 for males and 0.40 for females. The hypothesis that women are more susceptible to non-transmissible environmental factors is supported. Shared environments are found to increase the similarity between brothers to the same degree as between sisters or between opposite sexed pairs.

Data obtained in a Danish adoption study were integrated with data from a St. Louis sample to obtain a genetic heritability of alcoholism of 0.51 in males and 0.29 in females. The amount of variance explained by transmissible non-genetic factors is 0.13 in males and 0.08 in females. Finally, the within person genic-cultural correlations are 0.20 for males and 0.07 for females. Examining these data, we conclude that both genetic and non-genetic factors are important in the transmission of alcoholism and that the relative importance of both types of transmissible factors is less for women.

REFERENCES

Cavalli-Sforza, L. L. and Feldman, M. W.: Cultural versus biological inheritance: Phenotypic transmission from parents to children. (A theory of the effect of parental phenotypes on children's phenotypes). *Am. J. Hum. Genet.*, 25:618-637, 1973.

Chakraborty, R. and Schull, W. J.: Workshop on the genetics of common disease. Snowbird, Utah, 1978.

Cloninger, C. R., Christiansen, K., Reich, T., and Gottesman, I.: Implications of sex differences in the prevalences of antisocial personality, alcoholism, and criminality for familial transmission. *Arch. Gen. Psychiatry*, 35:941-951, 1978.

Cloninger, C. R., Rice, J., and Reich, T.: Multifactorial inheritance with cultural transmission and assortative mating. II. A general model of combined polygenic and cultural inheritance. *Am. J. Hum. Genet.*, 31:176-198, 1979.

CLONINGER, C. R., RICE, J., and REICH, T.: Multifactorial inheritance with cultural transmission and assortative mating. III. Family structure and the analysis of separation experiments. *Am. J. Hum. Genet.*, 31:366-368, 1979.

CLONINGER, C. R. Personal communication, 1978.

CURNOW, R. N. and SMITH, C.: Multifactorial models for familial diseases in man. *J. R. Statist. Soc.*, A, 138: 131-169, 1975.

ELANDT-JOHNSON, R. C.: *Probability Models and Statistical Methods in Genetics.* New York: Wiley, 1971.

ELSTON, R. C. and YELVERTON, K. C.: General models for segregation analysis. *Amer. J. Hum. Genet.*, 27:31-45, 1975.

FALCONER, D. S.: The inheritance of liability to certain diseases estimated from the incidence among relatives. *Ann. Hum. Genet.*, 29:51-76, 1965.

FALCONER, D. S.: The inheritance of liability to disease with variable age of onset with particular reference to diabetes mellitus. *Ann. Hum. Genet.*, 31:1-20, 1967.

FEIGHNER, J. P. et al.: Diagnostic criteria for use in psychiatric research. *Arch. Gen. Psychiat.*, 26:57-63, 1972.

FELDMAN, M. W. and CAVALLI-SFORZA, L. L.: Models of cultural inheritance: A general linear model. *Ann. Hum. Biol.*, 2:215-226, 1975.

GOODWIN, D. W., SCHULSINGER, F., HERMANSEN, L. et al.: Alcohol problems in adoptees raised apart from alcoholic parents. *Arch. Gen. Psychiat.*, 28:238-243, 1973.

KAPLAN, E. B. and ELSTON, R. C.: A subroutine package for maximum likelihood estimation (MAXLIK), Institute of Statistics Mimeo Series No. 823. Univ. of N.C., Chapel Hill, 1972.

KENDALL, M. G. and STUART, A.: *The Advanced Theory of Statistics*, Vol. 2: *Inference and Relationship*. New York: Hafner, 1973.

LI, C. C.: *Path Analysis—A Primer*. Pacific Grove, Ca.: The Boxwood Press, 1975.

MORTON, N. E.: Analysis of family resemblance. I. Introduction. *Am. J. Hum. Genet.*, 26:318-330, 1974.

NANCE, W.: A note on assortative mating and maternal effect. Workshop on the Genetics of Common Disease. Snowbird, Utah, 1978.

RAO, D. C., MORTON, N. E., and CLONINGER, C. R.: Path analysis under generalized assortative mating: Theory. *Genet. Res.*, 33:175-188, 1979.

RAO, D. C., MORTON, N. E., and YEE, S.: Resolution of cultural and biological inheritance by path analysis. *Am. J. Hum. Genet.*, 28:228-242, 1976.

RAO, D. C. and MORTON, N. E.: Path analysis of family resemblance in the presence of gene-environment interaction. *Am. J. Hum. Genet.*, 26:767-772, 1974.

REICH, T., JAMES, J. W., and MORRIS, C. A.: The use of multiple thresholds in determining the mode of transmission of semi-continuous traits. *Ann. Hum. Genet.*, 36:163-184, 1972.

REICH, T., CLONINGER, C. R., and GUZE, S. B.: The multifactorial model of disease transmission. I. Description of the model and its use in psychiatry. *Brit. J. Psychiat.*, 127:1-10, 1975.

REICH, T., WINOKUR, G., and MULLANEY, J.: The transmission of alcoholism. In: R. Fieve, D. Rosenthal, and H. Brill (Eds.), *Genetic Research in Psychiatry*, 1975.

REICH, T., RICE, J., CLONINGER, C. R., WETTE, R., and JAMES, J.: The use of multiple thresholds and segregation analysis in analyzing the phenotypic heterogeneity of multifactorial traits. *Ann. Hum. Genet.*, 42:371-390, 1979.

RICE, J., CLONINGER, C. R., and REICH, T.: Multifactorial inheritance with cultural transmission and assortative mating. I. Description and basic properties of the unitary models. *Am. J. Hum. Genet.*, 30:618-643, 1978.

RICE, J., REICH, T., CLONINGER, C. R., and WETTE, R.: An approximation to the multivariate normal integral: Its application to multifactorial qualitative traits. *Biometrics,* 35:451-459, 1979.

RICE, J., CLONINGER, C. R., and REICH, T.: General causal models for sex differences in the familial transmission of multifactorial traits: An application to human spatial visualizing ability. *Social Biology,* 1980, in press.

RICE, J., CLONINGER, C. R., and REICH, T.: The analysis of behavioral traits in the presence of cultural transmission and assortative mating: Applications to IQ and SES, *Behav. Genet.,* 1980, in press.

RICE, J., SUAREZ, B., CLONINGER, C. R., and REICH, T.: The application of segregation analysis and path analysis to multifactorial inheritance. I. Quantitative traits, 1980. In preparation.

SLATER, E. and COWIE, V.: *The Genetics of Mental Disorders.* London: Oxford University Press, 1974.

WINOKUR, G., REICH, T., RIMMER, J., and PITTS, F.: Alcoholism III. Diagnosis and familial psychiatric illness in 259 alcoholic probands. *Arch. Gen. Psychiat.,* 23:104-111, 1970.

WRIGHT, S.: On the nature of size factors. *Genetics,* 3:367-374, 1918.

8

Family Formation by Schizophrenics

L. ERLENMEYER-KIMLING, PH.D.,
ROBIN A. WUNSCH-HITZIG, M.A.
and
SERENA DEUTSCH, M.A.

For nearly 170 years, people have been asking questions about various aspects of family formation by the psychiatrically ill. As early as 1809, Phillipe Pinel reported statistics on the marital status of patients in a French mental hospital, and, somewhat later, other investigators followed suit with data on patients elsewhere in Europe and the United States. Although empirical data on reproductive rates were not collected before 1907, opinions about the fertility of the mentally ill were advanced long before then. Recall, for example, Benedict Morel's (1857) proposal that, while psychopathology intensified in each succeeding generation of families that he labeled "degenerate," fertility declined from generation to generation, until the family line eventually became extinct through biological sterility.

The opposite notion about the relationship between mental disorder and fertility began to prevail around the turn of the century. Higher, rather than lower, reproductive rates were attributed to psychiatrically disturbed persons and their relatives, compared to other members of society, and the early social Darwinists sounded alarms about possible dysgenic effects and sociocultural deterioration resulting from the overbreeding of the "insane."

In reality, the data from the more than 50 investigations that have been conducted on marriage and fertility of affected individuals support neither of these simplistic views. The research findings have never validated the claim that psychiatric patients produce an excess of offspring. Indeed, most of the studies have shown the reproductive rates of mentally ill persons to be below those of their general population peers, although biological infertility, which was postulated by Morel, turns out not to be the cause of the lowered reproductivity. To complicate matters, too, there are sizeable differences among diagnostic categories with respect to marriage and fertility rates, so that it is not appropriate to speak of figures for *the* mentally ill, but only for designated diagnostic groups.

Perhaps most important, however, it has become clear that reproductive differentials between patients and members of the general population are not static; in fact, they have changed substantially over the course of this century, at least for some diagnostic groups. Such changes are probably compounded of the same trends that have shaped the marriage and birth rates of the general population at various periods, together with the major social and medical innovations that have dramatically affected the lives of psychiatric patients and that have improved opportunities for marrying and establishing families.

Changes in the reproductive rates of psychiatric patients may be either of two kinds: a differential change in relation to the general population's reproductive rates or the same degree of change that is experienced by the general population, so that previously existing reproductive differentials between patients and their general population peers are maintained. Changes in the differential reproductive rates were long considered to have significant impact on the gene pool of succeeding generations, and early interest in the fertility of mentally ill persons arose primarily out of concerns about possible genetic and eugenic implications. It has gradually become clear, however, that any changes in the reproductive rates of psychiatric patients relative to those of the general population would have only minor genetic effects in the short run and would probably be too unstable to have important long-term effects.

At the same time, it has become evident that there are a number of aspects of family formation by mentally ill persons that may have social consequences other than those that concerned the earlier workers in this area. For example, it may be of considerable importance to know: how many individuals enter into a marriage or enduring sexual liaison with a former or prospective psychiatric patient; how many family units are formed by patients and what is the stability of these family units; how many children are born to and brought up by a disturbed parent; and how is the placement of the children handled when the family unit dissolves. The answers to such questions may provide pointers that are valuable in determining the service needs of the families of patients, as well as the needs of the patients themselves.

Our focus here is on schizophrenic* patients and the recent trends in their marriage, divorce, and reproductive rates that seem to indicate a need for greatly expanded services of several kinds for the various family members. The recent data show a substantially altered picture with respect to differentials that formerly existed between schizophrenics and the general population. We will begin with a summary of the general findings on several of the components of family formation in schizophrenic patients and will then consider the trends and some of their implications.

GENERAL FINDINGS

Marital Data

Despite the claim of the turn-of-the-century eugenicists that the mentally ill were producing more than their share of offspring, it could be easily seen from the investigations that began to be undertaken on psychiatric patients, and on schizophrenics especially, that they certainly were not as likely to marry as were the members of the general population. Data are now available from 21 investigations of schizophrenic patients from the 1920s to the 1970s (omitting the most recent study of reproducivity by Burr et al., 1979, for which marital data have not yet been reported). As Table 1 shows, virtually every one of these studies reported the proportion of schizophrenic patients who had ever married to be considerably lower than the proportion of individuals in the relevant general population who had married. In all of the patient samples where male-female comparisons were possible—except for the Berlin sample admitted around the turn of the century (Kallmann, 1938)—the marriage rates of the male schizophrenics were well below those of the female schizophrenics.

Several of the studies (Erlenmeyer-Kimling et al., 1969; Essen-Möller, 1935; Stevens, 1969) have demonstrated that the marriage rate of people who are going to become schizophrenic is well below the expected rate for same-aged members of the general population even before the illness becomes manifest, and that there is an even sharper curtailment in the number of marriages contracted after onset or first admission, as might be expected.

* We have accepted the diagnosis assigned by the investigators in the various studies.

TABLE 1

Marriage Rates of Schizophrenics as Percentage of Marriage Rates of General Population or Control Group

Investigators	Location	Period Studied	Schizophrenics' Marriage Rate as Percentage of Rate in General Population or Control Group				
			Males & Females	Males		Females	
Kallmann	Germany	1893-1902	< 100%		m = f		
Lindelius	Scandinavia	1900-10		25%		39%	
Essen-Möller	Germany	1904-27	< 100%		m < f		
Böök	Scandinavia	1902-49		31%		78%	
Gibbs	U.S.A.	1923	< 100%		m < f		
Brugger	Germany	1931	< 100%				
Nissen	Scandinavia	1932	< 100%				
Landis & Page	U.S.A.	1933		38%		57%	
Erlenmeyer-Kimling, et al.*	U.S.A.	1934-36		38%		78%	
Ødegaard	Scandinavia	1931-45	< 100%		m < f		
Ødegaard**	Scandinavia	1934-46		40%		49%	
Essen-Möller	Scandinavia	1947	< 100%				
Norris	England	1947-49	< 100%		m < f		
Ødegaard**	Scandinavia	1946-55	< 100%	35%		57%	
Farina et al.	U.S.A.	1949-54	< 100%		m < f		
Erlenmeyer-Kimling, et al.*	U.S.A.	1954-56		47%		82%	
Gregory	Canada	1954-58		35%		73%	
Slater et al.	England	1952-66	< 100%		m < f		
Stevens	England	1955-63				73%	
MacSorley	England	1958-60	< 100%				
McNeil & Kaij	Scandinavia	1958-60				60%	(process Sz)
						96%	(Sz-like)
Price	England	1965-66	< 100%		m < f		
El-Islam & El-Deeb	Egypt	1966		78%		85%	

* Sample from two time periods
** Sample from two time periods

Married patients have been found to have a higher rate of release from hospital, a shorter duration of hospitalization, and a lower return rate (Farina et al., 1963; Gittelman-Klein and Klein, 1968; Norris, 1956; Person, 1964; Stevens, 1969). While it has been suggested that the association between marriage and good prognosis might depend on various advantages, such as better home care, conferred by the married state, it is more likely that both prognosis and the probability of entering into marriage are related to other personal characteristics of the patient, including the diagnostic subtype of schizophrenia. Thus, poor premorbid adjustment and schizoid personality—which are not socially conducive to courtship and marriage and which lead to very much reduced marriage rates—also tend to be associated, possibly on biological grounds, with poor prognosis, while the reverse is true of good premorbid adjustment and nonschizoid personality (El-Islam and El-Deeb, 1968; Farina et al., 1963; Gittelman-Klein and Klein, 1968; Norris, 1956; Ødegaard, 1946; Stevens, 1969). A similar distinction apparently holds for hebephrenic and catatonic early onset patients versus paranoid, later onset patients (Kallmann, 1938).

Schizophrenics with lower IQ scores are also less likely to marry and more likely to have a poor prognosis than patients with higher IQ (Jones, 1973; Jones and Offord, 1975). Thus, there appears to be some degree of positive selection—whether in the social or the biological sense—for nonschizoid personality, IQ, and less severe forms of the disorder among schizophrenics who marry and who, therefore, are the most likely to become parents—the current "sexual revolution" notwithstanding.

Although the mean age at first marriage has been reported to be about the same for schizophrenics as for members of the general population (Goldfarb and Erlenmeyer-Kimling, 1962; Stevens, 1969), the average duration of the marriages contracted by schizophrenics has been found to be substantially less. For instance, in a survey of patients admitted to The Bethlem-Maudsley Hospitals in London (Slater et al., 1971), the mean number of years spent in the married state between ages 20 and 44 years was 7.5 and 12 years for schizophrenic males and females, respectively, contrasted with 18 and 20 years for general population males and females, respectively.

The shortened duration of the marriages of the schizophrenic patients is attributable to a greatly elevated rate of divorces and permanent separations. Psychiatric patients of all diagnostic categories, and schizophrenic patients in particular, appear to be more prone to marital breakdown than are their peers in the general population. For example, in a study of schizophrenic patients admitted to State hospital facilities throughout

New York in 1954-56 (Erlenmeyer-Kimling et al., 1969), 60 percent of the ever-married males and 40 percent of the ever-married females were found to be divorced or permanently separated by follow-up in 1962. In a sample of 68 women with process schizophrenia admitted to Östra Psychiatric Hospital in Mälmo, Sweden, between 1958 and 1960, 51 percent had terminated in divorce (McNeil and Kaij, 1974). In Egypt—a country of low divorce rates—among schizophrenics at a Cairo outpatient clinic, El-Islam and El-Deeb (1968) found that 19 percent of the ever-married males and 30 percent of the ever-married females had divorced, in contrast to 2 percent and 6 percent of ever-married males and females, respectively, in a sample of medical control cases. El-Islam and El-Deeb (1968) and Stevens (1969), in England, concluded that the excess of divorces and separations observed in schizophrenic patients occurs mainly in those cases with poor premorbid adjustment and schizoid personality who *do* manage to marry. Thus, patients with the least positive characteristics seem to have not only a greater likelihood of remaining unmarried but also an increased probability of having a marriage terminated by divorce or separation if they do marry.

Assortative Mating

Who marries people who are or are going to become mental patients? A number of studies have been concerned with the question of assortative mating, which is especially important to the understanding of morbidity risks in the offspring and to the evaluation of such risks in terms of genetic hypotheses. Several studies (Gregory, 1959; Hagnell and Kreitman, 1974; Hall et al., 1971; Kreitman, 1962; Nielsen, 1964; Penrose, 1944; Pond et al., 1963; Ryle and Hamilton, 1962) have indicated that the frequency of married pairs in which both partners are treated for mental problems at some time in their lives substantially exceeds the frequency expected on the basis of random or noncontingent admissions into treatment facilities. Concordance between the spouses for diagnosis or symptoms has been reported to be high in some studies, ranging between 29 percent and 64 percent (see Kreitman, 1968 for review). Most of these studies, however, include a wide range of mental problems of varying degrees of severity.

When the investigation is confined to schizophrenic patients only and to the search for schizophrenia in the spouses, there is much less evidence for concordance of diagnosis. Leistenschneider (1938) and Früh (1943) were unable to identify any spouses of schizophrenic patients who had a schizophrenic psychosis themselves, although 4 percent and 8 percent, respectively, of the spouses were considered by the investigators to be schizoid. Stevens (1969) and Reed et al. (1973) also obtained low rates of diagnostic concordance but reported that there was a significant increase in other types of diagnoses among the spouses of schizophrenics compared to chance expectations. In a study by Egger (1942) and in two large samples examined by Erlenmeyer-Kimling et al. (1966), however, the frequency of assortative mating specific to schizophrenia was found to be about 2 percent.

All of the foregoing studies used a criterion of psychiatric hospitalization or treatment on the part of the spouse. Fowler and Tsuang (1975), on the other hand, evaluated spouses on the basis of psychiatric interviews and found that 39 percent of the spouses of schizophrenics and 17 percent of the spouses of patients with affective disorders were classified as being psychiatrically disturbed. Diagnostic concordance was low in this study, too, with alcoholism and personality disorders accounting for 70 percent of the disturbed spouses. Psychiatric interviews were also used by Rosenthal (1974) to obtain diagnoses of spouses in the Danish research on adopted-away offspring of schizophrenic parents. One-third of the spouses of the schizophrenic parents received a diagnosis of schizophrenia spectrum disorder, and 22 percent received a diagnosis of psychopathic personality disorder. The interview approach evidently identifies a great deal of psychopathology in the spouses that would be overlooked if hospitalization or treatment were used as the sole criterion for mental disturbance. The data from the several studies combined indicate that, while marriages between two schizophrenics are relatively rare, the spouses of schizophrenics frequently have some kind of mental disturbance.

Fertility Computations

Although a number of investigators have reported on the fertility of schizophrenic patients, the data are difficult to pool because of major differences in methodology and in the treatment of the data. Some investigators, for example, have studied fertility rates in married patients only. Some have reported both illegitimate and legitimate children, but not in such a way that the figures can be combined for an overall estimate of reproduction. Similarly, pre- and post-hospitalization rates of reproduction are frequently presented separately in such a way that it is not possible for readers to compute cumulative figures.

It is unfortunate that many investigators have failed to appreciate the importance of calculating the total reproductivity of their probands for comparison with that of the general population. Total reproductivity is the child-per-person rate for all individuals—married and never-married combined—in the sample or population under study. Reports confined to marital fertility alone can be extremely misleading if the marriage rate of schizophrenic patients differs greatly from that of the general population. Total reproductivity is *the* rate needed to estimate contributions to the gene pool of the next generation and to plan for the needs of patients and their children.

Marital Fertility

Table 2 shows data from 11 studies in which the marital fertility of schizophrenic patients is reported for comparison with marital fertility rates in the general population. Schizophrenic patients, as a group, have had lower rates of reproduction than persons in the general population primarily because the marriage rate of the schizophrenics has been low. It is clear from the data on fertility within marriage that biological fertility is not diminished in schizophrenic individuals; while some of the investigators have found the marital fertility of the schizophrenics to be below that of the general population, other workers have noted no important differences. Most of the reduction in marital fertility that does occur is the result of a greatly decreased birth rate following onset and admission to a mental hospital, although Essen-Möller (1935, 1959) pointed out that in marriages contracted after onset, there is no diminution in family size.

Certain inconsistencies can be seen among the various studies. For example, fertility within marriage has sometimes been reported to be lower for male than for female schizophrenics (Kallmann, 1938; Ødegaard, 1960, for patients first admitted in 1936-45), sometimes to be higher for males than for females (Essen-Möller, 1935; Böök, 1953; Ødegaard, 1960, for patients first admitted in 1946-55), and sometimes to be the same for the two sexes (Goldfarb and Erlenmeyer-Kimling, 1962, for samples admitted in 1934-36 and in 1954-56; Slater et al., 1971). Similarly, childless marriages have sometimes been found to be more frequent among schizophrenics than in the general population (Kallmann, 1938; Garrone, 1962; MacSorley, 1964, for female, but not male, patients), and sometimes have been found not to differ (Goldfarb and Erlenmeyer-Kimling, 1962, for both time samples and both sexes). In Lindelius' (1970) study of Swedish patients first admitted in 1900-1910, there was actually a smaller percentage of childless marriages among preschizophrenic individuals than among their general population peers.

TABLE 2

Marital Fertility of Schizophrenics as Percentage of Marital Fertility of General Population or Control Group

Investigators	Period Studied	Fertility of Married Schizophrenics as Percentage of Fertility of Married General Population or Control Group: Males & Females	Males	Females	Childless Marriages: Schizophrenics/ General Population
Kallmann	1893-1902	100% (Paranoid)			
		50% (Hebephrenic & Catatonic)	m < f		> 100%
Lindelius	1900-10	94% (pre-onset)			
		80% (at follow-up)			
Essen-Möller	1904-27	100%	m > f		
Garrone	1901-50			50%	
Böök	1902-49	< 100%	m > f		
Goldfarb & Erlenmeyer-Kimling*	1934-36	100%	m = f		300%
Ødegaard**	1936-45	< 100%	m < f		
Ødegaard**	1946-55	100%	m > f		100%
Goldfarb & Erlenmeyer-Kimling*	1954-56	100%	m = f		
Slater et al.	1952-66	73%			
Stevens	1955-63			< 100%	100%
McNeil & Kaij	1958-60			< 100%	
El-Islam & El-Deeb	1966	< 100%			

* Sample from two time periods
** Sample from two time periods

While some of the discrepancies across studies may be attributable to relatively small sample sizes or to local social factors; other differences are possibly due to differences in the composition of the various samples. For instance, Essen-Möller (1935) and Kallmann (1938) observed that marital fertility was low in hebephrenic and catatonic patients but nearly normal in paranoid patients; since diagnostic subtypes have not been specified in most of the other investigations, it isn't possible to determine whether or not their proportions of paranoid and nonparanoid patients are similar. Stevens (1969) has pointed out that religion and social class are also important variables that affect comparisons of the marital fertility of schizophrenics with that of the general population. Differences in the composition of samples with respect to these variables could be responsible for some of the discrepancies among the studies.

Illegitimate Fertility

As is the case for marital fertility, the findings on out-of-wedlock births appear to be inconsistent across studies. German patients hospitalized between 1893 and 1902 (Kallmann, 1938) and between 1904 and 1927 (Essen-Möller, 1935) had low rates of illegitimacy compared to their relevant general populations even prior to onset, and then showed further reductions after onset. Böök (1953) found somewhat less illegitimate fertility among schizophrenic women than among normal controls in a North Swedish isolate population from 1902 to 1949, although the difference between the schizophrenic and normal women was not as great as in the earlier German studies. In Ødegaard's (1960) investigation of first admissions to psychiatric hospitals in Norway, the rate of illegitimate births among schizophrenic women compared to general population women was slightly reduced for first admissions during 1936-45 and was almost identical for first admissions in 1946-55 (4 percent versus 4.25 percent for schizophrenic and general population women, respectively). Erlenmeyer-Kimling (unpublished data) obtained similar results: illegitimacy was slightly lower for white schizophrenic women admitted to State hospitals in New York in 1934-36 and slightly higher for those admitted in 1954-56 in comparison with illegitimacy figures for the white general population in the same time periods.

Stevens (1969, 1970) reported exceptionally high illegitimate fertility in schizophrenic women hospitalized in London in 1955-63—12 percent of the unmarried patients had one or more illegitimate births before admission and 6 percent did so after admission, in contrast to an expectancy of about 2 percent in the general population. In part, the very high rate for the patients was attributable to the inclusion of Jamaican patients (with a 44 percent illegitimacy rate) in the sample, but even when the British white patients were considered alone, the percentage having an illegitimate child was 7 percent before admission and a further 3 percent after admission. McNeil and Kaij (1974) also found an elevated illegitimacy rate in schizophrenic women born after 1912 and admitted to a Swedish psychiatric hospital during 1958-60: 16 percent of all births to the schizophrenic women were illegitimate, compared to 10 percent of all births in the general population.

The progression of findings from the early studies to the more recent ones suggests that, as sexual freedom has expanded and the exposure of unmarried women to the risk of illegitimate conceptions has risen in Western societies, this risk may have been even further increased in schizophrenic women.

TABLE 3

Total Reproductivity of Schizophrenics as Percentage of Total Reproductivity of General Population or Control Group

Investigators	Period Studied	Reproductivity of Schizophrenics as Percentage of Reproductivity of General Population or Control Group: Males & Females	Males	Females
Lindelius	1900-10	37%		
Essen-Möller	1904-27	40%		
Böök	1902-49	70%	39%	105%
Erlenmeyer-Kimling, et al.*	1934-36			58% (at admission)
				46% (at follow-up)
Ødegaard**	1936-45		32%	44%
Ødegaard**	1946-55		39%	53%
Erlenmeyer-Kimling, et al.*	1954-56			70% (at admission)
				54% (at follow-up)
MacSorley	1958-60		39%	32%
McNeil & Kaij	1958-60			36%
El-Islam & El-Deeb	1966	57%	51%	36%
Burr	1976			100%

* Sample from two time periods
** Sample from two time periods

Total Reproductivity

As noted earlier, total reproductivity refers to the number of children ever-born per person. Table 3 presents the total reproductivity of schizophrenic patients as a percentage of the total reproductivity of the comparable general population as reported in, or calculated from, eight studies. Unfortunately, two of the larger studies of fertility in schizophrenia—those of Kallmann (1938) and Stevens (1969)—did not present data that would allow this comparison to be made. Stevens did not consider total reproductivity at all and did not combine her data on legitimate and illegitimate fertility or on pre- and post-admission fertility. It can be estimated, however, that the total reproductivity of the schizophrenic women was low compared to that of the general population.

Kallmann (1938) reported the total reproductivity of his schizophrenic probands but not of the general population. Nevertheless, it is clear that the hebephrenic and catatonic patients, with low rates of marriage and marital fertility, were greatly surpassed by the general population with respect to total reproductivity. The paranoid patients, however, probably had about the same overall reproductive rates as did members of the general population, because they exceeded the latter with respect to marriage rates (76 percent of the paranoid probands and 71 percent of the Berlin population were married) and had at least as high a marital fertility rate.

As can be seen in Table 3, in every study where direct comparisons have been made—except for the females in Böök's (1953) study—schizophrenic patients have been found to have child-per-person rates which are far below those of their psychiatrically normal peers. In Böök's investigation of schizophrenics and selected controls in a North-Swedish isolate population, the schizophrenic women had a higher rate of legitimate and illegitimate fertility than did the controls, did better than schizophrenics usually do with respect to marriage (viz., they had 78 percent as great a marriage rate as the controls), and accordingly achieved a slightly increased rate of total reproductivity compared to the controls. Schizophrenic men in that study showed a higher marital fertility rate than their controls (6.9 children per married schizophrenic male opposed to 4.7 per married control male) but lower illegitimate fertility and a vastly depressed marriage rate (25 percent versus 81 percent ever-married for schizophrenics and controls, respectively), so that their total reproductivity was low. El-Islam and El-Deeb's (1968) sample of outpatients in Cairo is the only one in which schizophrenic men have a higher rate of reproduction relative to normals than do schizophrenic women.

In a study of patients admitted to Bethlem and Maudsley Hospitals (London) during 1952 through 1966, Slater et al. (1971) calculated estimates of total reproductivity for schizophrenic women by age at admission in comparison with census data on women of the same age.

Women admitted at age 20 had 22 percent as many children as expected for their age, women admitted at 65 had 96 percent the expected reproductive rate compared to general population women of their age. Figures for other ages, between 25 and 55 years, ranged from 38 percent to 67 percent of expected reproductivity. Thus, the total reproductivity of the schizophrenic women was depressed below that of the general population regardless of age at admission, but approached parity as age of admission of the women increased.

TRENDS IN MARRIAGE AND FERTILITY RATES

There have been vast changes in the fertility rates and smaller changes in the marriage rates of most Western populations since the latter part of the last century. Essen-Möller (1935) pointed out some years ago that the marital and reproductive rates of individuals with psychiatric disorders must be evaluated over the course of time with reference to trends in the general population. His own data collected on patients admitted to a Münich institution between 1904 and 1924—a period in which the general population birth rate was falling sharply—showed that schizophrenic men had approximately the same rate of marital fertility as the rest of the population at the beginning of the period when fertility was high and failed to reduce their birth rate as rapidly as did the general population when the latter began to practice contraception. Schizophrenic women in Essen-Möller's study began with a lower rate of marital fertility than women in the general population, but, as the birth rate of the general population declined, it eventually approached that of the schizophrenic women. Thus, the net effect of the lowered fertility rates in the general population was to decrease the magnitude of the differential between schizophrenic and normal individuals. Kallmann (1938), examining both the schizophrenic and the normal relatives of his Berlin probands, also concluded that "schizophrenics have participated far less in the generally diminished birth rate than the average population" (p. 71).

A similar finding has been reported by Ødegaard (1960) who compared the relative reproduction (i.e., the total reproductivity of patients relative to that of the general population) of patients admitted to psychiatric hospitals in Norway during 1936-45 with that of patients admitted in 1946-55. Between the two periods, the marital fertility of the general population decreased, but the relative reproduction of the psychotics (all diagnoses combined) increased. Ødegaard noted that the "most likely explanation is that the patients have maintained their fer-

TABLE 4

Marriage and Fertility of Schizophrenic Probands at "Survey" Admission to New York State Hospitals in 1934-36 or 1954-56*

	Males		Females	
Number of probands	1934-36 (546)	1954-56 (383)	1934-36 (572)	1954-56 (398)
Marriage:				
% ever married	24.2	40.6	53.1	60.0
% childless marriage	28.7	24.1	34.2	26.1
Reproductivity:				
child/person	0.4	0.7	0.9	1.1
child/marriage	1.9	1.6	1.8	1.8
child/fertile marriage	2.6	2.2	2.7	2.5
% with one or more children	17.3	30.8	35.0	44.4

* Adapted from Erlenmeyer-Kimling, 1976

tility upon very much the same level, without following the decreasing trend in the general population" (1960, p. 29). It should be mentioned, however, that, unlike patients of all other diagnoses, schizophrenic and manic-depressive women did not show significant increases in their relative rates of reproduction from the earlier to the latter period.

With the introduction of drug therapy, the initiation of "open door" policies, and, subsequently, the move toward full-scale community care, mentally ill individuals in recent years have had increased opportunities for marriage and reproduction. Shearer et al. (1968), for example, reported an increase of 366 percent in the birth rate within state mental hospitals in Michigan over a 30-year period (i.e., 1935-64), an increase attributed to the open-door policy. In a study (Erlenmeyer-Kimling et al., 1966, 1969) comparing marriage and fertility in a sample of schizophrenic patients admitted to New York State hospitals in 1934-36 and a sample admitted in 1954-56, marriage rates were found to have increased substantially in the later sample, especially for males, as can be seen in Table 4. The time span under study was one of rising birth rates in the general population, in contrast to the investigations cited above. Table 4 shows that the schizophrenics actually experienced a decline in the average family size per fertile marriage, but the proportion of marriages remaining childless also declined. Most important, because of the increased percentage of probands who married in the 1954-56 sample, the total reproductivity of this group and the proportion of probands who became parents was considerably higher than for the 1934-36 sample. As noted earlier (see Table 3 and text), the total reproductivity of the 1954-56 schizophrenic women was 70 percent as high as that of the general population women while in the earlier period, the schizophrenic women had only 58 percent as large a total reproductivity rate as the general population. (Population figures are not available for men for comparison with the male schizophrenics.)

The reproductive gains made by the probands of the later sample were attributed by Erlenmeyer-Kimling et al. (1969) to the effect of shorter hospitalizations, increased community care and maintenance on drug therapy, and possibly to a more relaxed social climate in which the mentally ill suffer less stigma than formerly. Stevens (1969), too, concluded that fertility differentials between schizophrenics and members of the general population have lessened—and perhaps largely disappeared—with the spread of birth control and the impact of community care, although her own data did not actually document such a conclusion.

A recently completed study by Burr et al. (1979) also suggests that there has been a striking decrease in the reproductive differential that had been found earlier to exist between schizophrenics and the general population. In this study, the total reproductivity of women admitted to psychiatric services in a large public hospital in Atlanta, Georgia, during a six-month period in 1976 was found to be no different from the total reproductivity of Atlanta women who had participated in a household survey of fertility. The mean number of live births per woman aged 25-44 was 2.24 ± 1.86 for women of all psychiatric diagnoses combined and 2.62 ± 1.97 for the Atlanta survey women. Further, no differences were found among women in different diagnostic categories. Thus, the trend that was suggested by the comparison of the 1934-36 and 1954-56 samples of schizophrenic patients in New York State (Erlenmeyer-Kimling et al., 1966, 1969) now appears to have been borne out in the study of the Atlanta patients.

Data from an ongoing, prospective study of children of schizophrenic parents (Erlenmeyer-Kimling, 1970, 1975; Erlenmeyer-Kimling et al., 1979) point to further trends that have an impact on the families formed by schizophrenic patients. First, although earlier studies were consistent in showing that most of the births to schizophrenic patients occurred before first admission, the data from the current high-risk study show that of the 113 children born to 32 schizophrenic parents, 29 percent were born after first admission. The percentage of births after first admission is higher—32 percent—for the schizophrenic women than for the schizophrenic men, 24 percent. At least one child was born following hospitalization in 39 percent of the families of the schizophrenic women and in 44 percent of the families of the schizophrenic men.

Second, the frequency of unplanned births is high in this sample: 58 percent of the children are reported to have been unplanned births in the families in which a parent is schizophrenic, as compared to 39 percent in comparison families, in which neither parent has been treated for a psychiatric illness. The percentage of unplanned births is 61 percent in families of schizophrenic men and 56 percent in families of schizophrenic women. Burr et al. (1979) have reported much lower frequencies of unplanned or unwanted births in the recent Atlanta study: 39 percent of the pregnancies to schizophrenic women were unplanned or unwanted compared to 36 percent of the pregnancies of the Atlanta survey women. The figure for the Atlanta survey women is similar to that for the normal comparison families in the high-risk study, but the large discrepancy between the figures for the schizophrenic patients in the two studies remains to be explained. It should be noted that the Burr et al. (1979) sample contained 223 schizophrenic women, while our high-risk sample contains only 32 families with a schizophrenic parent.* On the other hand, data in the former study may have been obtained under conditions that were less conducive to discussion of confidential material than was the case in the high-risk study where family members were interviewed in their own homes.

Finally, the current divorce rate among the parents in our high-risk study is of some interest because the families were selected, at the start of the study in 1971, for a high degree of stability. One of the criteria for including a family in the study was that the marriage be intact, with both biological parents of the children living in the home. Yet, after seven years of follow-up, 31 percent of the families with one schizophrenic parent have undergone a divorce or permanent separation, in contrast to 5 percent of the comparison families with two psychiatrically normal parents. Thus, even in a sample that was deliberately biased toward marital stability, the marriages of the schizophrenic patients do not seem to endure.

SOME IMPLICATIONS OF THE RECENT TRENDS

The assembled data from the recent studies indicate: 1) that schizophrenic individuals are more likely to marry than they were in earlier periods; 2) that their marriages are likely to be broken by divorce or

---

* We have omitted here the families in which both parents are schizophrenic.

separation; 3) that they have fewer childless marriages than was formerly so; 4) that their total reproductive rate—or at least the reproductive rate of schizophrenic women—is now very similar to that of the general population, in contrast to the large differential that previously existed; 5) that a substantial proportion of the children are being born after first admission; and 6) that a sizeable proportion of the births before and after admission are unplanned.

We translate these findings to mean, first, that more people are involved in a potentially unsettled and unsettling marriage with a schizophrenic spouse than at any earlier period of time that has been studied. Of course, research by Fowler and Tsuang (1975) and by Rosenthal (1974) demonstrates that many of the spouses of the schizophrenic patients suffer from other types of psychiatric disorders themselves and may therefore contribute to the turbulence of the family unit. Second, the number of children who are experiencing the distress of living with one or two emotionally disturbed parents has increased. Furthermore, many of these children are unplanned and, possibly, unwanted, a fact that may exacerbate the poor interpersonal relationships that are usual in such families. Some 10 to 15 percent (Erlenmeyer-Kimling, 1977; Zerbin-Rüdin, 1967) of the children are expected to develop a schizophrenic psychosis in adolescence or adulthood as a product of interactions between a genetic predisposition and environmental stresses, but even those children who do not possess the genotype, and hence are unlikely to become schizophrenic, may bear lifetime scars from emotional traumas inflicted in the course of being brought up in a home with a mentally ill parent.

The recent trends with respect to family formation point to the need for at least three types of services that are currently not available in most mental health facilities. The first is family planning services for patients and their spouses. Abennethy and Grunebaum (1972) have previously emphasized that there is a place for family planning programs in psychiatric settings, and Burr et al. (1978) have recently reiterated this view. The data reviewed here on unplanned pregnancies and on the relatively high proportion of children born after first admission suggest that hospitals and clinics should introduce family planning services into the programs offered to schizophrenic patients. As Burr et al. (1979) have observed, these services should not be in any way coercive and should be individually tailored for the needs of each patient and his or her spouse and other family members.

The family planning services could impart information not only about contraception, in the tradition of such services, but also about the problems of parenthood in families of mental patients and some of the possible difficulties for children in these families. Such services should therefore provide a basis for informed decision-making on the part of the patient and spouse.

The second need is for coordinated supportive services for the spouses of the patients. There are evidently relatively more people who are marrying schizophrenics nowadays than in earlier years. The spouses are frequently confronted with the tensions of managing the home and breadwinning roles single-handedly, coping with the children's problems, and dealing with a sometimes disruptive patient. Very often the marriage does not last. The children usually go with the spouse of the patient (according to data from our high-risk study), so that the spouse's struggle to manage is apt to continue. Moreover, the spouse may feel guilty about "deserting" the patient because of the illness, so that counseling, as well as social, services are indicated. While a variety of services are available in many communities, they tend to be difficult to locate and to put together. Our experience with the families of schizophrenic patients in the course of the longitudinal high-risk study mentioned earlier suggests that the members of such families are especially inept at finding and utilizing services on their own and that they rarely receive much assistance from the patient's treatment facility. We propose that attention to the needs of the spouse and family is a legitimate part of the services to be offered by psychiatric clinics and hospitals. The role of the clinics and hospitals might be limited to an evaluation of the family problems created by the mental illness and coordination of referrals to appropriate services.

Lastly, the increasing number of children with one or two schizophrenic parents deserves special attention. In our high-risk study, we are observing that many of the children of schizophrenic parents begin to show serious emotional problems at quite young ages. Some of these may be early manifestations of schizophrenia, while others may be reflections of a disturbed home which can be expected to have a more benign outcome, particularly if the children receive attention at the right time. As is the case with the needs of spouses of patients, however, the needs of the children tend to fall between the cracks in the network of existing services. Again, we urge that the children of mentally ill parents might be greatly helped if their situation were routinely evaluated as a part of the psychiatric services provided to the patient and if a subsequent follow-through were offered to ensure that those children requiring services of any type actually came together with appropriate sources of assistance.

REFERENCES

ABENNETHY, V. D. and GRUNEBAUM, H.: Toward a family planning program in psychiatric hospitals. *Am. J. Pub. Health,* 62:1638-1640, 1972.

BÖÖK, J. A.: A genetic and neuropsychiatric investigation of a North-Swedish population with special regard to schizophrenia and mental deficiency. *Acta Genet.,* 4:1-139 and 315-414, 1953.

BRUGGER, C.: Versuch einer Geisteskrank-enzählung in Thüringen. *Z. ges. Neurol. Psychiat.,* 133:351, 1931.

BURR, W. A., FALEK, A., STRAUSS, L. T., and BROWN, S. B.: Fertility in schizophrenic outpatients. *Hos. Com. Psychiat.,* 30:527-531, 1979.

EGGER, H.: Zum Problem der Gattenwahl Schizophrenen. *Z. ges. Neurol. Psychiat.,* 174: 353-385, 1942.

EL-ISLAM, M. F. and EL-DEEB, H. A.: Marriage and fertility of psychotics. *Soc. Psychiat.,* 38:24-27, 1968.

ERLENMEYER-KIMLING, L.: A prospective study of children of schizophrenic parents. United States Public Health Service, Grant #MH 19560, 1970.

ERLENMEYER-KIMLING, L.: A prospective study of children at risk for schizophrenia: Methodological considerations and some preliminary findings. In: R. Wirt, G. Winokur, and M. Roff (Eds.), *Life History Research in Psychopathology,* Vol. 4. Minneapolis: University of Minnesota Press, 1975.

ERLENMEYER-KIMLING, L.: Schizophrenia: A bag of dilemmas. *Soc. Biol.,* 23:123-134, 1976.

ERLENMEYER-KIMLING, L.: Issues pertaining to prevention and intervention in genetic disorders affecting human behavior. In: G. W. Albee and J. M. Joffe (Eds.), *Primary Prevention in Psychopathology.* Hanover, N.H.: University Press of New England, 1977.

ERLENMEYER-KIMLING, L., CORNBLATT, B., and FLEISS, J.: High-risk research in schizophrenia. *Psychiatric Annals,* 9:79-102, 1979.

ERLENMEYER-KIMLING, L., NICOL, S., RAINER, J. D., and DEMING, W. E.: Changes in fertility rates of schizophrenic patients in New York State. *Am. J. Psychiat.,* 125: 916-927, 1969.

ERLENMEYER-KIMLING, L., RAINER, J. D., and KALLMANN, F. J.: Current reproductive trends in schizophrenia. In: P. H. Hoch and J. Zubin (Eds.), *Psychopathology of Schizophrenia.* New York: Grune & Stratton, 1966.

ESSEN-MÖLLER, E.: Untersuchungen über die Fruchbarkeit gewisser Gruppen von Geisteskranken. *Acta psychiat. neurol.* (Kbh), Suppl. 8, 1935.

ESSEN-MÖLLER, E.: Mating and fertility patterns in families with schizophrenia. *Eugen. Quart.,* 6:142-147, 1959.

FARINA, A., GARMEZY, N., and BARRY, III, H.: Relationship of marital status to incidence and prognosis of schizophrenia. *J. Abnorm. Soc. Psychol.,* 67:624-630, 1963.

FOWLER, R. C. and TSUANG, M.: Spouses of schizophrenics: A blind comparative study. *Comprehensive Psychiatry,* 16:339-342, 1975.

FRÜH, L.: Über die Belastung von Ehegatten Schizophrenen. *J. ges. Neurol. Psychiat.,* 174:353-396, 1943.

GARRONE, G.: Étude statistique et génétique de la schizophrénie à Genève de 1901 à 1950. *J. Génétique Humaine,* 11:91-219, 1962.

GIBBS, C. E.: Sex development and behavior in female patients with dementia praecox. *Arch. Neurol. Psychiat.,* 11:179-194, 1924.

GITTELMAN-KLEIN, R. and KLEIN, D. F.: Marital status as a prognostic indicator in schizophrenia. *J. Nerv. Ment. Dis.,* 147:289-296, 1968.

GOLDFARB, C. and ERLENMEYER-KIMLING, L.: Mating and fertility trends in schizophrenia. In: F. J. Kallmann, L. Erlenmeyer-Kimling, E. V. Glanville, and J. D.

Rainer (Eds.), *Expanding Goals of Genetics in Psychiatry*. New York: Grune & Stratton, 1962.

GREGORY, I.: Husbands and wives admitted to mental hospital. *J. Ment. Sci.*, 105:457-462, 1959.

HAGNELL, O. and KREITMAN, N.: Mental illness in married pairs in a total population. *Brit. J. Psychiat.*, 125:293-302, 1974.

HALL, D. J., BALDWIN, J. A., and ROBERTSON, N. C.: Mental illness in married pairs: Problems in estimating incidence. In: J. A. Baldwin (Ed.), *Aspects of the Epidemiology of Mental Illness*. Boston: Little, Brown & Co., 1971.

JONES, M. B.: I.Q. and fertility in schizophrenia. *Brit. J. Psychiat.*, 122:689-696, 1973.

JONES, M. B. and OFFORD, D. R.: Independent transmission of I.Q. and schizophrenia. *Brit. J. Psychiat.*, 126:185-190, 1975.

KALLMANN, F. J.: *The Genetics of Schizophrenia*. New York: J. J. Augustin, 1938.

KREITMAN, N.: Mental disorder in married couples. *J. Ment. Sci.*, 108:438-446, 1962.

KREITMAN, N.: Married couples admitted to mental hospital. *Brit. J. Psychiat.*, 114:699-708 and 709-718, 1968.

LANDIS, C. and PAGE, J. D.: *Modern Society and Mental Disease*. New York: Farrar & Rinehart, 1938.

LEISTENSCHNEIDER, P.: Beitrag zur Frage des Heiratskreises der Schizophrenen. *J. ges. Neurol. Psychiat.*, 1962:289-326, 1938.

LINDELIUS, R.: A study of schizophrenia. *Acta. psychiat. Scand. Suppl.*, 216, 1970.

MACSORLEY, K.: An investigation into the fertility rates of mentally ill patients. *Ann. Hum. Genet.*, 27:247-254, 1964.

MCNEIL, T. F. and KAIJ, L.: Rates of reproduction, illegitimate birth, marriage and divorce for hospitalized Swedish female psychiatric patients. Unpublished manuscript, 1974.

MOREL, B.: *Traité des dégénerscences physiques, intellectuelles et morales de l'espèce humaine*. Paris: Bailliere, 1857.

NIELSEN, J.: Mental disorders in married couples (Assortative mating). *Brit. J. Psychiat.*, 110:683-697, 1964.

NISSEN, A. J.: Om de schizophrenes fruktbarhetsforhold. *Nord. Med. Tidskr.*, 4:929, 1932.

NORRIS, V.: A statistical study of the influence of marriage on the hospital care of the mentally sick. *J. Ment. Sci.*, 102:467-486, 1956.

ØDEGAARD, O.: Marriage and mental disease: A study in social psychopathology. *J. Ment. Sci.*, 92:35-59, 1946.

ØDEGAARD, O.: Marriage rate and fertility in psychotic patients before hospital admission and after discharge. *Int. J. Soc. Psychiat.*, 6:25-33, 1960.

PENROSE, L.: Mental illness in husband and wife. *Psychiat., Quart. Suppl.*, 18:161-166, 1944.

PERSON, JR., P. H.: *Hospitalized Mental Patients and the Outcome of Hospitalization*. Washington, D.C.: U.S. Government Printing Office, 1964.

PINEL, P.: *Traité de l'Aliénation Mentale*, 2nd Edition. Paris: 1809.

POND, D. A., RULE, A., and HAMILTON, M.: Marriage and neurosis in a working-class population. *Brit. J. Psychiat.*, 109:592-598, 1963.

PRICE, J. S., SLATER, E., and HARE, E. H.: Marital status of final admissions to psychiatric beds in England and Wales in 1965 and 1966. *Soc. Biol.*, 18 *Suppl.* S74-94, 1971.

REED, S. C., HARTLEY, C., ANDERSON, V. E., PHILLIPS, V. P., and JOHNSON, N. A.: *The Psychoses: Family Studies*. Philadelphia: W. B. Saunders Co., 1973.

ROSENTHAL, D.: The concept of subschizophrenic disorders. In: S. A. Mednick, F. Schulsinger, J. Higgins, and B. Bell (Eds.), *Genetics, Environment and Psychopathology*. Amsterdam: North-Holland Publishing Co., 1974.

RYLE, A. and HAMILTON, M.: Neurosis in 50 married couples. *J. Ment. Sci.*, 108:265-273, 1962.

SHEARER, M. L., CAIN, A. C., FINCH, S. M., and DAVIDSON, R. T.: Unexpected effects of an "open door" policy on birth rates of women in state hospitals. *Am. J. Orthopsychiat.*, 38:413-417, 1968.

SLATER, E., HARE, E. H., and PRICE, J. S.: Marriage and fertility of psychiatric patients compared with national data. *Soc. Biol.*, 18 Suppl. S60-73, 1971.

STEVENS, B. C.: *Marriage and Fertility of Women Suffering from Schizophrenia or Affective Disorders.* Maudsley Monograph No. 19. London: Oxford University Press, 1969.

STEVENS, B. C.: Illegitimate fertility of psychotic women. *J. Biosoc. Sci.*, 2:17-30, 1970.

ZERBIN-RÜDIN, E.: Endogene Psychosen. In: P. E. Becker (Ed.), *Humangenetik. Ein kurzes Handbuch in fünf Bänden.* Stuttgart: George Thieme Verlag, 1967.

IV

THE CONSEQUENCES OF PSYCHIATRIC DISORDER FOR LIFE STRESS AND INTERPERSONAL RELATIONSHIPS

Introduction by Norman Kreitman, M.D.

The five papers in this group have overlapping areas of interest, but in general are so diverse that it would be simpler to consider each in turn.

Research into the social isolation of the elderly has been in progress for at least 30 years, but, as Professor Cooper and Dr. Sosna remind us, clear answers to the most basic questions are still not available. These authors usefully underline that the concept of isolation needs to be carefully defined and that in practice the term has at least three different usages. The first and simplest refers to the physical situation of an individual, particularly whether he lives alone. The second concerns the array of social interactions which he enjoys; these can be enumerated given a suitably sensitive instrument such as a detailed interview, with the implication that normative data should be collected with equal care and expense. The third variation represents the subjective satisfaction or distress of the individual with the quality and variety of the social transactions in which he engages, or, in Weiss' terms, his social provisions.

Cooper and Sosna report elegant work which is still at an early stage but it is to be hoped that they will eventually give us data on how these three variables are related not only to psychiatric illness but also to each other. How the correlations should be interpreted, however, is by no means obvious, the main problem being that subjective satisfaction may itself vary according to the presence or absence of symptoms. Thus, a family once viewed as caring and supportive may be seen by a respondent as harsh and unsympathetic after a depressive syndrome has developed, without there having been any detectable change in the behavior of the other family members. Issues of this kind arise in connection with other studies in the section, notably that by Professor Henderson, and will require some further comment.

The substantive data presented by Cooper and Sosna are very preliminary, and the authors point out that they have not included individuals identified in their survey as already in institutions and hospitals. Clearly these will require to be added before any general conclusions can be attempted. By the same token, the implications of their findings for the provision of care for the elderly, a topic modestly omitted from their discussion, can only be addressed once these more severely debilitated individuals have been included. It will be particularly fascinating to see if the Mannheim survey supports the conclusions of other researchers to the effect that the provision of care for the chronically disabled and the organically psychiatrically ill depends little upon the formal diagnosis and very much upon the level of social dependency which the individuals manifest.

The paper by Drs. Arey and Warheit is contentious, and might be considered to claim more than it demonstrates. They present a rather lengthy introduction covering a variety of only marginally related themes. These range from Freudian theories of childhood maturation to the impact of a sick member upon the mental health of the rest of the family. Nor is it easy to avoid being perplexed by statements that certain health problems may not be of "neurotic nature or magnitude" but may be situational and reactive. However, the substance of the communication is contained in the data. The authors demonstrate that respondents in a sample survey who reported having a psychologically disturbed member of the family had higher scores on anxiety and depression scales than those reporting that their families were all normal. They also show that this effect holds true within groups stratified by sex, race or socioeconomic status, and that having a number of sick family members appears to have a greater impact than having only one. Unfortunately, the design of the study does not permit anything to be said about just what these sick family members are like, but since personality disorders and minor neurotic symptoms are the commonest forms of psychiatric abnormality, presumably for the most part the respondents were talking about people they have difficulty getting on with. Moreover, respondents who are anxious or depressed may well ascribe their feelings to the behavior of others, and what could be more convenient than to label these others as sick?

A further tabulation illustrates the effect on the respondents of "having" a disturbed wife, child, sibling and so forth. It is contended that having a sick child poses especially difficult problems, but the figures quoted for depression and symptom scores for those reporting a disturbed sibling are only fractionally lower. Similarly, the data from parents attending child health centers do not on the face of it buttress the authors' arguments. It is amply established that there are vastly more disturbed children in the community than ever reach treatment facilities, and it would be no surprise to learn that a major determinant of declaration to agencies was parental depression and anxiety. In the community sample mothers who were particularly tense or gloomy may have been inclined to describe their children as problematic. Without data on the children themselves it is very difficult to draw any conclusions. Nevertheless, the general conclusion that the current fashion of community care for psychiatric patients imposes formidable psychological burdens upon families is one amply demonstrated by a growing body of research.

Professor Henderson and his colleagues present us with only a brief report of work in progress concerning the relation between an individual's social integration, the effect of life events or adversity, and the development of neurotic symptoms. The findings refer only to the cross-sectional data obtained at the beginning of what is planned as a protracted follow-up study.

Work on this general theme is preoccupying a number of researchers at the present time; one could almost speak of a life events industry. Lack of space precludes discussion of the many complex methodological issues that arise in enquiries of this kind, such as the difficulties of avoiding contamination of reports by individuals who are anxious or depressed at interview, and of distinguishing between the objective and subjective components of life events. There are, however, two points which might be noted in connection with Professor Henderson's study.

The first is that, according to the analysis so far, both adversity and social integration are independently associated with the presence of symptoms. This differs from the findings of other workers reporting that a lack of social support is essentially a potentiating factor in the face of adversity and of little consequence by itself. It would seem on the face of it that these two positions are quite clear-cut and should be susceptible to empirical testing. Unfortunately, now that issues of this kind have come to the fore it appears that the statistical models which might be used to test such hypotheses are much less obvious than one might have supposed. Workers are currently arguing not about the rival findings from different studies but as to how the results of a single investigation should properly be tested and interpreted. The nub of the problem appears to be that the term interaction means all things to all statisticians. The fault lies, however, not with the mathematicians but with ourselves. We are going to be required to specify in advance and in very much greater detail than has been the custom precisely what we mean by a vulnerability factor, or more generally, what we mean by saying one factor potentiates another. If we consider both A and B to carry risks for a particular disorder, do we expect a group of individuals exposed to both to show a rate of the disorder equivalent to the sum of the two risk factors? Or do we alternatively expect the rate to be the product of the risks? How do we handle situations where the two factors may act concordantly only at higher levels? What if none of the relationships are linear? Let us hope that we can find good answers to these good questions.

The second feature of the paper by Dr. Henderson and his colleagues is their statement that they have demonstrated associations rather than causality. This, alas, is a common enough situation in social enquiries, but they propose that a solution might be obtained to questions of causality by using serial interviews of the same sample over a period of several months. The outcome will be awaited with interest, but the design itself presupposes that each of the variables under question will have a distinct temporal course; in other words, events and changes in social integration will vary at different rates so that the precedence of one over the other can be demonstrated. This may or may not turn out to be the case, but, as the preacher says, let us pray.

The paper by the Dohrenwends is again concerned with the problem of teasing out directions of causality and of testing alternative models. They set up the problem by presenting a general paradigm of the relationships between external events, individual characteristics and ensuing psychological changes, pathological or otherwise. They further distinguish two main groups of events. The first approximates to the conditions of extreme situations such as battle combat and is represented by major loss events, physical illness or injury or severe disruption of social supports. It seems that the authors do not anticipate there being any great likelihood of people being exposed to independent events of lesser degree of severity than, say, being bombed. The reason for this supposition is not clear, especially as their data show that "objective" happenings, especially losses, occur in about a quarter of the population sample. The second group of behaviors could be reflections of a disturbed mental state. These are frequent and may be the kinds of happenings reported in the numerous research studies which have demonstrated an excess of recent life events among "patients" in comparison with controls.

They then proceed to discuss two hypotheses. The first is that individuals who are mentally ill or showing symptoms have been exposed to life events at a frequently greater than would have been expected from matched normal subjects. This they term the "proneness" hypothesis, and it is to be understood as increased exposure to events. They present data on a variety of types of events drawn from five separate samples and conclude that the frequency of events increases as one considers groups with increasing psychopathology, and secondly, that the steepest trends are found for those events which can be interpreted as due to the patient's own behavior. Their data are robust in the sense of producing the same general conclusions using alternative definitions of psychopathology and after controlling for educational status.

The conclusions drawn seem unexceptionable; psychopathology may be a consequence of stressful circumstances but it also carries with it an appreciable likelihood of illness-linked behaviors which lead the patient into further difficulties. The only ambiguity here—apart from technical problems which the authors themselves point out—may be that individuals located in certain kinds of social roles may be both more liable to develop illness and to generate, through custom or for other reasons, events which are clearly within their own agency, without these two phenomena being causally linked. This possibility the authors recognize at the outset, but prefer to omit from their discussion.

They then proceed to consider the hypothesis of vulnerability, by which is meant the likelihood of psychiatric breakdown given an undesirable life event. Here they draw on data from studies on the relapse of schizophrenics during a drug-placebo maintenance trial reported by Leff and others. Presumably, here one has to guard against the too-ready assumption that processes responsible for the recurrence of an illness also contribute to its etiology. Evidence from disorders as diverse as tuberculosis, parasuicide and, indeed, schizophrenia itself suggest that this may not always be the case.

The overall conclusions are that both proneness (in the special sense employed) and vulnerability are likely to be important factors but that the existing literature portraying the positive relationship between a number or magnitude of recent stressful life events and various types of pathology is difficult to interpret, since many of the events included in these studies could as easily be consequences of illness as causes. This point would bear underlining. Studies which fail to distinguish as sharply as possible between events which are outside the patient's control and those which probably or certainly are within it can only add to an area of confusion which is already dense enough, and the only remedy would be to set aside perhaps half the existent literature in this difficult area. Surely we should all have learned by now that unless control and outcome variables are so specified that no contamination occurs at the point of definition, no conclusions are possible.

Finally in this group, Dr. Muhangi presents a descriptive account of psychiatric disorders among African refugees. Besides drawing our attention to the political and psychological plight of many thousands of such individuals, the paper may also serve to remind us that migration studies could perhaps contribute to life event theory. The classical papers in the massive literature on migration were written before current awareness of the importance of distinguishing different types of events, a theme amply borne out in this volume. Maybe some of the old questions about the psychiatric consequences of migration could be tackled afresh using newer techniques.

9

Family Settings of the Psychiatrically Disturbed Aged

BRIAN COOPER, D.M.
and
UTE SOSNA

In this paper, no general description or analysis of the family situation of mentally ill old people will be attempted. Instead, we shall be concerned with the family setting only insofar as it bears on a particular issue—namely, to what extent mental disorders in the senium are associated with a reduced level of social contacts, or with inadequacies in the standards of social support and reinforcement which are maintained by means of such contacts.

These questions are central to the design and method of a study of old people in the city of Mannheim, West Germany, which is currently being undertaken as part of a special research program in psychiatric epidemiology, based at the Central Institute of Mental Health in that city (Häfner, 1978). The present chapter falls into two parts: first a short review of the research background, highlighting conceptual and methodological problems; secondly, a report of selected findings from the research program in Mannheim, including some preliminary data from the current field study.

SOCIAL ISOLATION, OLD AGE AND MENTAL DISORDER

Among the age-related characteristics found in association with mental disorders of late life, social isolation occupies a prominent position. It has been postulated as a central feature of the condition of old people in modern urban society (Parsons, 1942). Changes of social role in old age, marked by a reduction both in frequency of social contacts and in intensity of personal relationships, have been reported from a number of studies (Phillips, 1957; Blau, 1961; Tunstall, 1966). The general observation that with increasing age an individual tends to withdraw to some extent from the activities and social roles of his earlier life has been interpreted according to a number of different theories (Cumming & Henry, 1961; Havighurst et al., 1964; Welford & Birren, 1965). So far, research has left open the question as to how far social disengagement in late life should be seen as the result of a biological aging process, and how far it is imposed upon the elderly by artificial constraints in our society. The psychiatric significance of social isolation, whether developing in old age or forming part of a life-long pattern of adjustment, also remains largely unclear.

From the time of Durkheim (1951), such interrelated concepts as "anomie," "alienation" and "social isolation" have been postulated as determinants of suicide (Sainsbury, 1975). In the investigation of schizophrenia (Cooper, 1978) and of psychogeriatric disorders (Grad de Alarcon, 1971), clinical and statistical associations with isolation have been reported from many countries. In all empirical research in this field, however, the concept of isolation has proved difficult to define in operational terms. The definitions employed can be grouped into five main categories, which correspond to a number of different levels of analysis (Table 1).

1. *Urban Ecological Studies*

Up to now, most evidence in favour of a connection between social isolation and occurrence of mental illness in the elderly has come from

TABLE 1

Criteria of Social Isolation, at Different Levels of Analysis

Level of Analysis	Criteria of Social Isolation
Social interaction	1. Characteristics of local population (e.g. % of single-person households)
Psychological	2. Living alone
	3. Having few family and social contacts
Ecological	4. Emotional isolation (feeling lonely, neglected)
	5. Being cut off from group norms (alienation, "anomia")

ecological studies, in which isolation has been measured as a characteristic, not of individuals, but of urban areas. It was in this sense that Faris and Dunham (1939) used the concept to explain the observed distribution of schizophrenic psychoses in Chicago. They did not examine the rates for mental disorder in old age as a whole but, in discussing the distributions for senile and arteriosclerotic psychoses, pointed to the contrast, rather than the similarities, with that for schizophrenia—perhaps because they wished to emphasize a basic difference between organic and "functional" mental disorders. Actually, the distributions were not so dissimilar, as Table 2 illustrates for schizophrenia and senile psychoses. However, both distributions were more obviously related to socio-economic characteristics of the urban areas concerned than to isolation as a variable.

Whereas most subsequent ecological surveys have tended to confirm Faris and Dunham's findings for schizophrenia, the distributions reported for senile and arteriosclerotic psychoses have been less consistent, and permit of no firm conclusions (Gruenberg, 1954; Hare, 1956; Hardt, 1959; Levy & Rowitz, 1970; Reimann & Häfner, 1972). Moreover, very little information is provided by these studies as to the distribution of depressive and other "functional" syndromes in old age.

2. *Household- and Living-group*

In ecological research, demographic variables, such as the proportion of single-person households, or of widowed and divorced persons, in in-

TABLE 2

Area Rates for Schizophrenia and Senile Psychoses, Chicago, 1922-34

Type of Area	Schizophrenia*	Senile Psychoses**
1. Single home $50+	20.7 (1)	32.9 (3)
2. Single home $50—	26.4 (3)	30.3 (1)
3. Two-flat $50+	26.9 (4)	35.6 (5)
4. Two-flat $50—	32.5 (6)	43.9 (7)
5. Apartments (native-born)	23.4 (2)	36.0 (6)
6. Hotels, etc.	27.1 (5)	33.0 (4)
7. Apartments & two-flat	38.4 (7)	46.6 (8)
8. Apartment (foreign-born)	44.6 (8)	31.8 (2)
9. Apartment (negroes)	50.4 (9)	106.8 (11)
10. Tenements	54.9 (10)	66.9 (9)
11. Rooming houses	93.3 (11)	104.3 (10)

Source: Faris & Dunham (1939)
* Rate per 100,000 population
** Rate per 100,000 over 65

dividual wards or city districts must be employed as indices of social isolation. The appropriateness of household type as an indicator of social isolation has been confirmed by direct investigations of samples of old persons: those who live alone are at increased risk for social isolation. Tunstall (1966), in a survey of four areas in England, found that 68 percent of old people living alone could be categorized as isolated according to his criteria, which were based on frequency of family and other social contacts. The proportion of all old people in the survey who were isolated according to these criteria amounted to only 22 percent, so that the association between living alone and being isolated appeared to be very strong.

In a comparative study in three countries—Denmark, England and the United States (Townsend & Tunstall, 1968)—the proportion of old persons living alone who complained of loneliness ranged from 73 percent to 88 percent among men and from 68 percent to 74 percent among women. The corresponding proportions of those living with marital partners or children, who complained of loneliness, were very much lower and in no country above 20 percent. Whether defined by subjective or objective criteria, therefore, social isolation in late life does appear to be largely characteristic of old people living alone.

The psychiatric significance of such findings has still to be established. Undoubtedly, psychiatric hospital admission rates, as well as total inpatient rates, for the elderly are higher among single, widowed and divorced persons than among the married. Investigations in a number of countries have shown that those who live alone have increased psychiatric admission rates, and are overrepresented among residents of geriatric homes—a group with high mental illness rates. These findings could, however, be due to a selective process of referral and admission to institutions. There is no firm evidence that the true incidence or prevalence of mental disorder is increased among old people who live alone. On this point, findings of field studies are inconclusive. Nielsen (1963), in a survey of the Danish island of Samsø, found a non-significant trend towards lower psychiatric rates among married old people, and higher rates among the widowed and single; however, those living alone did not show any increased prevalence. Roth and his co-workers, in their Newcastle survey (Kay, Beamish & Roth, 1964), also failed to discover any connection between psychiatric prevalence and type of family setting. They pointed out that, in a cross-sectional field survey, many old people who have been taken into geriatric wards or nursing homes outside the survey area may be missed, and that this could result in serious bias. On the other hand, both Bellin and Hardt (1958) in Syracuse and Lowenthal and Berkman (1967) in San Francisco reported markedly higher rates of psychiatric impairment among the widowed and single than among the married groups in their community samples.

3. *Frequency of Family and Social Contacts*

Living alone is an imperfect criterion of isolation. In Tunstall's study, for example, one-third of the "living alone" group could not be classed as isolated. Many old people living alone are members of extended family groups or social networks, which provide them with regular opportunities for personal contact. Attempts have been made to measure social isolation more precisely, in terms of frequency of person-to-person contacts made in a defined time period. Isolation then becomes a relative concept, which can be reduced to a dichotomy by means of a fixed cutting score on a scale representing frequency.

The best-known example of this type of approach in psychiatry is the San Francisco study of Lowenthal and her co-workers (Lowenthal, 1964, 1965). Members of a community sample of 600 elderly persons were first assigned to three groups, according to their reported patterns of social contact, termed respectively "isolates," "reactors," and "intermediates." The true isolates proved to be a small group, amounting to only 5 percent of the sample, who did not display any excess of psychiatric morbidity. Frequency of mental disorder was actually highest in the large intermediate group, which presumably included many persons with milder degrees of isolation. That this was indeed the case may be inferred from a subsequent analysis of the data, in which the sample as a whole was divided into two sub-groups: those judged to be "deprived," in terms of social activities, and the rest (Lowenthal & Berkman, 1967). The deprived group showed a much higher rate of psychiatric impairment than the remainder. Broadly speaking, therefore, the survey findings indicated a positive association between psychiatric prevalence and mild, though not severe, forms of isolation.

4. *Subjective Aspects of Isolation*

In the studies so far discussed, social isolation was defined, explicitly or implicitly, as an objectively verifiable lack of family and social contacts. This type of definition could leave important qualitative aspects out of the reckoning (Lowenthal & Haven, 1968; Bungard, 1975). Subjective isolation, growing out of a sense of loneliness and neglect, may be only partially correlated with objective isolation. Moreover, there is a risk of confusing isolation regarded as a *condition,* observed at one point in time, with isolation viewed as a *process,* which develops over the years and may in part represent an underlying inability of the individual to make or to maintain adequate, lasting relationships. Lowenthal (1964) found that the so-called "pure isolates" in her survey—persons with a longstanding pattern of very infrequent social contacts—did not complain of loneliness and did not appear to carry any increased risk of becoming mentally ill. She concluded that:

> While such an alienated life-style might in itself be culturally defined as a form of mental illness, lack of interpersonal relationships, which is one of its main characteristics, may help to prevent the development of overt psychogenic disorder (or to prevent its detection if it does develop).

The San Francisco findings were broadly consistent with those of Sheldon (1948) in Wolverhampton and Roth and his co-workers in Newcastle (Kay et al., 1964); all three surveys indicated that lack of social contacts in old age is frequently one expression of a form of adaptation which relates to personality factors, and that supervening mental illness should then be regarded as a product of the individual's personality and life-style, rather than of his current social environment. These findings underline the need to investigate the role of loneliness and emotional isolation, independently of the frequency of social contacts.

5. *Alienation and "Anomia"*

Finally, a number of workers, notably Dean (1961) and Seeman (1959), have employed the term social isolation in the rather different sense of alienation from cultural or group norms. This concept is closely linked to Durkheim's notion of "anomie" which, according to DeGrazia (1948) includes: "A painful uneasiness or anxiety, a feeling of separation from the group or of isolation from group standards, and a feeling of pointlessness, or that no certain goal exists."

Although most sociologists regard anomie as a feature of the social system, which must be measured in terms of collectives, it seems clear that a social condition of this kind must be reflected in individual perceptions, attitudes and modes of behavior. These personal characteristics, which were grouped by Srole (1956) under the generic label of "psychological anomie," or "anomia," may serve as links in a causal chain connecting the nature of the social environment, and the individual's roles in society, to the emergence of mental disorder. Thus, feelings of helplessness, futility and separation, generated or reinforced by social isolation, may form a matrix in which depressive illness can develop.

Plausible though the hypothesis may be, there appears as yet to be no evidence that Srole's concept of anomia is of heuristic value in psychiatric research. Leighton and his associates discussed the question briefly in their reports on the Stirling County Study (Hughes et al., 1960; Leighton et al., 1963), but could reach no conclusion on the basis of their own survey data. We have not found any work dealing with the possible relevance of anomia to mental disorders in the elderly, the group which one might expect, *a priori*, to be most closely affected.

This short review suggests that the concept of social isolation, as employed in psychiatric research, is still rather poorly defined and of uncertain significance. The correct strategy in empirical research, therefore, must be to try to measure different aspects independently of one another and to test their correlations with one another, as well as with the dependent variable of illness.

FAMILY SETTINGS OF MENTALLY ILL OLD PEOPLE IN MANNHEIM

1. *Psychiatric Inpatients*

The immediate background to the current field study in Mannheim is provided by two sets of data, taken from other epidemiological research projects carried out from the Central Institute of Mental Health. The first derive from the Psychiatric Case Register, which systematically monitors all contacts made by Mannheim residents with psychiatric inpatient or outpatient services. Table 3 shows the distribution of psychiatric inpatients over 65, by marital status, on a given day in 1977. In comparison to the general population of the city in this age-range, there is a marked excess of single and widowed persons over the married.

TABLE 3

Marital Status of Mannheim Psychiatric Inpatients Over 65, Compared with Base Population

Marital Status	Psychiatric Inpatients, Over 65 %	Mannheim Population, Over 65 %
Single	14.9	7.6
Married	32.2	47.8
Widowed	47.9	40.1
Divorced	5.0	4.5
Total	100.0	100.0
No. of persons	121	50,217

In this respect, the Mannheim data correspond well with those reported from many other cities and countries. It may be remarked that the number of psychiatric inpatients is low for a city with over 300,000 inhabitants, corresponding to only 0.4 per 1,000 total population, or 2.6 per 1,000 over 65 years. The hint of an explanation is to be found in Table 4, which shows the distribution of psychogeriatric inpatients according to type of living group at admission. Many have come from old people's homes or nursing homes, and it seems clear that such institutions must contain a high proportion of all the mentally ill old people who are in residential care. The Table also reveals a marked excess of persons from single-person households.

TABLE 4

Psychiatric Inpatients, Over 65 Years
(Mannheim Case Register, 15.01.77)

Type of Living Group	Male	Female	Both Sexes
	%	%	%
Private household, living alone	17.5	55.7	42.9
Private household, living in group	42.5	32.9	36.1
Living in institution or hostel	40.0	11.4	21.0
Total	100.0	100.0	100.0
No. of patients	40	79	119
Unknown	5	8	13

2. *Patients Consulting in General Practice*

The second set of data is taken from a recent survey of psychiatric illness in general medical practice in Mannheim (Zintl-Wiegand et al., 1978; Zintl-Wiegand & Cooper, 1979). A sample was drawn from the patients who consulted during a two-week period in each of 13 Mannheim practices. All patients in the sample were interviewed, during normal consulting hours, by two psychiatrists using a semi-structured clinical interview. Of a total of 1,026 interviewed patients, 30.4 percent were over the age of 65. Table 5 summarizes the distribution of the sample, by marital status and by psychiatric status.

Widowed persons are overrepresented and married persons underrepresented among the psychiatrically ill group. To this extent, the general practice sample conforms in its distribution to that of the inpatient sample illustrated in Table 3. However, deviation from the general population is much less pronounced than in the inpatient sample, especially as

TABLE 5

Mannheim General Practice Sample,
Patients Over 65

Marital Status	Psychiatric Illness (Cases)	No Psychiatric Illness (Normals)
	%	%
Single	6.5	8.8
Married	41.6	48.3
Widowed	49.1	37.6
Divorced	2.8	5.4
Total	100.0	100.0
No. of patients	108	204
Unknown	—	—

regards the proportion of single persons. The well-marked gradient across all three groups, in the ratio of married persons to other categories, suggests that rates of specialist referral and hospital admission among the elderly mentally ill vary with marital status.

Corresponding differences between mentally ill and other patients in the general practice sample were found in respect of the type of living group, as can be seen from Table 6.

TABLE 6

Mannheim General Practice Sample,
Patients Over 65

Type of Living Group	Psychiatric Illness (Cases)	No Psychiatric Illness (Normals)
	%	%
Living alone	44.4	32.4
Living in household groups	54.6	64.7
Living in institution or home	1.0	2.9
Total	100.0	100.0
No. of patients	108	204
Unknown	—	1

While Table 6 reveals an excess among the mentally ill group of persons living alone, the distribution is much less skewed than that for psychiatric inpatients, shown in Table 4, largely because residents of old people's homes and nursing homes do not figure prominently in the general practice samples; indeed, they are underrepresented.

Taken in conjunction, these two sets of data suggest that the main influence of family setting relates not to frequency of morbidity, but rather to the probability of hospital referral, admission and retention, and that investigation of a community sample would reveal at most only weak associations between family setting and frequency of mental illness.

3. *A Field Survey Sample*

The current field study of old people in Mannheim has been designed in part to permit a more detailed analysis of this problem, by systematic assessment of the various aspects of social isolation. In all, a stratified sample of 500-600 old people will be investigated. To permit estimation of rates for individual wards of Mannheim, the survey is being restricted to a small number of these wards, each with a sample-size adequate for at least simple statistical analyses. Three central wards and four on the city periphery have been selected, providing a total elderly population of 11,000. The proportion of single-person households is relatively high in the central wards and relatively low in the suburbs. In addition, the central wards can be subdivided into two groups of roughly equal size, one characterized by high, and one by low, socioeconomic status.

All members of the survey sample in these seven contrasting districts of Mannheim are investigated with the help of two semistructured interviews. The first is undertaken by a medical research worker with psychiatric training. The main aim is to ascertain whether or not a psychiatric disorder is present, according to the operational criteria employed. The interview is based on a standard schedule, which generates a series of 23 clinical ratings of psychiatric symptoms and observed abnormalities, each on a 5-point scale, together with an over-all clinical severity rating. In addition, the interviewer checks systematically for any physical or sensory handicaps and also rates the person's capacity for self-care and any general disability. The interview procedure has been modified for this psychogeriatric project from one used in a number of earlier studies (Goldberg et al., 1970; Cooper, 1972; Cooper et al., 1975; Zintl-Wiegand & Cooper, 1978). It is known to be highly reliable when used by psychiatrists trained in its use.

The social interview is also based on a semistructured schedule, the Interview for Measurement of Social Isolation (IMSI), which was constructed specially for use in this project. This instrument has been based on consideration of the various aspects of social isolation, previously discussed. Its structure is shown schematically in Table 7.

At the first, ecological level of analysis, we rely upon published statistical data for the districts of Mannheim, together with special extractions from the current register of inhabitants. All other relevant information must be obtained at interview. Information on social and family contacts is gathered by means of detailed questioning about the period of seven days immediately preceding interview. The scoring system is taken, with some modifications, from that used by Tunstall (1966).

In investigating the subjective aspects of isolation, two scales are used. The first of these was developed *ad hoc* for the survey, and is a measure of the extent to which an individual's family and social contacts fulfill his basic psychological needs for sharing, support and reassurance of worth.*

TABLE 7

Operational Measures of Social Isolation

Level of Analysis	Isolation Index		Operational Criteria
Ecological (collective)	I	objective	1. % single-person household
Social Interaction (individual)	II	↓	2. Household group
			3. Frequency of contacts
Psychological (individual)	III		4. Rating of support from social contacts (*ad hoc* scale)
	IV	subjective	5. Social isolation subscale from Dean's Alienation Scale

The second scale is a translation of part of a standardized attitudinal measure: the subscale "social isolation" from Dean's Alienation Scale (1961).

Finally, the interview includes a battery of questions on occupation or previous occupation, educational level, income and housing conditions, designed to enable the social class and socio-economic status of each proband to be assessed as accurately as possible.

PRELIMINARY FINDINGS

We have recently carried out a preliminary analysis of data collected in the first three survey wards. Of 206 sample members confirmed as being resident during the survey, 15 were in hospitals or old people's homes, and have not yet been investigated; 34 definitely refused to be

* Since constructing this scale, we have learned that its items correspond quite closely to the list of "provisions of social relationships" described by Weiss (1974), and to the framework of a structured questionnaire on social bonds developed by Henderson and his co-workers in Canberra (Henderson et al., 1978).

interviewed, or have persistently avoided any contact. The following report is based on 157 completed investigations.

The proportion diagnosed as having a psychiatric disorder, according to the survey criteria, is 26.8 percent, a figure which corresponds closely to the estimates made by Sheldon (1948) and by the Newcastle group (Kay, Beamish & Roth, 1964) in England, as well as by Essen-Möller et al. (1956) in Sweden. The psychiatric group was characterized by a high frequency of associated physical ill health and handicaps, 55 percent being rated as moderately or severely disabled, in contrast to only 11 percent of the remaining probands. The group as a whole comprised two main diagnostic categories with widely differing features. Organic psychosyndromes, associated with cognitive disorders, were found in 12.1 percent of the sample, mostly in persons over 75. Functional mental disorders, with predominantly affective and neurotic symptoms, were present in 14.7 percent. The distribution by psychiatric status and by marital status is shown in Table 8.

TABLE 8

Field Study Sample, Psychiatric Status by Marital Status

Marital Status	Psychiatric Cases %	Normals %
Single	4.8	10.4
Married	40.0	39.1
Widowed	52.4	47.8
Divorced	2.4	2.6
Total	100.0	100.0
No. of persons	42	115

No significant difference was found, in respect of marital status distribution, between the mentally ill and normal groups. (The distribution for the mentally ill group as a whole approximated to that for the corresponding group of general practice patients, shown in Table 5.) Within the mentally ill group, however, the distribution differed markedly between organic and functional syndromes: 69 percent of those with organic mental disorders were widowed, compared with only 39 percent of those with functional mental disorders. The differences were clearly related to the age-structures of the two diagnostic categories.

Similar findings appeared with respect to the types of living group to

TABLE 9

Field Study Sample, Psychiatric Status by Living Situation

Living situation	Psychiatric Cases Organic %	Functional %	Mentally Normal %
Living alone	15.8	43.5	36.5
Living in group	84.2	56.5	63.5
Total	100.0	100.0	100.0
No. of persons	19	23	115

which the old people belonged. Here again, no over-all difference was detected between the mentally ill and normal groups; yet within the mentally ill group, those with organic syndromes differed from those with functional disorders. The point is illustrated by Table 9.

Only 15.87 percent of the "organic" subgroup were living alone, compared with 43.5 percent of the "functional" group. Among persons living in household groups, the majority of those who had organic mental disorders were widowed and lived with sons, daughters or other relatives, whereas most of those suffering from functional disorders were living with their spouses.

The next step in the analysis was to examine the relationship between corresponding mental disorders and frequency of social contact. In Table 10, social contact scores have been allocated to three subgroups, representing degrees of social isolation. It appears that, while the mentally ill group as a whole was *not* characterized by social isolation, milder forms of isolation were present in excess among the old persons with functional mental disorders.

A similar analysis was carried out on the psychological indices of social isolation. The distribution of scores indicated that very few of the probands with organic syndromes were suffering from a lack of sharing, support or reassurance of worth. While the problems of assessment involved in applying such measures to persons with dementing conditions are obvious enough, these initial findings strongly suggested that such conditions will be found relatively seldom in co-existence with social isolation among old people living in private households. It may be inferred that such a combination of biological and social handicaps is so disabling that a high proportion of the affected persons are admitted to institutions at an early stage of the morbid process: a point which will be explored in the further course of the present investigation.

TABLE 10

Field Study Sample: Psychiatric Status by Frequency of Social Contact

Social Contact Score	Organic Psycho-syndromes	Functional Psychiatric Illness	Mentally Normal
	%	%	%
0-9 (severe isolation)	5.3	8.7	8.6
10-24 (mild isolation)	10.5	43.5	21.7
25+ (no isolation)	84.2	47.8	69.7
Total	100.0	100.0	100.0
No. of persons	19	23	115

Scores for sharing, support and reassurance of worth were on average lower among persons with functional mental disorders than among the mentally normal group (39 percent vs. 22 percent having total scores below a fixed cutting-score for "isolation"). This difference appeared to derive chiefly from a predominance in the functionally mentally ill group of those depending on a single significant other person, whereas the mentally normal group tended to have close relationships with more persons, including some outside the household.

The pattern of scores on the subscale of Dean's Alienation Scale differed from that found with other indices of social isolation. Here, the mentally ill group as a whole manifested a higher frequency of high scores for isolation than did the mentally normal group, and this excess of high scores was found equally among the organically and functionally ill subgroups. Since, however, one-quarter of the "organic" group had been unable to answer the questions and, in general, the validity of this type of measure when applied to persons with severe cognitive impairment is dubious, the findings are difficult to interpret.

Finally, brief mention should be made of the current situation as regards medical and social care of this elderly population. Of 42 mentally ill persons so far identified, none was under psychiatric treatment or supervision at the time of interview, and in only two instances were earlier episodes of psychiatric treatment reported. After allowance for underreporting, it still seems evident that we are dealing here with a section of the population who make few demands on psychiatric services, until or unless admission to a hospital or other institution becomes unavoidable. The contribution of social services to the care of this group also appeared to be small, only 10 persons (6.4 percent) reporting any visits by social workers or community nurses.

A very different picture was obtained with regard to general medical care: 78 percent of the sample had consulted a general practitioner within the three months prior to interview and, in addition, 39 percent had consulted non-psychiatric medical specialists of various kinds, mostly in office practice, during the same period.

DISCUSSION

This preliminary analysis was undertaken as an exercise in method, and in order to discern trends in the survey data which might be predictive for the findings of the completed investigation. They must, therefore, be interpreted with caution. The most striking finding so far is that social isolation, whether gauged by type of living group or by frequency of social contacts, appears to carry a different significance for each of the two broad categories of psychogeriatric disorder. Persons with "chronic brain syndrome" living in the community are as a rule widowed, but are in close contact with relatives, from whom they receive a good level of support; hence, they can seldom be classed as isolated—less often, indeed, than members of the normal elderly population. This suggests that the chief importance of social isolation in this group is as a factor in selective admission and retention in hospital chronic wards and old people's homes. Probably the combination of social isolation with a dementing process, or with chronic physical disability, is particularly likely to result in long-term institutional care. A systematic approach to secondary and tertiary prevention will therefore call for effective methods of identifying such high-risk individuals at an early stage of the morbid process: a type of monitoring for which, at present, the general hospital and general medical practice appear to offer the most valuable strategic points.

Old persons with some degree—though not an extreme degree—of social isolation have been found in this study, as in the earlier surveys here cited, to have increased rates of functional mental disorders—principally affective disturbances. The cause-and-effect relationship behind this association is by no means clear, and can be explored only with the help of prospective studies, commencing in the presenium. Thus it is doubtful that screening of isolated old people for affective or other non-organic mental disorders would be a useful preventive strategy, since those who are most isolated do not seem to constitute an especially high-risk group for mental illness. A more promising approach to preventive action would appear to be the psychiatric screening of old people known to suffer from chronic physical disease or disability.

REFERENCES

BELLIN, S. S. and HARDT, R. H.: Marital status and mental disorders among the aged. *Am. Sociol. Rev.*, 23:155-162, 1958.

BLAU, I. S.: Changes in status and age identification. *Am. Sociol. Rev.*, 21:198, 1961.

BUNGARD, W.: *Isolation und Einsamkeit im Alter. Eine sozial-psychologische Studie.* Cologne: P. Hanstein, 1975.

COOPER, B.: Clinical and social aspects of chronic neurosis. *Proceedings of the Royal Society of Medicine*, 65:509, 1972.

COOPER, B.: Epidemiology. In: J. K. Wing (Ed.), *Schizophrenia, Towards a New Synthesis.* New York and London: Academic Press, 1978.

COOPER, B., HARWIN, B. G., DEPLA, C., and SHEPHERD, M.: Community mental health care: An evaluative study. *Psychol. Med.*, 5:372, 1975.

CUMMING, E. and HENRY, W. E.: *Growing Old. The Process of Disengagement.* New York: Basic Books, 1961.

DEAN, D. G.: Alienation: Its meaning and measurement. *Am. Sociol. Rev.*, 26:723, 1961.

DEGRAZIA, S.: *The Political Community.* Chicago: Chicago University Press, 1948.

DURKHEIM, E.: Le suicide. J. A. Spaulding and G. Simpson (Transl.), *Suicide: A Survey in Sociology.* Glencoe, Illinois: Free Press, 1951.

ESSEN-MÖLLER, E., LARSSON, H., UDDENBERG, G. E., and WHITE, G.: Individual traits and morbidity in a Swedish rural population. *Acta Psychiatrica Neurologica Scandinavica*, Supp. 100, Copenhagen, Munksgaard, 1956.

FARIS, R. E. L. and DUNHAM, H. W.: *Mental Disorders in Urban Areas. An Ecological Study of Schizophrenia and Other Psychoses.* Chicago: Chicago University Press, 1939. (Reprinted New York: Hafner, 1960).

GOLDBERG, D. P., COOPER, B., EASTWOOD, M. R., KEDWARD, H. B., and SHEPHERD, M.: A standardized psychiatric interview for use in community surveys. *Brit. J. Prev. Soc. Med.*, 24:18, 1970.

GRAD DE ALARCON, J.: Social causes and social consequences of mental illness in old age. In: D. W. K. Kay and A. Walk (Eds.), *Recent Development in Psychogeriatrics.* British Journal of Psychiatry, Special Publication No. 6. Ashford, Kent, U.K.: Headley, 1971.

GRUENBERG, E. M.: Community conditions and psychoses of the elderly. *Am. J. Psychiat.*, 110:888, 1954.

HÄFNER, H. (Ed.): *Psychiatrische Epidemiologie.* Berlin, Heidelberg, New York: Springer, 1978.

HARDT, R. H.: The ecological distribution of patients admitted to mental hospitals from an urban area. *Psychiat. Quart.*, 33:126, 1959.

HARE, E. H.: Mental illness and social conditions in Bristol. *J. Ment. Sci.*, 102:349, 1956.

HAVIGHURST, R. J., NEUGARTEN, B. L., and TOBIN, S. S.: Disengagement, personality and life satisfaction in the later years. In: P. F. Hansen (Ed.), *Age with a Future.* Copenhagen: Munksgaard, 1964.

HENDERSON, S., DUNCAN-JONES, P., MCAULEY, H., and RITCHIE, K.: The patient's primary Straighton group. *Brit. J. Psychiat.*, 132:74, 1978.

HUGHES, C. C., TREMBLAY, M.-A., RAPOPORT, R. N., and LEIGHTON, A. H.: *People of Cove and Woodlot.* The Stirling County Study, Vol. II. New York: Basic Books, 1960.

KAY, D. W. K., BEAMISH, P., and ROTH, M.: Old-age mental disorders in Newcastle-upon-Tyne, Part II: A study of possible social and medical causes. *Brit. J. Psychiat.*, 110:668, 1964.

LEIGHTON, D. C., HARDING, J. S., MACKLIN, D. B. et al.: *The Character of Danger: Psychiatric Symptoms in Selected Communities.* The Stirling County Study, Vol. III. New York: Basic Books, 1963.

LEVY, L. and ROWITZ, L.: The spatial distribution of treated mental disorders in Chicago. *Soc. Psychiat.*, 5:1, 1970.

LOWENTHAL, M. F.: Social isolation and mental illness in old age. *Am. Sociol. Rev.*, 29:54-70, 1964.

LOWENTHAL, M. F.: Antecedents of isolation and mental illness in old age. *Arch. Gen. Psychiat.*, 12:245-254, 1965.

LOWENTHAL, M. F. and BERKMAN, P.: *Aging and Mental Disorders in San Francisco. A Social Psychiatric Study*. San Francisco: Jossey-Bass, 1967.

LOWENTHAL, M. F. and HAVEN, C.: Interview and adaptation: Intimacy as a critical variable. *Am. Sociol. Rev.*, 33:49, 1968.

NIELSON, J.: Gerontopsychiatric period-prevalence investigation in a geographically delimited population. *Acta Psychiatrica Scandinavica*, 38:307, 1963.

PARSONS, T.: Age and sex in the social structure of the United States. *Am. Sociol. Rev.*, 7:604, 1942.

PHILLIPS, B. S.: A role theory approach to adjustment in old age. *Am. Sociol. Rev.*, 22:212, 1957.

REIMANN, H. and HÄFNER, H.: Psychische Erkrankungen alter Menschen in Mannheim. *Soc. Psychiat.*, 7:33, 1972.

SAINSBURY, P.: Suicide and attempted suicide. In: K. P. Kisker, J.-E. Meyer, C. Müller, and E. Strömgren (Eds.), *Psychiatrie der Gegenwart*, Band III. Soziale und angewandte Forschung, 2. Auflage, Berlin, Heidelberg, New York: Springer, 1975.

SEEMAN, M.: On the meaning of alienation. *Am. Sociol. Rev.*, 24:783, 1959.

SHELDON, J. H.: *The Social Medicine of Old Age. Report of an inquiry in Wolverhampton*. London: Oxford University Press, 1948.

SROLE, L.: Social integration and certain corollaries. *Am. Sociol. Rev.*, 21:709, 1956.

TOWNSEND, P. and TUNSTALL, J.: Isolation, desolation and loneliness. In: E. Shanas et al. (Eds.), *Old People in 3 Industrial Societies*. New York: Atherton Press, 1968.

TUNSTALL, J.: *Old and Alone*. London: Routledge, 1966.

WEISS, R. S.: The provisions of social relationships. In: Z. Rubin (Ed.), *Doing Unto Others*. Englewood Cliffs, New Jersey: Prentice Hall, 1974.

WELFORD, A. T. and BIRREN, J. E.: *Behavior, Aging and the Nervous System*. Springfield, Illinois: Charles C Thomas, 1965.

ZINTL-WIEGAND, A. and COOPER, B.: Psychische Erkrankungen in der Allgemeinpraxis: eine Untersuchung in Mannheim. *Der Nervenarzt*, 50:352, 1979.

ZINTL-WIEGAND, A., SCHMID-MAUSHART, C., LEISNER, R., and COOPER, B.: Psychische Erkrankungen in Mannheimer Allgemeinpraxen. Eine klinische und epidemiologische Untersuchung. In: H. Häfner, 1978, Op. cit. pp. 111-133.

10

Psychosocial Costs of Living with Psychologically Disturbed Family Members

SANDRA AREY, PH.D.
and
GEORGE J. WARHEIT, PH.D.

The systematic inquiry regarding the relationships between familial structures and environments and their impact on the mental health and social well being of family members has a long history of clinical observations, case studies, and empirical investigations. Over the last 50 years, Freudian and other psychodynamic theories of individuation have been particularly influential. In essence, these theories have generated the pervasive view of human development which suggests that early socialization experiences exert a disproportionate influence upon later psychosocial development. For example, Freud suggested that even forgotten impressions leave deep traces in our psychic life, and act as determinants for future development (1962). He further argued that neuroses are acquired only during early childhood even though their symptoms may not make their appearance until much later (1949).

The vital long-term importance attributed to early socialization experiences explicit in Freudian thought has been echoed by others. Social learning, behavioral and sociological theorists have emphasized the importance of parents as sources for role modeling and for the development and reinforcement of attitudes and behaviors in their children. Logically, these perspectives have led many researchers to focus on the etiological role of the family in the development and/or transmission of mental disorders and related social pathologies.

Examples of research which have emphasized the importance of *family structures* as causal agents in the etiology of mental disorders and social pathologies include: Bowlby, 1953, 1960, 1961, 1969; Brown, 1961, 1966; Pitts et al., 1965; Monroe, 1966a, 1966b; Goode, 1956, 1963; Burchinal, 1964; Birtchnell, 1970a, 1970b, 1970c; Burchinal, Hawkes & Gardner, 1957; and Arey, 1978. Studies which have focused on family *dynamics* as etiologic factors in the development of mental disorders include: Lidz, Fleck & Cornelison, 1965; Lidz, 1973; Wynne & Singer, 1963a, 1963b; Singer & Wynne, 1965a, 1965b; Wynne, Singer & Toohey, 1976; Mishler & Wáxler, 1968; Goldstein & Rodnick, 1975; a topical issue of the Schizophrenia Bulletin, 1976; Rosenthal, 1970.

Overall, these studies indicate that strong relationships exist between family variables, e.g. structures, functions and interactions and mental disorders. These findings are important and have had a great influence on our knowledge of the etiology and epidemiology of mental illness. At the same time, it must be emphasized that these findings are correlational in character and as such do not represent definitive causal statements. For example, it can be argued that non-normative family structures and aberrant interaction and communication patterns are the consequences of having a seriously disturbed person living in the family. It is, of course, vitally important to understand the genetic-environmental interaction if we are to understand the etiology of mental illness. It is also important to understand the impact that mentally ill persons have on the family structures and on the mental well-being of those living in the same household. Not all mental health problems found in relatives of probands are of a psychotic or neurotic nature or magnitude; some are situational and reactive.

Evidence regarding the reactive nature of psychiatric symptoms in members of families of mental patients has been provided by scholars addressing the same issues from a variety of perspectives. The 1955 work of Clausen, Yarrow, and colleagues remains a classic example of impact studies. They reported findings on 33 families of men hospitalized for schizophrenia. Their work traced impact from the husbands' first manifestation of problems, to the early stages of the wives' recognition and acceptance of the problems as psychiatric, through periods prior to, during, and after hospitalization (Clausen & Yarrow, 1955a, 1955b, 1955c; Clausen, Yarrow, Deasy, & Schwartz, 1955). Their findings suggest the consequences of such ordeals were costly to the wives and children of the patients and also to their extended families.

Such consequences have been labeled the "subjective burden" on the family (Freeman & Simmons, 1963; Hoenig & Hamilton, 1969) as opposed to the "objective burden" which includes economic (money and employment) costs, physical health costs, social and familial disruption. The subjective burden is the family's perception of duress and oppression caused by the patient's presence in the home. In a study of 125 lower socioeconomic families who were maintaining a discharged psychiatric patient in their homes, Doll (1976) found that family members had a significant subjective burden. Families "paid a price" for maintaining these relatives in their homes in the form of emotional pain and social isolation.

In a discussion of their genetic adoption study, Wender and colleagues (1971) made the following observations about finding a higher level of psychopathology in the adoptive parents of schizophrenics than in the adoptive parents of normals:

> It must be mentioned in passing that the evaluation of psychopathology in the adoptive parents of the schizophrenics was complicated by the fact that some of their psychopathology appeared to the raters to be reactive to pathology in their children. Many of these parents presented a picture of depression, apathy, social withdrawal, preoccupation, anxiety, and feelings of futility and guilt. In about one-half of the couples these symptoms seem clearly related to the onset of severe problems in their offspring (1971, p. 1016).

Similar emotional states have been found to be common among relatives of adult schizophrenics. Creer & Wing (1974), reporting the findings of two surveys conducted in England, suggest emotions such as constant anxiety, depression, guilt, disappointment, frustration, and anger may be normal reactions to living with psychiatrically disturbed family members. They suggest, "it is not necessary to regard these emotional reactions as 'abnormal' or in some sense pathological in themselves. They can be seen simply as reactions to a confusing, incomprehensible, distressing, and apparently unmodifiable situation" (1974, p. 33).

These surveys showed that more than half the relatives claimed their own well-being had been severely or very severely affected by the presence of a schizophrenic relative in their household. Such negative consequences were defined by relatives as being in response to the unpredictability of the patients' moods, behaviors, and habits and concern about the patients' future and long-term care. In addition to the personal negative consequences exemplified by these emotional states, relatives frequently reported familial conflicts and problems with the wider community. Although family conflicts usually centered on the unequal amount of attention required by the mentally ill family member, it was noted family conflicts were not restricted to the direct care of the schizophrenic nor to the nuclear family. The mere presence of the schizophrenics created a disruptive atmosphere that encompassed extended family members and sometimes resulted in the "total breakup of the family unit" (Creer & Wing, 1974). Moreover, it was noted:

> Whilst some families did seem able to cope with all this (conflict) they tended to be those where the patient had had a long history of illness and had also become relatively stable and manageable, and where the relatives, through various fortunate circumstances had been able to devise a regime within which the patient could function satisfactorily (1974, p. 35).

Similar findings were reported from a study of the families of 226 adult schizophrenics in the United States. In a test of the efficacy of mainstreaming schizophrenic patients to their homes for community based treatment, Pasamanick, Scarpitti and Dinitz (1967, p. viii) found the "ability and willingness of families to tolerate deviant or asocial family members" to be one of the best predictors of success. Their findings suggested that in cases where home care failed, "either patient behavior was bizarre or dangerous, or the responsible relative could no longer cope with the patient's needs."

The impact of mental illness on families is a timely research issue for two reasons. First, in recent years clinicians have emphasized the need to incorporate family members into the treatment process if the progress made in therapy sessions or in therapeutic environments is to be maintained in the daily life of the patient. And, second, the demands on the families of patients are being increased since the current emphasis on deinstitutionalization is regularly returning more and more psychiatric patients to their families. It is our opinion that if the goals of community based treatment and short-term hospitalizations are to be realized the needs of the families which serve as the daily caretakers of released patients must be identified and met as part of any comprehensive program of intervention and treatment. It is, therefore, incumbent upon students of the issue to provide an empirically based understanding of the social and psychosocial costs associated with caring for mental patients in family settings. By using preliminary but relevant data, this paper attempts to address this issue.

METHODS

The data presented in this paper come from two sources: cross-sectional field surveys and clinical interviews. The field survey data were gathered as part of a series of epidemiological assessments of mental health problems, service needs, and utilization patterns in the southeastern United States. The clinical interviews were conducted with parents who either were seeking or had sought admission for their children to a residential psychiatric treatment center.

Epidemiologic Surveys

Data from the epidemiological field surveys represent information on 4,202 adults residing in six counties. In each county, electric utility listings were used to provide the household sampling frame. Once a statistical probability sample of households was identified, individual respondents within them were selected via the Kish (1965) technique for randomizing respondents within households. Only persons 18 years of age and older were selected for the samples. The refusal rate was low, ranging from 8 percent to 12 percent in the various field surveys.

This multistaged probability sampling method produced samples which closely approximated the social and demographic characteristics of the research counties as enumerated by the U.S. Bureau of the Census. Of the sample of 4,202, 83 percent were white and 17 percent black; 43 percent male and 57 percent female. The age distribution fell into five rather equal categories with persons 60 years of age and older representing 29 percent of the sample; persons in the 30-44 age group represented 23 percent; persons in the 45-59 age group represented 22 percent; persons 23-30 represented 14 percent; followed by those under 22 years of age (12 percent). The overwhelming majority were married (66 percent); 13 percent were widowed; 5 percent divorced and 3 percent were separated. Thirteen percent had never married. The socioeconomic status (SES) of respondents was determined by combining income, education, and occupation scores as suggested by Nam et al. (1975). The sample's SES characteristics were as follows: 29.3 percent were in the 2 lowest quintiles; 51.9 percent were in the 3rd and 4th quintiles, and 18.8 percent in the highest (5th) quintile. For our purposes, respondents have been placed into one of three categories: low, moderate, or high on the basis of their SES scores.

Each respondent in the epidemiologic study was interviewed in his/her home using a 317-item questionnaire. One of 10 major subcomponents if the questionnaire was a comprehensive mental health inventory consisting of approximately 100 different questions constituting seven scales designed to measure psychiatric symptoms and dysfunctions. Three of these scales are used in the analyses presented here. These are: an 18-item depression scale; a 12-item anxiety scale; and an 11-item psychosocial dysfunction scale (Appendix 1). A description of these scales and their reliability and validity have been reported elsewhere and will not be outlined here (Cf. Schwab et al., 1979; Warheit et al., 1979; Warheit et al., 1976; Warheit, Holzer & Arey, 1975.)

For purposes of analysis, a statistical distribution of scores for each scale was prepared. Respondents with scores one or more standard deviations above the sample mean are identified as being in a high category. This method, while appearing arbitrary, has been validated by extensive comparisons of scores with high-risk groups in the general population and with carefully selected samples of psychiatric patients (Warheit et al., 1979).

All respondents were also asked whether they had a family member with serious nervous or emotional problems. For those who responded affirmatively, answers to questions of how many and who were pursued. This information permits exploration of the differential impact of various family members (e.g. child, spouse, or parent) and also of the number of problematic family members present in the home.

Clinical Interviews

In addition to data from the epidemiologic surveys, results from clinical interviews are included. The interviews were conducted as part of an ongoing study of the relative psychosocial impact on families of mentally ill children who are maintained in the home rather than in institutional settings. Data are presented on 118 persons, all of whom were parents who had sought admission for their children into the residential treatment center of a Department of Psychiatry at a University Teaching Hospital. Forty-eight mother/father couples and 21 single mothers were interviewed at the treatment center while their children were receiving preadmission evaluations. In addition, mothers of ten children whose preadmission evaluations had resulted in staff recommendations not to admit the children to the residential treatment center were interviewed in their homes. All ten children were still in the home at the time of the mothers' interview. Also interviewed in their homes were 39 mothers whose children had in the past four years been inpatients at the residential treatment center and currently were inpatients at other residential psychiatric programs.

TABLE 1

Percent of Respondents with High Psychiatric Symptom/Function Scores by Presence of Family Member with Mental Health Problem

		Depression		Anxiety		Psychosocial Dysfunction	
Problematic Family Member	Total N	N	%+	N	%+	N	%+
Yes (19%)	779	244	31.3	222	28.5	209	26.8
No (81%)	3,356	412	12,3	383	11.4	274	8.2

All differences between "no" and "yes" groups significant at $p < .001$.

The analyses presented in Tables 1-4 have the respondents' mental health as the dependent variable and the absence or presence of a family member with serious nervous or emotional problems as the independent variable. The empirical questions addressed are: 1) are psychiatric symptoms more prevalent among respondents with mentally ill family members than among those without; 2) does the race, sex, or socioeconomic status of the respondent affect the impact of having a mentally ill family member in the home; 3) if the respondent has more than one mentally ill family member, is the impact on his own mental health increased; and 4) does the impact on the respondents vary according to which family member is identified as mentally disturbed, e.g. child versus spouse versus parent?*

FINDINGS

As indicated in Table 1, 81 percent (N = 3356) of the sample reported no mentally disturbed family members. The percentage of persons in the No group scoring more than one standard deviation above the sample mean was significantly lower than for persons who did report a mentally ill family member. In the No group, only 8-12 percent scored high on the three measures of mental health while no fewer than 26 percent of the Yes group scored high on each of the same scales. The percentage of respondents with high levels of anxiety and depressive symptomatology was twice as high in the Yes group as in the No group. On the measure of psychosocial dysfunction, the percentage in the Yes group was three times that of the No group.

Prior research in psychiatric epidemiology has reported that blacks, females, and members of the lower socioeconomic groups have signifi-

* Persons naming self as having mental health problems are excluded from all analyses except those reported on the bottom of Table 4.

TABLE 2

Percent of Respondents with High Psychiatric Symptom/Function Scores by Presence of Family Members with Mental Health Problems Controlling for Race and Sex

Presence of Family Member with Mental Health Problems Controlled for Race of Respondent	Total N	Depression N	Depression %+	Anxiety N	Anxiety %+	Psychosocial Dysfunction N	Psychosocial Dysfunction %+
White	3,423	474	13.8	447	13.1	377	11.0
No	2,759	282	10.2	275	10.0	208	7.5
Yes	664	192	28.9	172	25.9	167	25.5
Black	686	180	26.2	156	22.7	105	15.3
No	572	128	22.4	106	18.5	65	11.4
Yes	114	52	45.6	50	43.9	40	35.1
Presence of Family Member with Mental Health Problems Controlled for Sex of Respondent							
Male	1,782	195	10.9	195	10.9	147	8.2
No	1,487	122	8.2	132	8.9	89	6.0
Yes	295	73	24.7	63	21.4	58	19.7
Female	2,353	461	19.6	410	17.4	336	14.3
No	1,869	290	15.5	251	13.4	185	9.9
Yes	461	171	35.3	159	32.9	151	31.2

All differences between "no" and "yes" groups significant at $p < .001$.

cantly higher percentages of persons scoring high on measures of mental health problems than whites, males and those in upper socioeconomic statuses (cf. Dohrenwend & Dohrenwend, 1969; Gove & Tudor, 1973; Schwab et al., 1979). The data in Tables 2 and 3 corroborate these earlier findings in the process of making both between-group and within-group comparisons. Table 2 shows that although blacks and females in general have greater percentages scoring high on the various scales, the increase in symptoms associated with the presence of a disturbed family member is similar to that of whites and males.

The same interpretation can be applied to the distributions shown in Table 3. In general, the lowest socioeconomic groups have three times the percentage of persons scoring in the high range on the three measures of mental health than do the highest socioeconomic groups, and twice the percentage of those in the middle range socioeconomic groups. However, as with the race and sex controls, the presence of a mentally disturbed family member produces higher scores for those in all socioeconomic groups.

TABLE 3

Percent of Respondents with High Psychiatric Symptom/Function Scores by Presence of Family Members with Mental Health Problems Controlling for Socioeconomic Status

Presence of Family Member with Mental Health Problems Controlled for SES of Respondent	Total N	Depression N	Depression %+	Anxiety N	Anxiety %+	Psychosocial Dysfunction N	Psychosocial Dysfunction %+
SES—Low	1,201	338	28.1	339	27.5	181	15.1
No	943	222	23.5	211	22.4	102	10.8
Yes	258	116	45.0	128	48.1	79	30.6
SES—Moderate	917	144	15.7	129	13.2	115	12.5
No	740	86	11.6	85	11.5	62	8.4
Yes	177	58	32.8	44	21.0	53	29.9
SES—High	2,014	173	8.6	135	6.5	185	9.2
No	1,671	104	6.2	86	5.1	109	6.5
Yes	343	69	20.1	49	13.1	76	22.2

All differences between "no" and "yes" groups significant at $p < .001$.

The distributions in Table 1-3 show statistically significant differences in the percentage of persons reporting psychiatric symptoms based on the presence or absence in the home of a person with serious mental health problems. The data reported in Table 4 represent refinements of the basic question, i.e., does it matter how many family members have mental health problems; and, does it make any difference which family member has the problems? The data shown in Table 4 indicate a consistent pattern of progressive increases in percentages of high scale scores for those with more mentally disturbed family members. The rates for those with one disturbed family member are two to three times higher than for those with no mentally disturbed family members. The rates for those with more than one disturbed family member are approximately three to five times as great as those in the None category.

Table 4 also reports findings designed to answer the question: are mental health consequences of living with a disturbed person altered by the structure of the relationship, i.e., parent, spouse and so forth? Only respondents reporting one emotionally disturbed family member are included in this analysis. The purpose of excluding respondents living with more than one mentally ill family member is to avoid confounding the analysis by the possible effects of particular combinations of relatives. For example, among persons reporting two ill family members, certain combinations might be more stress producing: living with two mentally ill children might have significantly different stress consequences than living with a mentally ill parent and a mentally ill sibling. There were too few patterned combinations in our sample to permit statistical comparisons of these interactions; therefore, the analysis presented in the lower half of Table 4 is limited to respondents living with only one mentally ill family member.

The kinship statuses identified by respondents were parent, spouse, child, sibling and self. In addition, various members of the extended family, such as aunt, uncle or grandparent were grouped together and labeled other. Respondents who identified themselves as the family member with serious mental health problems had by far the largest percentage of high scores on all three scales. The percentage of this group in the high category on the three scales ranged from 55.6 percent to 63.9 percent. When those in the self category are excluded from the analysis, respondents reporting a mentally ill child in the home had the largest percentage scoring high on the depression and anxiety measures. The largest percentage scoring high on psychosocial dysfunction was in the group with a mentally ill parent in the home, although respondents identifying a parent as the mentally ill family member had the lowest percentage of high depression and anxiety scores.

The impact of having a child with serious mental health problems in the home is further explored in Table 5. Data from the community

TABLE 4

Percent of Respondents with High Psychiatric Symptom/Function Scores by Presence of Family Members with Mental Health Problems Controlling for Number and Relationship

Number of Family Members with Mental Health Problems	Total N	Depression N	Depression %+	Anxiety N	Anxiety %+	Psychosocial Dysfunction N	Psychosocial Dysfunction %+
None	3,356	412	12.3	383	11.4	274	8.2
One	682	198	29.0	186	27.3	170	24.9
Two-three	97	46	47.4	38	39.2	40	41.2
Which Family Member has Mental Health Problems							
Parent Only	153	36	23.5	24	15.7	43	28.1
Spouse Only	140	36	25.7	37	26.4	23	16.4
Child Only	136	44	32.4	46	33.8	32	23.5
Sib Only	109	33	30.3	34	31.2	26	23.9
Other Only	108	27	25.0	25	23.1	23	21.3
Self Only	36	22	61.1	20	55.6	23	63.9

All differences between "no" and "yes" groups significant at $p < .001$.

samples are compared with data from the clinical interviews. The small cell sizes for some groups make statistical tests of significance inappropriate and at the same time limit the generalizability of the findings. However, the overall patterns are basically consistent and suggest some important areas for further study. Since all respondents in the clinical interviews were white, data used to compare them with respondents from the community samples were limited to white parents whose children were living at home at the time of interview. The comparisons are predominantly for mothers since too few fathers of inpatients or fathers who had unsuccessfully sought admission for their children were available for interviews. Clinical interview data for fathers seeking their child's first psychiatric admission are available, however, and are presented in the lower half of Table 5.

The top of Table 5 represents data on mothers. Mothers from the community sample reporting children with serious mental health problems had twice the percentage scoring high on all three scales than did the community sample mothers without a mentally ill child. While more than half the mothers seeking their child's first psychiatric admission scored high on the depression and anxiety scales, the scores of mothers of inpatients were relatively low, resembling those of the community

TABLE 5

Percent of Respondents with High Psychiatric Symptom/Function Scores for Community and Non-Community Samples which Include Family Members with Mental Health Problems

		Depression		Anxiety		Psychosocial Dysfunction	
	Total N	N	%+	N	%+	N	%+
Community Sample Mothers	830	143	17.6	123	14.8	127	15.3
Community Sample Mothers: Child with M. H. Problems	100	37	37.0	36	36.0	29	29.0
Mothers Seeking Child's 1st Admission	69	38	55.1	44	63.8	15	21.8
Mothers Who Unsuccessfully Sought Child's Admission	10	4	40.0	4	40.0	3	30.0
Mothers of Inpatients	39	9	23.1	7	18.0	6	15.4
Community Sample Fathers	63	54	8.5	43	6.8	40	6.3
Community Sample Fathers: Child with M. H. Problems	32	6	18.8	7	21.9	5	15.6
Fathers Seeking Child's 1st Admission	48	12	25.0	8	16.7	3	6.3

sample mothers without a mentally ill child. The scores for mothers who had sought inpatient admission for their children but had not succeeded were similar to those of the community sample mothers who reported having a mentally disturbed child in the home.

The small percentage of community sample fathers scoring high on the three scales reflects the sex related differences in baseline scores noted earlier. Very few community fathers were known to have children with mental health problems and there were very few fathers seeking admission for their child in the clinical sample. However, the few community fathers who did report the presence of a mentally disturbed child in the home were twice as likely to score high on the three scales as were the community sample, and those seeking admission for their children had elevated rates of depression and anxiety, but not more psychosocial dysfunction.

DISCUSSION

Mental illness is costly. Federal mandates to provide care and treatment for the mentally ill, the associated training programs for mental health professionals, the recycling of old mental institutions, and the construction of new community based treatment facilities and programs add up to a multibillion dollar industry. Every citizen is affected financially by the problem of mental illness in that tax monies provide the bulk of financial support for such endeavors. And, every citizen is affected socially and personally by philosophical, political, and scientific assumptions that together determine the current patterns of care.

The "state of the art" which determines methods of identification and diagnosis, intervention policies and procedures, and the medical and social outcomes of treatment has been dramatically influenced by the 1963 Community Mental Health Center Act and its subsequent amendments. The enactment of this legislation was hailed by some as the "third major revolution" in the field of mental illness: the first being the ideological switch from a theological to a medical etiology of mental illness, and the second being the introduction of chemotherapy in the form of psychoactive drugs. Of relevance to the research reported in this paper, it is important to note that the Community Mental Health Center Act represented a philosophical shift in the locus of treatment and care. The concomitant development of social models of mental disorder (nurture over nature, problems in living, residual deviance), new intervention and therapy modalities (therapeutic milieu, therapeutic community), and the growing successes of the psychoactive drugs, created an atmosphere that condemmed long-term custodial institutionalization and urged replacement with short-term community based treatment. Implicit is the goal of "mainstreaming" discharged psychiatric patients.

Consequently, the nation's large mental institutions began emptying their wards of chronic patients. There has been a steady annual decrease in patient populations and in the average length of stay. In 1970, 21 percent of hospitalized mental patients remained more than six months, with the average length of stay being 473 days. In 1974, only 11 percent stayed more than six months, and the average length of stay dropped to 178 days (GAP Report #436, July 1977).

Three trends have resulted: 1) a radical reduction in the number of mental patients being housed in institutions at any one time; 2) a radical increase in readmissions (revolving door phenomenon); and 3) a significant increase in the use of outpatient clinics. Of crucial importance to the issues addressed in this paper is the associated increase in the number and frequency of patients returned to their families. Follow-up studies of discharged mental patients have found that 72 percent were released from hospital to a relative's household: 50 percent to a spouse; 30 percent to parents; and 20 percent to other relatives (GAP Report #436, July 1977). (These statistics apply only to adults; children with mental health problems are not represented in these figures.)

Whether the patient is a child or an adult, one of the major determinants of his future psychiatric history (readmissions) is the patient's family. Family characteristics found to be significant predictors of readmissions are: 1) negative expressed emotions by relatives at the time of the patient's hospitalization (Brown, Birley & Wing, 1972; Leff, 1976; Vaughn & Leff, 1976); 2) objective and subjective family burden (Hoenig & Hamilton, 1969; Freeman & Simmons, 1963; Doll, 1976); 3) incongruence between patient's and family's expectations regarding patient's performance after discharge (Serban et al., 1976); 4) and the availability of social support systems (Lindenthal, Thomas, & Myers, 1971; Nuckolls, Cassel, & Kaplan, 1972; Caplan, 1974; Cobb, 1976; Kaplan, Cassel, & Gore, 1977).

Although few studies have directly investigated the impact of mentally ill children on families, our findings support the logical assumption that the early age of onset exacerbates the problems faced by families of adults with mental disorders. Parents of young mentally ill children are in an extraordinarily complex situation. Not only must they deal with the direct problems of their child's disorder, they must also cope with the consequences of the mental disorder on other maturational and developmental processes of childhood (e.g., sleep disturbances, psychomotor retardation, prolonged dependence on others for personal safety and personal hygiene).

Some studies have compared the differential stress for parents of mentally retarded versus emotionally disturbed children (Ricci, 1970; Holroyd, 1974, 1975, 1976) and found that mothers of the emotionally disturbed described themselves as "less able to experience personal development or freedom, more limited in how they can use their time, poorer in health and mood, more sensitive to how the child fits into the community, and more aware of disharmony within the family" (Holroyd, 1974, p. 94).

Our preliminary findings suggest that the psychosocial costs associated with maintaining a mentally ill child or adult in the home are significant. Descriptions of lives such as the one noted above make understandable the high rates of depression, anxiety, and psychosocial dysfunction. Perhaps the next step is to determine the effect on such symptoms of various social support systems, family therapies, and respite care programs.

REFERENCES

AREY, S.: A break in the family life cycle. Presented at the American Sociological Association, San Francisco, 1978.

BIRTCHNELL, J.: Early parent death and mental illness. *Brit. J. Psychiat.*, 116:281-288, 1970a.

BIRTCHNELL, J.: Recent parent death and mental illness. *Brit. J. Psychiat.*, 116:289-297, 1970b.

BIRTCHNELL, J.: Depression in relation to early and recent parent death. *Brit. J. Psychiat.*, 116:299-306, 1970c.

BOWLBY, J.: *Child Care and the Growth of Love*. Baltimore: Penquin Books, 1953.

BOWLBY, J.: Grief and mourning in infancy and early childhood. *Psychoanal. Study Child*, 15:9-52, 1960.

BOWLBY, J.: Childhood mourning and its implications for psychiatry. *Am. J. Psychiat.*, 118:481-498, 1961.

BOWLBY, J.: *Attachment*. New York: Basic Books, 1969.

BROWN, F.: Depression and childhood bereavement. *J. Ment. Sci.*, 107:754-777, 1961.

BROWN, F.: Childhood bereavement and a subsequent psychiatric disorder. *Brit. J. Psychiat.*, 112:1036-1041, 1966.

BROWN, G., BIRLEY, J., and WING, J.: Influence of family life in the course of schizophrenic disorders: A replication. *Brit. J. Psychiat.*, 121:241-258, 1972.

BURCHINAL, L.: Characteristics of adolescents from unbroken, broken, and reconstituted families. *J. Mar. Fam.*, 26, 1 (February):44-51, 1964.

BURCHINAL, L., HAWKES, G., and GARDNER, B.: Marriage adjustment, personality characteristics of parents and the personality adjustment of their children. *J. Mar. Fam.*, Vol. 19, No. 4 (November):366-372, 1957.

CAPLAN, G.: *Support Systems and Community Mental Health*. New York: Behavioral Publications, 1974.

CLAUSEN, J. and YARROW, M.: Introduction: Mental illness and the family. *J. Soc. Issues*, Vol. 11, No. 4:3-5, 1955a.

CLAUSEN, J. and YARROW, M.: Paths to the mental hospital. *J. Soc. Issues,* Vol. 11, No. 4:25-32, 1955b.

CLAUSEN, J. and YARROW, M.: Further observations and some implications. *J. Soc. Issues,* Vol. 11, No. 4:61-65, 1955c.

CLAUSEN, J., YARROW, M., DEASY, L., and SCHWARTZ, C.: The impact of mental illness: Research formulation. *J. Soc. Issues,* Vol. 11, No. 4:6-11, 1955.

COBB, S.: Social support as a moderator of life stress. *Psychosom. Med.,* 38:300-314, 1976.

CREER, C. and WING, J.: *Schizophrenia at Home.* London: Institute of Psychiatry, 1974.

DOHRENWEND, B. P. and DOHRENWEND, B. S.: *Social Status and Psychological Disorder.* New York: John Wiley, 1969.

DOLL, W.: Family coping with the mentally ill: An unanticipated problem of deinstitutionalization. *Hosp. Com. Psychiat.,* 27:183-185, 1976.

FREEMAN, H. and SIMMONS, O.: *The Mental Patient Comes Home.* New York: John Wiley & Sons, 1963.

FREUD, S.: *An Outline of Psychoanalysis.* Translated by J. Strachey, London: Hogarth Press, 1949.

FREUD, S.: Infantile sexuality. Translated by A. Brill, *Nervous and Mental Disease Monographs,* No. 7, 1962.

GOLDSTEIN, M. and RODNICK, E.: The family's contribution to the etiology of schizophrenia: Current status. *Schizoph. Bull.,* Issue No. 14, Fall: 48-63, 1975.

GOODE, W.: *After Divorce.* Glencoe, Ill.: Free Press, 1956.

GOODE, W.: *World Revolution and Family Patterns.* New York: The Free Press of Glencoe, 1963.

GOVE, W. and TUDOR, J.: Adult sex roles and mental illness. *Am. J. Sociol.,* 78 (Jan.): 812-835, 1973.

GROUP FOR THE ADVANCEMENT OF PSYCHIATRY (GAP): The chronic mental patient in the community. Circular Letter No. 436: July, 1977.

HOENIG, J. and HAMILTON, M.: *The Desegregation of the Mentally Ill.* London: Routledge and Kegan, 1969.

HOLROYD, J.: The questionnaire on resources and stress: An instrument to measure family response to a handicapped family member. *J. Com. Psychiat.,* 2:92-94, 1974.

HOLROYD, J.: Stress in families of institutionalized and non-institutionalized autistic children. *J. Com. Psychol.,* 3:26-31, 1975.

HOLROYD, J.: Mental retardation and stress on the parents: A contrast between Down's syndrome and childhood autism. *Am. J. Ment. Defi.,* 80:431-436, 1976.

KAPLAN, B., CASSEL, J., and GORE, S.: Social support and health. *Medical Care,* Vol. XV, No. 5, May, Supplement: 47-58, 1977.

KISH, L.: *Survey Sampling.* New York: John Wiley & Sons, Inc., 1965.

LEFF, J.: Schizophrenia and sensitivity to the family environment. *Schizoph. Bull.,* Vol. 2, No. 4, 1976.

LIDZ, T.: *The Origin and Treatment of Schizophrenic Disorders.* New York: Basic Books, Inc., 1973.

LIDZ, T., FLECK, S., and CORNELISON, A. R.: *Schizophrenia and the Family.* New York: International Universities Press, 1965.

LINDENTHAL, J., THOMAS, C., and MYERS, J.: Psychological status and the perception of primary and secondary support from the social milieu in time of crisis. *J. Nerv. Ment. Dis.,* Vol. 153, No. 2:92-98, 1971.

MISHLER, E. G. and WAXLER, N. E.: *Family Processes and Schizophrenia.* New York: Science House, Inc., 1968.

MONROE, A.: Some familial and social factors in depressive illness. *Brit. J. Psychiat.,* 112: 429-441, 1966a.

MONROE, A.: Parental deprivation in depressive patients. *Brit. J. Psychiat.,* 112:443-457, 1966b.

NAM, C., LAROCQUE, J., POWERS, M., and HOLMBERG, J.: Occupational status scores: Stability and change. American Statistical Association: Proceedings of the Social Statistical Section: 570-575, 1975.

NUCKOLLS, K., CASSEL, J., and KAPLAN, B.: Psychosocial assets, life crisis and the prognosis of pregnancy. *Am. J. Epidemiol.*, Vol. 95, No. 5:431-441, 1972.

PASAMANICK, B., SCARPITTI, F. R., and DINITZ, S.: *Schizophrenics in the Community: An Experimental Study in the Prevention of Hospitalization.* New York: Appleton-Century-Crofts, 1967.

PITTS, F., MEYER, J., BROOKS, M., and WINOKUR, G.: Adult psychiatric illness assessed for childhood parental loss, and psychiatric illness in family members. *Am. J. Psychiat.*, Suppl. 121:i-x, 1965.

RICCI, C.: Analysis of child-rearing attitudes of mothers of retarded, emotionally disturbed, and normal children. *Am. J. Ment. Defic.*, 74:756-761, 1970.

ROSENTHAL, D.: *Genetic Theory and Abnormal Behavior.* New York: McGraw-Hill, 1970.

Topical issue devoted to genetics of schizophrenia. *Schizoph. Bull.*, 2:3, 1976.

SCHWAB, J., BELL, R., WARHEIT, G. J., and SCHWAB, R. B.: *Social Order and Mental Health.* New York: Brunner/Mazel, 1979.

SERBAN, G., GIDYNSKI, C., and ZIMMERMAN, A.: Informants' post-discharge expectations of the schizophrenic's community adjustment. *Psychiat. Digest*, September: 14-19, 1976.

SINGER, M. and WYNNE, L.: Thought disorder and family relations of schizophrenics: III. Methodology using projective techniques. *Arch. Gen. Psychiat.*, 12:187-200, 1965a.

SINGER, M. and WYNNE, L.: Thought disorder and family relations of schizophrenics: IV. Results and implications. *Arch. Gen. Psychiat.*, 12:201-212, 1965b.

VAUGHN, C. and LEFF, J.: The influence of family and social factors on the course of psychiatric illness. *Brit. J. Psychiat.*, 129:125-137, 1976.

WARHEIT, G., HOLZER, C., and AREY, S.: Race and mental illness: An epidemiologic update. *J. Hlth. Soc. Behav.*, 16(4):243-256, 1975.

WARHEIT, G., HOLZER, C., BELL, R., and AREY, S.: Sex, marital status and mental health: A reappraisal. *Social Forces*, 55 (2):459-470, 1976.

WARHEIT, G., HOLZER, C., ROBBINS, L., and BUHL, J.: Planning for mental health services: Needs assessment approaches. Forthcoming: National Institute of Mental Health: Rockville, Maryland.

WENDER, P., ROSENTHAL, D., ZAHN, T., and KETY, S.: The psychiatric adjustment of the adopting parents of schizophrenics. *Am. J. Psychiat.*, 127:1013-1018, 1971.

WYNNE, L. and SINGER, M.: Thought disorder and family relations of schizophrenics: I. A research strategy. *Arch. Gen. Psychiat.*, 9:191-198, 1963a.

WYNNE, L. and SINGER, M.: Thought disorder and family relations of schizophrenic: II. A classification of forms of thinking. *Arch. Gen. Psychiat.*, 9:199-206, 1963b.

WYNNE, L., SINGER, M., and TOOHEY, M.: Communication of the adoptive parents of schizophrenics. In: J. Jorstad and E. Ugelstad (Eds.), *Schizophrenia 75, Psychotherapy, Family Studies, Research.* Oslo: University of Oslo Press, 1976.

APPENDIX

DEPRESSION SCALE

Affect—Mood

1. Do you feel in good spirits?
2. How often do you have crying spells or feel like it?

3. How often do you feel you don't enjoy doing things anymore?
4. How often do you feel alone and helpless?
5. How often do you feel that people don't care what happens to you?
6. How often do you feel that life is hopeless?

Body Complaints—Somatic

7. Do you tend to feel tired in the mornings?
8. Do you feel that you are bothered by all sorts of ailments in different parts of your body?

Psychological Patterns

9. Have you ever had periods of days or weeks when you couldn't take care of things because you couldn't get going?
10. Do you have any trouble getting to sleep and staying asleep?
11. How often do you have trouble with sleeping?
12. Do you ever have loss of appetite?

Negative Self Evaluation (Cognition)

13. When things don't turn out, how often would you say you blame yourself?
14. How often do you think about suicide?
15. Life has changed so much in our modern world that people are powerless to control their own lives. (Would you: strongly agree, agree, undecided, disagree, strongly disagree.)

Future Outlook

16. Do you sometimes wonder if anything is worthwhile anymore?
17. How often would you say that things don't turn out the way you want them to?
18. How does the future look to you?

(Cronbach's alpha = 0.84)

ANXIETY SCALE

1. Do your hands ever tremble enough to bother you?
2. Are you ever troubled by your hands or feet sweating so that they feel damp and clammy?
3. Have you ever been bothered by your heart beating hard?
4. Have you ever been troubled by "cold sweats"?
5. Do you feel that you are bothered by all sorts (different kinds) of ailments in different parts of your body?
6. Do you ever have loss of appetite?
7. Has any ill health affected the amount of work (housework) you do?
8. Do you ever feel weak all over?
9. Do you ever have spells of dizziness?
10. Have you ever been bothered by shortness of breath when you were not exerting yourself?
11. For the most part, do you feel healthy enough to carry out the things that you would like to do?
12. Have you ever had periods of days or weeks when you couldn't take care of things because you couldn't get going?

(Cronbach's alpha = 0.82)

PSYCHOSOCIAL DYSFUNCTION SCALE

1. During the last year did worry or nervousness get you down physically?
2. During the last year, did worry or nervousness cause problems with your family life?

3. During the last year, did worry or nervousness interfere with your social activities?
4. During the last year, have you ever had to stay at home or in bed because of worry or nervousness?
5. During the last year, were you unable to do your usual work because of worry or nervousness?
6. In the last year, how often did you feel that you might have a nervous breakdown or that you might lose your mind?
7. Does this feeling get you down physically?
8. In the last year has this feeling caused problems with your family/personal life?
9. Does this feeling interfere with your social activities?
10. In the last year have you ever had to stay at home or in bed because of this feeling?
11. In the last year were you unable to do your usual work at any time because of feeling that you might have a nervous breakdown?

(Cronbach's alpha = 0.88)

11

Social Bonds, Adversity and Neurosis

SCOTT HENDERSON, D.M., PAUL DUNCAN-JONES,
D. G. BYRNE, PH.D., RUTH SCOTT
and
SYLVIA ADCOCK

We have been investigating the possible contribution to the causes of neurosis made by the lack of social bonds. The aim of our studies has been to explore the immediate social environment for factors which afford protection from non-psychotic disorder and to develop methods for this task. The background to the work has been described elsewhere (Henderson, 1977; Henderson et al., 1978a; Henderson et al., 1978b).

Two hypotheses are being tested:

1) that a deficiency in social bonds in the current environment is a causal factor in neurosis; and
2) that this effect holds in its own right, and not only under the stress of adverse experiences, as Brown and his colleagues have suggested (Brown & Harris, 1978).

METHOD

To investigate these hypotheses, we are using the following methods in a population study:

1. *Morbidity*. Morbidity is assessed by three instruments—the PSE,

the Zung depression scale, and the Goldberg GHQ. In the present paper, we will be reporting only on the 30-item GHQ (Goldberg, 1972).

2. *Social Bonds.* Bonds to the individual's primary group and immediate social environment are assessed by the Interview Schedule for Social Interaction (ISSI). This instrument investigates attachment, social integration, opportunity for nurturing others, reassurance of worth, a sense of reliable alliance, and the obtaining of guidance. The 52 items are combined into variables developed by multivariate analysis of contingencies and analysis of covariance structures (Duncan-Jones, 1978). These four measures are:

i) the Availability of Attachment (AVAT)
ii) the Adequacy of Attachment (ADAT)
iii) the Availability of Social Integration (AVSI)
iv) the Adequacy of Social Integration (ADSI).

In the analyses reported here, we will use a composite derived from canonical correlation of these four summary indices with non-psychotic morbidity. The creation of this composite measure is explained in the Appendix.

3. *Adversity.* A scale of adverse life events was developed for an Australian population by Tennant and Andrews (1976) from Paykel et al.'s (1971) instrument. We have augmented this list of events and combined three summary measures to create a composite index of life events by canonical correlation analysis, as described in the Appendix.

The Sample. This was a systematic sample of the Electoral Roll of Canberra, the capital city of Australia. Since all Australian citizens are required by law to be registered on this Roll, the sample is representative of the population. A response rate of 85 percent was achieved, to yield a sample size of 753 persons.

Design. A longitudinal design is being employed, in which a subsample of 300 are being interviewed four times at four-monthly intervals. This, we hope, will allow us to investigate the direction of causality between social bonds, adversity, and morbidity. The present paper, however, reports only on the first wave of interviewing.

FINDINGS

The present paper presents associations found between morbidity, adversity and social bonds. The GHQ and ISSI scores are both skewed to the left (i.e., in the direction of no morbidity and ample supports). Their joint distribution is far from being bivariate normal, possibly depressing their correlation. We tried transforming the scores to make them more normally distributed. However, the resulting correlations were not greatly increased.

Morbidity and Adversity

Table 1 shows the mean GHQ score for those in the sample scoring low, medium and high on Adversity (unfavorable life events). There is a statistically significant increase in morbidity with increasing levels of reported adversity ($p < .001$). Adversity explains 10.3 percent of the variance in the GHQ score.

TABLE 1

Mean GHQ Score by an Index of Life Event Stress

	N	%	Mean GHQ
Low life events	448	59.5	1.95
Medium life events	191	25.4	4.64
High life events	114	15.1	5.41
Total	753	100.0	3.16

Explained Variance = 10.3%

Morbidity and Social Bonds

Table 2 shows the distribution of the mean GHQ score according to the respondents' score on the social bond scale. Social bonds explain 8.1 percent of the variance.

We conducted a three-way analysis of variance, including sex as well as social bonds and adversity, to learn their joint effect on GHQ scores. The results are shown in Table 3 and are based on hierarchical F-tests, in the order indicated.

TABLE 2

Mean GHQ Score by a Composite Index of Social Bonds

	N	%	Mean GHQ
Low social bonds	111	14.7	5.92
Medium social bonds	189	25.1	3.77
High social bonds	453	60.2	2.23
Total	753	100.0	3.16

Explained Variance = 8.1%

TABLE 3

Three-way Analysis of Variance of GHQ Score

		Significance
Main Effects:	Sex	N.S.
	Life Events	$p < .001$
	Social Bonds	$p < .001$
Interactions:	Sex by Life Events	N.S.
	Sex by Social Bonds	N.S.
	Life Events by Social Bonds	N.S.
	Three-way Interaction	N.S.

(Test Procedure: Hierarchical F Tests, in the order indicated above)

The main effects are not statistically significant for sex, but both life events and social bonds are significant at the .001 level. None of the interactions is significant, including the three-way interaction. We conclude that adversity and social bonds are independently associated with morbidity, for both sexes.

These results are illustrated in Table 4, where mean GHQ scores are shown for life events and social bonds considered jointly.

TABLE 4

Mean GHQ Score by Life Events and Social Bonds

	Low Events	Medium Events	High Events
Low Social Bonds	3.92	6.38	7.46
Medium	2.72	5.00	5.06
High Social Bonds	1.45	3.80	4.00

Explained Variance = 14.6%

Morbidity increases regularly with *either* more adversity or fewer social bonds. Our data therefore suggest that deficiencies in the primary group may do more than act as a vulnerability factor.

DISCUSSION

These cross-sectional findings point to an association, but one is well aware that they provide no evidence that adversity or lack of social bonds *caused* morbidity as we hypothesized. Considering only the morbidity/low social bond association, irrespective of the load of adversity, there are at least three categories of alternative explanations: The associations may have their origin in contamination between either of the independent variables and the morbidity measure, in distorted reporting by symptomatic respondents, or in an association between both variables and a third, such as competence in personal relationships or the personality trait of dependency.

The three-way analyses of morbidity, social bonds and adversity lead to the conclusion that an association exists between morbidity and the two independent variables, and that there is no significant interaction between them or with sex. Above all, the present findings in no way establish the direction of causality.

Our interest lies in disentangling the degree to which the association between poor social bonds and neurosis represents the *consequences* of neurosis for the ability to maintain social relationship *vs.* the lack of social relationships as a cause of neurosis. Completing the field work of the panel study will enable us to use data from the four Waves to investigate the direction of causal relationships.

REFERENCES

BLALOCK, H. M.: *Causal Inferences in Nonexperimental Research.* Chapel Hill: University of North Carolina Press, 1961.

BROWN, G. W. and HARRIS, T.: *The Social Origins of Depression.* London: Tavistock, 1978.

DUNCAN-JONES, P.: The interview measurement of social interaction. *Proceedings of the 1978 Congress of the International Sociology Association,* Uppsala, 1978.

DUNCAN-JONES, P. and HENDERSON, S.: The use of a two-phase design in a population survey. *Soc. Psychiat.,* 13:231-237, 1978.

GOLDBERG, D.: *The Detection of Psychiatric Illness by Questionnaire.* Institute of Psychiatry Maudsley Monographs No. 21. London: Oxford, 1972.

HENDERSON, S.: The social network, support and neurosis. *Brit. J. Psychiat.,* 131:185-91, 1977.

HENDERSON, S., DUNCAN-JONES, P., MCAULEY, H., and RITCHIE, K.: The patient's primary group. *Brit. J. Psychiat.,* 132:74-86, 1978a.

HENDERSON, S., BYRNE, D. G., DUNCAN-JONES, P., ADCOCK, S., SCOTT, R., and STEELE, G. P.: Social bonds in the epidemiology of neurosis. *Brit. J. Psychiat.,* 132:463-6, 1978b.

PAYKEL, E. S., PRUSOFF, B. A., and UHLENHUTH, E. H.: Scaling of life events. *Arch. Gen. Psychiat.,* 25:340-347, 1971.

TENNANT, C. and ANDREWS, G.: A scale to measure the stress of life events. *Aust. N.Z. J. Psychiat.,* 15:27-32, 1976.

WEISS, R.: The provisions of social relationships. In: Z. Rubin (Ed.), *Doing Unto Others.* Englewood Cliffs, N.J.: Prentice-Hall, 1974, pp. 17-26.

WING, J. K., COOPER, J. E., and SARTORIUS, N.: *The Measurement and Classification of Psychiatric Symptoms.* Cambridge University Press, 1974.

ZUNG, W. W. K.: A self-rating depression scale. *Arch. Gen. Psychiat.,* 12:63-70, 1965.

APPENDIX A: INDEX CONSTRUCTION

The foregoing analysis uses composite indices of social support and life events. Each of these indices is an "optimised" composite of several sub-indices, derived by canonical analysis.

The social support index was derived from the Interview Schedule for Social Interaction. A detailed structural analysis has shown that the data could be reasonably well summarized in just four dimensions (Duncan-Jones, 1978). Interview items from each dimension were dichotomized, and scores derived by counting positive items. The four indices are:

AVSI	A count of 16 items measuring AVailability of Social Integration
AVAT	A count of 8 items measuring AVailability of ATtachment
ADSI	A count of 17 items measuring perceived ADequacy of Social Integration
ADAT	A count of 18 items measuring perceived ADequacy of ATtachment.

A canonical correlation analysis was performed, with the above four indices forming one set of variables, and the other set consisting of

GHQ score (30 item)
Zung Self-rating Depression Scale (total score)
Symptom Index*

From the canonical analysis, an optimal weighted composite of the four social support measures was derived. This weighted composite was used in the analysis reported in the current paper. The correlations of the four support measures with this composite social support index are

AVSI	.50
AVAT	.33
ADSI	.72
ADAT	.88

The composite score clearly gives greater weight to perceived adequacy of social support than to its availability.

The *life events index* was based on administration of a life events list (an extended and somewhat modified form of the Paykel list) enquiring about experiences in the last 12 months. In addition, respondents rated

* A count of positive responses to whether four items (anxiety, depression, irritability, nervousness) had been suffered in the last month.

each event on ten scales covering the perceived emotional impact of the event and locus of responsibility for it. In the present analysis, three sub-indices were used to construct a composite index of life event impact. These were

Number of life events experienced in last twelve months (unweighted count).
Total weighted score for life events experienced in last twelve months.
Score for single most severe adverse event experienced in last twelve months.

Tennant and Andrews' (1976) weights were used in scoring life events. However the life events list included eight types of event not covered by Tennant and Andrews. For these types of event, weights were interpolated, using a regression of the Tennant and Andrews weights on mean scale scores for types of event.

A weighted composite of the three life event indices was derived by a canonical correlation analysis, in which the indices were related to the three morbidity measures listed above. The resulting composite index of life events correlated with the three sub-indices as follows:

Number of life events	.79
Total weighted score	.90
Maximum score	.35

It should be noted that in this index no allowance is made for recency of the event. An event eleven months prior to interview receives the same weight as a similar event the day before the interview. This is an *interim* treatment of the data which is almost certainly less than optimal.

12

Psychiatric Disorders and Susceptibility to Stress

BRUCE P. DOHRENWEND, PH.D.
and
BARBARA SNELL DOHRENWEND, PH.D.

To date, a wide variety of correlations between psychopathology and recent stressful life events have been reported. For example, Brown, Harris, and Peto (1973), Paykel (1974), and Cooper and Sylph (1973) have provided evidence that episodes of acute schizophrenia, depression, and neurosis may follow life events. The range of correlates has been expanded to include associations with symptom scales that measure various types of psychological distress, rather than outright disorder. Markush and Favero (1974), for example, found that symptoms of depressed mood as well as a symptom scale of less specific psychological distress were related to measures of life events. Uhlenhuth, Lipman, Balter, and Stern (1974) have reported similar findings. Myers, Lindenthal, and Pepper (1974) have shown with still another measure of symptomatic distress that symptom scores will fluctuate over time with fluctuations in the nature and number of life events experienced.

Unfortunately, however, the correlations are often only modest at best (cf. Rabkin & Struening, 1976). Moreover, some of the findings are extremely difficult to interpret due to a probable confounding of the measurement of life events with the measurement of psychopathology. Consider, for example, some of the events in the measure developed by Holmes and Rahe (1967) which has strongly influenced most others.

Subjective events on their list such as "sexual difficulties," "major change in number of arguments with spouse," and "major changes in sleeping habits," taken at face value, are more likely to be manifestations of or responses to underlying psychopathology than causes of such pathology. Moreover, the problem is not limited to subjective events of this type since negative objective events such as "divorce" and "being fired from work" are as likely to be consequences as causes of psychopathology. As a number of investigators have pointed out, this kind of bias in a sample of life events seriously limits the kind of inferences that can be drawn from a correlation between the number or magnitude of events experienced and illness (cf. Brown, 1974; B. P. Dohrenwend, 1974). The limitations apply even when data are available over time, since psychiatric disorders are often of insidious onset and long duration.

THE PROBLEM

For these reasons, a major problem has arisen about how to interpret such studies. Do the correlations indicate that individuals with various types of psychopathology are victims of fateful circumstances that expose them to unusually harsh and numerous stressful life events? Or, is it that such persons are more vulnerable than the average person to stressful life events that tend to build up or cluster without serious consequence in the lives of most of us at one time or another? Or, are these disordered persons neither more victimized nor more vulnerable but rather more "stress-prone" (Zubin & Spring, 1977, p. 110) in that they bring upon themselves an excess of stressful life events that serve to amplify or exacerbate their underlying pathology?

In accord with the theme of this symposium, our purpose in this paper will be to examine especially the evidence for the last two possibilities, those of vulnerability and proneness. In further keeping with the symposium theme, we shall narrow the focus still more to the possible sources of vulnerability and proneness in the individual's psychopathology or disposition to psychopathology.

A PARADIGM OF THE STRESS RESPONSE

We will start our inquiry within the framework of a general paradigm of the stress response that we have found useful in the past. The paradigm was adapted from Hans Selye's formulation (1956) and translated into social and psychological terms (B. P. Dohrenwend, 1961). Selye's paradigm consists of four main elements: an antecedent stressor—often a toxic agent or electric shock in Selye's experiments with animals; conditioning or mediating factors such as climate or diet that increase or decrease the impact of the stressor; the General Adaptation Syndrome of nonspecific physical and chemical changes, indicating the intervening state of stress in an organism over time; and consequent adaptive or, in cases where there is a "derailment" of the mechanism of adaptation, maladaptive responses in the form of what Selye calls "diseases of adaptation."

By stripping these four kinds of elements of particular examples from Selye's work on physical and chemical variables, it is possible to arrive at the general paradigm of the individual organism's stress response shown in Figure 1. This general paradigm, in turn, can be translated into social and psychological terms for its various elements. For example, stressors

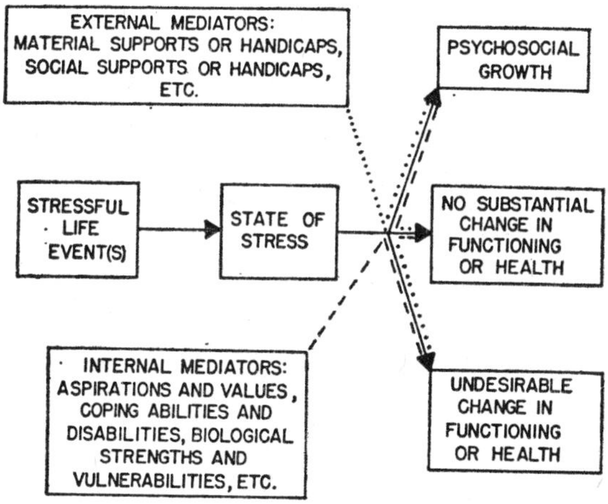

FIGURE 1. General paradigm of the stress process (based on B. P. Dohrenwend, 1961).

can range from extreme situations such as natural and man-made disasters to ordinary stressful life events such as birth of a first child, loss of a job, or death of a loved one. And mediating factors can be expanded to include both inner resources and deficits such as intellectual abilities, physical health, and, of particular interest here, inherited or acquired psychological vulnerabilities as well as external resources or deficits such as material wealth, social support in the form of family, friends, and community agencies, or the absence of such assets.

Whether there is a *General* Adaptation Syndrome of nonspecific physical and chemical changes has been questioned (Mason, 1975). The existence of anything directly analogous to it in social and psychological terms is even more of an open issue. We have, therefore, omitted reference to such a syndrome in Figure 1. Certainly, however, social psychological adaptation syndromes must have affective elements of adaptation rooted in the arousal responses of fear and anger; conative elements of adaptation involving change or reemphasis in activities—abandoning some activities, taking up others, increasing or decreasing still other activities; finally, adaptation is also likely to involve changes in orientation involving assimilation of new information, alteration of beliefs, and so on. Finally, when adaptation fails or the mechanisms underlying it become "derailed," we can look for maladaptive responses in the form of transient or persistent psychopathology. From accounts of symptoms observed in previously normal persons undergoing the stresses of extreme situations such as severe combat during wartime, it is apparent that these symptoms can run the gamut of those described in psychiatric nomenclatures (e.g., Kolb, 1973, pp. 436-438).

With regard to the antecedent conditions producing stress as portrayed in Figure 1, we can envision two extreme typological combinations of stressful life events on the basis of our previous analyses (B. S. Dohrenwend & B. P. Dohrenwend, 1978; B. P. Dohrenwend, 1979). At one extreme would be a pathogenic triad of recent life events that, we have hypothesized, would approximate the conditions of extreme situations such as combat. It would consist of fateful loss events, physical illness and injury, and other events that disrupt social supports. As a general rule, it will be rare that a member of the general population will have recently experienced the close occurrence of all three types of events. However, among some subgroups of the population, such as the aged, recent occurrence of the triad may appear with considerable frequency. Its impact would, we hypothesize, override internal and external mediating factors and, as in extreme situations such as those observed in combat, lead quite directly to derailment of the mechanisms of adaptation and consequent psychopathology in previously normal persons.

At the other extreme, by contrast, we can envision chronic psychiatric patients such as those whose admission to a Veterans Administration hospital was studied by Fontana and his colleagues (Fontana, Marcus, Noel, & Rakusin, 1972). For such persons, the types of stressors that differentiate them from control subjects are life events that are contingent upon their own actions and/or directly involved in the process of bringing them to the hospital. Such "contingent" and "involved" events—for example, quitting a job, provoking an argument with a spouse or an arrest from a policeman—are best interpreted not as antecedents to the patient's

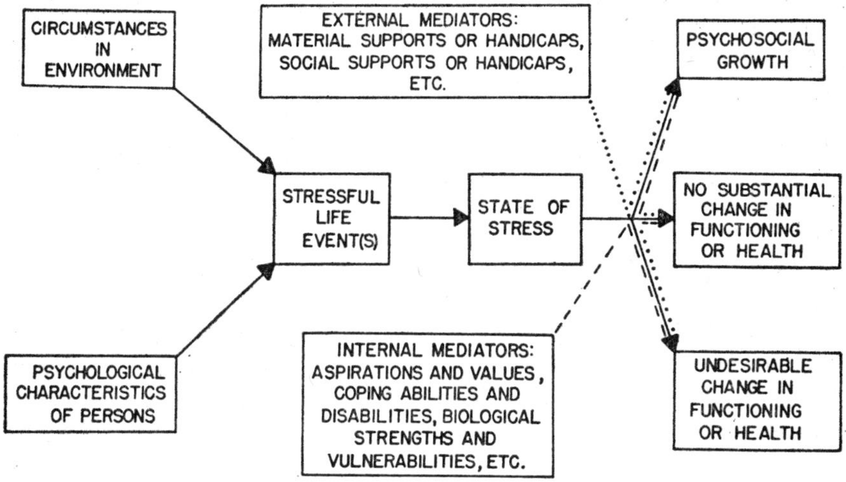

FIGURE 2. General paradigm of the stress process extended to include antecedents of stressful life events (based on Figure 1 in B. S. Dohrenwend, 1978).

disorder or to its exacerbation but rather, in Fontana's plausible view, as attempts to cope with onsets of exacerbations of disorder by behaving in such a way as to insure hospitalization.

Clearly, the paradigm in Figure 1 does not encompass the difference between such cases and those based on the pathogenic triad in extreme situations. In Figure 2, therefore, we present a more complete paradigm which takes into account the difference between the experimenter-generated stressors of laboratory studies, whose cause is external to the stress process under study, and the complex of environmental and personal factors that also generate stressful life events but which must be understood as part of the stress process.

THE QUESTION OF PRONENESS

Patients at Veterans Administration hospitals are likely to have chronic disorders, and multiple hospital admissions. They are hardly typical of psychiatric patients in general, much less of the substantial numbers of untreated psychiatric cases in the general population. To what extent do wider samples of psychiatric cases show similar proneness to stressful life events?

A few years ago we reported some study results that bear on this question (Dohrenwend, 1974). The more than 500 subjects interviewed were drawn from the Washington Heights Section of New York City. They consisted of 67 community leaders including, for example, state assemblymen, clergymen, and businessmen; a community sample of 257 (married and single adult heads of households of both sexes) drawn on a strict probability basis from the general population of Washington Heights; 118 outpatients from various psychiatric clinics in or adjacent to Washington Heights; 62 inpatients admitted to either of two mental hospitals; and 24 convicts at various city prisons. These subjects represent completion rates of 79 percent of the leaders we set out to interview; 67 percent of the community sample; 76 percent of the patients; and all of the prisoners. The interviewers were 15 psychiatrists who rated the presence or absence of psychiatric disorder and its severity in each subject. These ratings are described in more detail elsewhere (Dohrenwend, 1974). In addition to various questions about his or her symptomatology and functioning, each subject was asked a series of questions about the life events that he or she had experienced.

The sequence on life events started with the following open-ended questions:

> *"What was the last major event in your life that, for better or for worse, interrupted or changed your usual activities?"*
>
> If no response was forthcoming, the interviewer used the following standard probe:
>
> *"For example, events affecting your occupation, your physical health, your living arrangements, your relations with other family members, your friends, or your personal values or beliefs."*
>
> If a "major event" was recalled, the respondent was asked:
>
> *"When did this occur?"* Date (s) ....
> *"What happened?"*
>
> Several other questions were asked about additional events since then, but our main focus here is on the last major event. After these open-ended questions had been asked and the responses recorded, respondents were given a checklist and asked the following question:
>
> *"Some things happen to most people at one time or another. Other things happen to only a few people. Which of these events have you experienced during the last 12 months?"*
>
> The events on the checklist are as follows:
>
> Started to school, training program, etc.
> Graduated from school, training program, etc.
> Failed school, training program, etc.

Moved to better neighborhood
Moved to worse neighborhood
Engaged
Married
Widowed
Divorced
Separated
Other broken love relationship—Explain
Birth of first child
Birth of child other than first
Serious physical illness to self
Serious injury to self
Serious injury to loved one—Who?
Serious physical illness to loved one—Who?
Death of a loved one—Who?
Started to work on a job for the first time
Expanded business
Promoted or moved to more responsible job
Changed to more secure job
Business failed
Demoted or changed to less responsible job
Laid off
Fired

In this study, it was posible to range the different groups of subjects from most likely to be psychiatrically healthy (the community leaders) to most likely to have serious disorders or behavior problems (the psychiatric inpatients and prisoners) (Dohrenwend, 1974, p. 280). It was also possible to categorize the life events reported from those most likely to be consequences of psychiatric disorder, through those independently caused, to those most likely to be consequences of superior functioning as follows:

1. The respondent's subjective crises that are direct manifestations of psychiatric or emotional disturbance (e.g., a "nervous breakdown") and/or objective events such as hospitalization or imprisonment that are direct consequences of such disturbance.
2. The respondent's interpersonal conflicts.
3. Miscellaneous insignificant-seeming objective events and rare or unusual subjective events that are not clear in their relation to the respondent's psychiatric condition.
4. Objective loss events for whose occurrence the respondent is likely to share significant responsibility (e.g., divorce, separation).
5. Serious physical illness or injury to the respondent.

6. Objective loss events—other than serious physical illness or injury to the respondent—whose occurrence is likely to be outside the respondent's control (e.g., being widowed, husband's loss of job, spouse's physical illness).
7. Objective events that our own disagreeing judgments suggested to us that most people would see as representing mixtures of gains and losses in roughly equal proportions or mainly gains to some respondents and mainly losses to equal numbers of other respondents (e.g., birth of a child other than first).
8. Objective gain events (e.g., promotion, birth of a first child).

The first four types of events listed above are ordered in terms of likelihood of their being consequences of the individual's psychopathology (cf. Langner & Michael, 1963, pp. 117-146). The last two types, by contrast, are ordered in terms of likelihood of being consequences of generally superior functioning on the part of the individual. The remaining two types—serious physical illness and injury to the respondent and other objective loss events—are likely to be outside the person's control. Especially in the case of the latter type of fateful objective loss there is little reason to believe that such events are consequences of either the individual's psychopathology or of his or her superior functioning.

This ordering admittedly lacks precision. For example, some types of physical illness and injury are more likely to be consequences of psychopathology than others. Also, some types of gain events that occur to children of the respondents may only very indirectly be due to the respondents' own superior functioning (e.g., having children of whom they can be proud). Moreover, there are the ambiguous events in category 7, where normative definitions of gain and loss may be unclear or in conflict, and exceptions to the norm in other categories (e.g., the occurrence of a separation from one's spouse for which the individual bears no responsibility). Despite the grossness of the ordering, however, we found sharp differences in the events experienced by different groups of subjects. Consider first their responses to the open-ended questions about the last major event that they experienced. As Table 1 shows, there is clearly a positive relation between the ordering of the groups of subjects from most likely to be healthy to most likely to be disordered and the ordering of events from most likely to be confounded with good health to those most likely to be confounded with psychopathology.

For a majority of the subjects in each group, the last major event reported occurred a year or more before the interview; in a substantial minority of respondents, more than 10 years before. Moreover, since the question was open-ended, only events that were salient to the respondents were reported. Let us, therefore, turn to the results on the checklist of events for the preceding year where problems of salience and time of occurrence were better controlled.

Each of the items on the checklist described earlier is an objective event in the sense that its existence theoretically and often practically can be verified independently of the respondent's report of its occurrence. Moreover, all occurrences—be they objective events or subjective events—that involve descriptions of a subject's psychiatric disturbance or treatment for such disturbance have been excluded. Thus the range and variety of events related to positive functioning on the one hand and to psychopathology on the other is somewhat less for the checklist events than for the last major events, for which no such limitations were set. Nevertheless, as Table 2 shows, there is again a positive relationship between the health of the subject group and the types of events reported. Note especially that loss events for whose occurrence the subject may be responsible are more characteristic of patients and convicts than they are of community sample respondents and community leaders.

There is, however, some imbalance in the educational levels of the respondents from the leader, community, patient and prisoner samples. The leaders were disproportionately likely to have had college and graduate educations while very few of the patients and prisoners were college graduates, despite our efforts to oversample the college educated among them. To test whether these differences in educational levels could account for the differences in proneness among the groups, we repeated the analyses shown in Tables 1 and 2 separately for subjects at each of four educational levels: 0-7 grades; 8-11 grades; 12-15 grades; and 16 or more. Except for respondents at the 16 or more or college graduate level, the results remained statistically significant at the 0.05 level or better. At the college graduate level, the trend was in the right direction.

We conducted additional analyses of the relation of types of events to an index of severity of disorder based on the psychiatrists' ratings of each member of the community sample. Within this sample, there was a significant positive relationship between severity of disorder and likelihood that the events reported were consequences of the subjects' psychiatric condition (Dohrenwend, 1974, p. 292, p. 300).

It seems clear from these results that, to some extent, the stressful events accompanying psychopathology are a function of this proneness of the individual involved. This proneness is more pronounced for persons who have been frequently hospitalized for chronic disorders or imprisoned for problems of antisocial behavior than for cases discovered in

TABLE 1

Types of Last Major Event Reported by Respondents in Patient and Non-Patient Groups (in percent)

Type of Last Major Event	Respondent Groups: Leaders	Community Sample	Psychiatric Outpatients	Psychiatric Hospital Patients	Convicts
No last major event	7.6	16.5	21.1	18.9	10.5
Objective gain event	36.4	20.5	17.6	18.9	10.5
Objective event that may mix gain and loss	9.1	7.1	3.5	1.9	5.3
Objective loss event other than physical illness or injury—occurrence likely to be outside R's control	18.2	24.8	13.2	7.5	5.3
Objective loss event involving physical illness or injury to respondent	13.6	12.2	3.5	5.7	—
Objective loss event—occurrence likely to be R's responsibility	12.1	12.6	19.3	3.7	—
Miscellaneous event, insignificant objective event, or rare subjective event	3.0	2.4	0.9	13.2	—
Largely subjective events in the form of interpersonal conflicts involving respondent	—	1.5	0.9	5.7	—
Events which are direct manifestations of psychopathology or sociopathy and/or their dispositions	—	2.4	20.2	24.5	68.4
Total Percents	100.0	100.0	100.0	100.0	100.0
Base for percents = total respondents minus no answers	(66)	(254)	(114)	(53)	(19)

Note: With "no last major event" excluded and psychiatric outpatients, hospital patients and convicts combined, gamma = .37; $p < 0.001$.

community samples—a difference that raises some interesting questions about the role of labeling and secondary gain vs. severity of illness. Moreover, there may be sharp differences for different types of disorder quite apart from whether the disorder led to treatment or imprisonment. These are questions for further analysis and research. Meanwhile, the problem of proneness that a number of investigators have identified when reviewing the types of events included in inventories used to investigate the causal role of stressful life events is clearly not a trivial one, as these results show. And, in terms of the theme of this conference, it seems

TABLE 2

Types of Events Reported in Response to Checklist by Respondents in Patient and Nonpatient Groups (in Percent)

	Respondent Groups				
Type of Checklist Event	Leaders	Community Sample	Psychiatric Outpatients	Psychiatric Hospital Patients	Convicts
No checklist event	31.8	40.5	27.2	22.6	10.5
Gain events only or gain events plus mixed events only	30.3	17.7	21.1	18.9	5.3
Event that may mix gain and loss	—	1.6	—	—	—
Loss: occurrence unlikely to be R's responsibility and no other types of loss events	24.3	21.3	18.4	17.0	10.5
Loss: physical illness and injury and no loss: own responsibility	10.6	11.4	14.0	7.5	5.3
Loss: likely to be R's responsibility and any other types of events	3.0	7.5	19.3	34.0	68.4
Total Percent	100.0	100.0	100.0	100.0	100.0
Total respondents (minus no answers)	(66)	(254)	(114)	(53)	(19)

Note: With "no checklist events" excluded and psychiatric outpatients, hospital patients and convicts combined, gamma = .34; $p < 0.001$.

evident that however much psychopathology may be a consequence of stressful circumstances, it also carries with it a proneness to such circumstances as well.

THE QUESTION OF VULNERABILITY

There is now considerable evidence that individuals with some types of psychiatric disorders are more vulnerable to stressful life events than individuals with other types of psychiatric disorders. On the basis of case-control studies, for example, Brown, Harris and Peto (1973) and Paykel (1978) have estimated respectively that "brought forward time" and relative risk is greater for clinical depression than for schizophrenia. No one knows, however, what the true risk attached directly to stressful life events is for these or any other type of psychiatric disorder.

In view of the modest size of the associations reported thus far between life events and various types of psychopathology, there is general consensus that events must exert their impact in interactions with other factors such as the internal and external mediating factors described above in relation to Figure 2 (cf. Brown et al., 1973; Rabkin & Struening,

1976; Paykel, 1978). There is far less evidence about which of these mediating factors are the most important sources of vulnerability.

Certainly, one might expect that existing psychopathology would markedly increase vulnerability to subsequent stressful life events. The problem is that there are few investigations focused on this or any other sources of vulnerability possibility excepting early loss of parents (Langner & Michael, 1963; Brown, Harris & Copeland, 1977; Dohrenwend & deFigueiredo, in press) and lack of social supports (Nuckolls, Cassel, & Kaplan, 1972).

Some of the relevant data exist, however, and more could be developed without great difficulty. For example, Brown, Harris and Peto (1973) mention that they found that the current episode of depression was less often event-provoked when subjects had had a previous attack of depression than when they had not. This may suggest that the earlier attack left them with increased vulnerability, although it is also possible that the increased vulnerability was a treatment effect, or an effect of labeling. It should be possible to test the matter further in Brown and Birley's (1968) cases of acute schizophrenia collected for their earlier study, since some were first admissions while others were readmissions.

A particularly promising possibility might be to integrate life events research with psychotropic drug evaluation research, since the drugs could be expected to reduce both vulnerability to stress and proneness stemming directly from overt symptomatology. On the other hand, it is conceivable that a drug might induce vulnerability or proneness, and this could be tested as well.

There are results from a study by Leff and his colleagues that seem consistent with both possibilities (Leff, Hirsch, Gaind, Rohde, & Stevens, 1973). These investigators collected data on stressful life events from chronic and acute schizophrenics who were participating in placebo-controlled trials of maintenance phenothiazines. Drug treated patients who relapsed had more often experienced "independent" or fateful events in the prior five-week period than had placebo patients who relapsed, suggesting to us that for some patients, at least, the drugs reduced vulnerability to stress. An additional and even more pronounced finding, however, was that patients on drugs experienced more "possibly independent" events; that is, events that "are not so clearly out of . . . [the patient's] control but which seem unlikely to be produced by the unusual behavior of the subject himself" (p. 659). To the extent that these latter events actually were under the patients' control, this suggests that drugs increased proneness.

Returning to our paradigm in Figure 2 and its theoretical formulation, we would expect that any time psychopathology followed stressful life events differing in types and amounts from those contained in our pathogenic triad of fateful loss events, severe physical illness or injury, and other events that disrupt the subject's usual social supports, vulnerabilities stemming from various mediating factors could be found to play a part. Co-occurrence of events belonging to the pathogenic triad could be expected to override mediating factors even when these mediating factors were such as to reduce vulnerability to stress. Under the more common and less extreme stressful combinations of life events, we would expect mediating factors that induce varying types and amounts of vulnerability to play a part. At this point, however, we would still face the problem of isolating the role of prior psychopathology in creating vulnerability from that of other mediating factors.

CONCLUSION

We started with the question of how to interpret the results of a growing body of literature portraying a positive relationship between the number or magnitude of recent stressful life events and various types of psychopathology. The problem arises because many of the life events included in these studies could as easily be consequences as causes of psychopathology. We are more confident that they are causes when their occurrence is outside the control of the subject, when they clearly antedate the first occurrence of the psychopathology on which the study focuses, and when they are embedded in our hypothesized pathogenic triad of fateful loss events, severe physical illness or injury, and other events that disrupt the subject's usual social supports. Such events, we have argued, bring about approximations to the conditions of extreme situations that we know from studies of combat and other man-made and natural disasters will induce psychopathology in previously normal persons. However, the pathogenic triad is very uncommon in a community population living in normal circumstances, except possibly among the aged. To understand the observed relations between stressful life events and psychopathology, therefore, we look at innate and acquired personal factors and environmental factors that may exacerbate the impact of less extreme stressors, and innate and acquired personal factors that may affect the number or intensity of stressors to which particular individuals are exposed. The former set of factors is conceived as determining the vulnerability of the individual, the latter his or her proneness to stress.

It seems clear from the research that we have reviewed and from some of our own findings that psychiatric patients are both more vulnerable and more prone than the general population, as well as being victims of environmentally induced stressors to some extent. Beyond these important but nevertheless minimal facts, our knowledge becomes vague. We do not know in any precise sense, for example, to what extent different diagnostic types are victims of stressful events and to what extent vulnerable or prone to stressful events. Nor do we know to what extent the sources of their vulnerability and proneness are related to the underlying disorder as distinguished from some of the negative effects of the treatment process—the socialization in dependency involved for some, the debilitating side effects of drugs for others, and the stigma attached to the patient role by the wider society.

These questions will require programs of research that use complex designs, for example: elements of case-control studies to deal with the problem that major types of disorder are rare in the general population; samples of contrasting types of cases to deal with the problem that different types of stressors may be related to different types of disorders and that vulnerability and proneness to stress may vary with type of disorder as well; use of control groups sampled on a strict probability basis from the general population to increase generalizability of results and facilitate estimation of risk; contrasts of first admission cases with re-admissions as a step toward experimental trials in looking at possible treatment-related effects; collection of data on psychopathology in first-degree relatives to tests the relation between genetic risk and vulnerability to stress; provision for prospective features involving collection of data at multiple points in time to establish time sequences between stressful events and onsets or exacerbations of psychopathology. Research to date, much of it relatively simple in design, has made great advances in clarifying the questions about relations between stressful life events and psychopathology but has not given us many answers to these complex questions.

REFERENCES

Brown, G. W.: Meaning, measurement, and stress of life events. In: B. P. Dohrenwend and B. S. Dohrenwend (Eds.), *Stressful Life Events: Their Nature and Effects.* New York: Wiley, 1974.

Brown, G. W. and Birley, J. L. T.: Crises and life changes and the onset of schizophrenia. *J. Hlth. Soc. Behav.*, 9:203-214, 1968.

Brown, G. W., Harris, T., and Copeland, J. R.: Depression and loss. *Brit. J. Psychiat.*, 130:1-18, 1977.

Brown, G. W., Harris, T. O., and Peto, J.: Life events and psychiatric disorder: 2. Nature of the causal link. *Psychol. Med.*, 3:159-176, 1973.

Cooper, B. and Sylph, J.: Life events and the onset of neurotic illness: An investigation in general practice. *Psychol. Med.*, 3:421-435, 1973.

DOHRENWEND, B. P.: The social psychological nature of stress: A framework for causal inquiry. *J. Abnorm. Soc. Psychol.*, 62:294-302, 1961.

DOHRENWEND, B. P.: Problems in defining and sampling the relevant population of stressful life events. In: B. P. Dohrenwend and B. S. Dohrenwend (Eds.), *Stressful Life Events: Their Nature and Effects.* New York: Wiley, 1974, pp. 275-310.

DOHRENWEND, B. P.: Stressful life events and psychopathology: Some issues in theory and method. In: J. E. Barrett (Ed.), *Stress and Mental Disorder.* New York: Raven Press, 1979.

DOHRENWEND, B. P. and DEFIGUEIREDO, J. M.: Remote and recent life events. In: D. L. Ricks and B. S. Dohrenwend (Eds.), *Origins of Psychopathology: Research and Public Policy,* Cambridge University Press, in press.

DOHRENWEND, B. S. and DOHRENWEND, B. P.: Some issues in research on stressful life events. *J. Nerv. Ment. Dis.*, 166:7-15, 1978.

FONTANA, A. F., MARCUS, J. L., NOEL, B., and RAKUSIN, J. M.: Prehospitalization coping styles of psychiatric patients: The goal-directedness of life events. *J. Nerv. Ment. Dis.*, 155:311-321, 1972.

HOLMES, T. H. and RAHE, R. H.: The social readjustment rating scale. *J. Psychosom. Med.*, 11:213-218, 1967.

KOLB, L. C.: *Modern Clinical Psychiatry.* Philadelphia: W. B. Saunders, 1973.

LANGNER, T. S. and MICHAEL, S. T.: *Life Stress and Mental Health.* London: The Free Press of Glencoe, 1963.

LEFF, J. P., HIRSCH, S. R., GAIND, R., ROHDE, P. D., and STEVENS, B. C.: Life events and maintenance therapy in schizophrenic relapse. *Brit. J. Psychiat.*, 123:659-660, 1973.

MARKUSH, R. E. and FAVERO, R. V.: Epidemiologic assessment of stressful life events, depressed mood, and psychophysiological symptoms—a preliminary report. In: B. S. Dohrenwend and B. P. Dohrenwend (Eds.), *Stressful Life Events: Their Nature and Effects.* New York: Wiley, 1974, pp. 171-190.

MASON, J. W.: A historical view of the stress field. *J. Human Stress,* 1:6-12, 1975.

MYERS, J. K., LINDENTHAL, J. J., and PEPPER, M. P.: Social class, life events, and psychiatric symptoms: A longitudinal study. In: B. S. Dohrenwend and B. P. Dohrenwend (Eds.), *Stressful Life Events: Their Nature and Effects.* New York: Wiley, 1974, pp. 191-205.

NUCKOLLS, K., CASSEL, J., and KAPLAN, B.: Psychological assets, life crisis, and the prognosis of pregnancy. *Am. J. Epidemiol.*, 95:431-441, 1972.

PAYKEL, E. S.: Life stress and psychiatric disorder: Application of the clinical approach. In: B. S. Dohrenwend and B. P. Dohrenwend (Eds.), *Stressful Life Events: Their Nature and Effects.* New York: Wiley, 1974.

PAYKEL, E. S.: Contribution of life events to causation of psychiatric illness. *Psychol. Med.*, 8:245-253, 1978.

RABKIN, J. G. and STRUENING, E. L.: Life events, stress, and illness. *Science,* 194:1013-1020, 1976.

SELYE, H.: *The Stress of Life.* New York: McGraw-Hill Book Company, 1956.

UHLENHUTH, E., LIPMAN, R. S., BALTER, M. B., and STERN, M.: Symptom intensity and life stress in the city. *Arch. Gen. Psychiat.*, 31:759-764, 1974.

ZUBIN, J. and SPRING, B.: Vulnerability—a new view of schizophrenia. *J. Abnorm. Psychol.*, 86:103-126, 1977.

13

The Nature and Extent of Psychiatric Disorders Among African Refugees

J. Muhangi, M.D.

Asuni (1975) and German (1972) have pointed out that Africa is neither a racial nor an ethnic entity. Those who do not live there often regard the continent as made up of discrete nations, but the truth is that the national boundaries are artificial. It is common for one ethnic group to spread across frontiers, with members, not only of the group but of the "family," on both sides. Mobility across borders is high. This means that it can be difficult to decide who is and who is not an "immigrant" or a "refugee." To complicate the matter further, poverty is a major cause of mobility (German, 1971). Many people cross borders in order to find a better standard of living and, if they fail, may take the opportunity offered by political conditions in their country of origin to class themselves as "refugees." On the other hand, some genuine refugees may not class themselves as such for fear that harm could come to their families, and others may find it relatively easy to pass themselves off as citizens of the "host" country.

Geopolitical factors, in any case, probably account for only a small part of the psychiatric problems of a "refugee" group. Culture and education are often much more important. Orley (1968), for example, described how the Baganda divided illnesses into two categories: those regarded as "traditional," susceptible only to traditional remedies, and those regarded suitable for western medical techniques. Many authors have emphasized the importance of cultural attitudes in determining the way

Africans experience and perceive psychiatric disorders (Lambo, 1955; Muhangi & German, 1975; Prince, 1960; Wittkower & Histon, 1968).

Psychiatric services are largely undeveloped in Black African countries and data on the frequency of psychiatric disorders are scarce. There is a small group of highly educated people whose ideas of psychiatric illness are much the same as those in Euro-American cultures. But the large majority of rural people are unlikely to be able to consult a doctor, let alone a psychiatrist, and they have their own subcultural views of the nature of psychological disorders. It is against this background that the problem of mental illness in refugees must be considered.

METHODS AND MATERIAL

The author is a Ugandan who taught psychiatry at Makerere University for five years before moving to Kenya three years ago when political conditions in Uganda became unpredictable and often life-threatening. He met refugees in clinical practice, at reception centres, at social gatherings and in the course of University teaching. Notes were made about 103 people seen between April 1975 and December 1977. About 70 percent were seen privately; the rest were seen at the Kenyatta National Hospital outpatient clinic.

The number of Ugandan refugees who moved to Kenya following the advent of the military government has been variously estimated as 20 to 40 thousand. Most, by African standards, were well educated, with a formal schooling of some 10 years. A smaller group of refugees from Somalia had quite different educational and cultural background and these were excluded from the study.

RESULTS

Most of the refugees seen were men (80:23), 16 being students. Most of the men (54) were aged between 21 and 35; 10 (all students) were under 21, and only one man was over 45. The 23 women were, in general, older, none being under 21; 12 were between 21 and 35, and eight were over 45. Approximately equal proportions of the men were married and single, whereas nearly all the women (19) were married. This may well be due to the fact that psychiatric consultation is regarded as a threat to the marriage prospects of women.

More than 86 percent of the group were adequately employed. This high proportion reflects the acceptability of Ugandans in Kenya and also their relatively high educational qualifications. At the time of this study, large numbers of refugees had not yet entered Kenya and employment

TABLE 1

Psychiatric Diagnoses

	Males	Females
Schizophrenia	1	1
Manic-depressive	1	—
Anxiety states	28	9
Reactive depression	40	11
Acute psychotic episode	7	—
Alcoholism	3	—
Hysterical states	—	1
Other	—	1
Total	80	23

Table 1 shows the distribution of diagnoses in the group. The large majority were reactive depressions and anxiety states. Only 10 out of the 103 had a history of previous mental disorder. The symptoms complained of are listed in Table 2. It is characteristic that psychosomatic rather than prospects have probably decreased since. Acuda (1978) who runs a clinic for refugees in Nairobi has suggested that the number of severely depressed patients, many of them suicidal, has recently increased.
psychological symptoms were the presenting complaints (Muhangi & German, 1975). Twenty subjects had few clinical symptoms but had psychosocial problems that required mainly personal or friendly solutions in connection with accommodation, money, employment or various everyday difficulties.

DISCUSSION

In European and American studies the question of the contribution of "forced" movement to the excess morbidity found in migrants remains largely unresolved (Faris & Dunham, 1939; Malzberg & Lee, 1956; Mezey, 1960; Ødegaard, 1945, 1956). Detailed studies of this kind have not been carried out in Africa. Bennett and Assael (1970), who studied Rwandan immigrants in rural Uganda, concluded that loss of family and material support appeared to contribute to an increased incidence of alcoholism and antisocial behavior. Forster (1972) studied the impact of political changes in Ghana which resulted in similar hardships to those found in immigrants and refugees. He observed that there was no increase in first admission rate though he thought there could have been an increase in aggressive behaviour.

TABLE 2

Frequency of Neurotic Symptoms
(complained of or admitted)

	No. of Subjects
Headache	90
General weakness	40
Inability to sleep well	50
Heat in the head	32
'Things' crawling under the skin	4
Decreased libido	10
Fearing going mad	24
Inability to relax	5
Abdominal pain	17
Palpitations	20
Constipation	31
Partial impotence	20
Frigidity	1
Visual disturbances	2

The present study is descriptive only and it is not possible to draw more than tentative conclusions. First, only two of the patients had schizophrenia and only one had a manic psychosis. One of the schizophrenic patients (a man in his early thirties) had become ill at least 10 years previously while he was in Uganda; the other (a girl of 20) had a positive family history on both sides. The manic patient had had a first episode of mania before leaving Uganda. Migration therefore played little part in the generation of psychotic conditions in this group.

Much attentions has been paid to the occurrence of brief psychotic states in African subjects (Carothers, 1953; Collomb, 1956; Faergeman, 1963; German, 1972; Harworth, 1968; Lambo, 1955, 1960; Rainault, 1958). Muhangi (1972) has argued that it is not always easy to separate organic from functional psychoses when subclinical avitaminosis, anaemia, and infestations are common. However, none of the subjects in the present series presented with psychotic conditions in which the aetiology was unclear and the diagnosis of *bouffée délirante* was not used.

The much commoner neurotic conditions did seem to be related, though often in subtle ways, to the refugee status. For example, marital problems could be exacerbated by the lower income now earned by husbands, and there was a general lowering of morale described in such terms as, "Things can't be the same. We are out of our country." It is surprising that so few diagnoses of alcoholism were made. (At Butabika mental hospital in Uganda, in the late sixties, two or three patients with delirium tremens were admitted per week.) There may have been a tendency not to report abuse of alcohol. In addition, a lowered income means that there was little cash to spend on alcohol.

Given the unstable nature of African politics it seems likely that the number of refugees will increase. Most of those in the present study were first-time migrants but we can expect increased numbers of second-, third- and even fourth-time refugees, with a cumulative adverse affect on employment, education and family life and an increasing state of demoralisation, quite apart from the difficulties inevitably caused as the host countries begin to see the immigrants as aliens. There is an urgent need to re-evaluate the longer-term psychosocial needs of refugees, not only at the level of international organisations but at the national level as well. The Helsinki and other declarations of rights remain, as far as many African countries are concerned, purely paper declarations. The chief means of preventing the refugee problem is to find political means of gradual change and progress.

REFERENCES

Acuda, S. W.: Personal communication, 1978.

Asuni, T.: Social, cultural and economic determinants of psychiatric services in Western Nigeria. *Afr. J. Psychiat.*, Vol. 1:3-15, 1975.

Bennett, F. J. and Assael, M. I.: The mental health of Rwanda immigrants and refugees at Kasangati, Uganda. *International Mental Health Research Newsletter,* XII, 1. New York: The Postgraduate Center for Mental Health, 1970.

Carothers, J. C.: The African mind in health and disease: A study of ethnopsychiatry. Monograph Series, Geneva WHO, No. 17, 1953.

Collomb, H.: Introduction a *'la psychiatriae tropicale.'* 16:141-51, 1956.

Faergman, P. M.: *Psychogenic Psychosis.* London, 1963.

Faris, R. E. L. and Dunham, H. W.: *Mental Disorders in Urban Areas.* Chicago: Chicago University Press, 1939.

Forster, E. B.: Mental health and political change in Ghana 1951-1971. *Psychopathologie Africaine,* VIII, 3:383-417, 1972.

German, G. A.: The psychiatry of poverty. *Psychopathologie Africaine,* Vol. 1, No. 1, 1971.

German, G. A.: Aspects of clinical psychiatry in sub-Saharan Africa. *Brit. J. Psychiat.,* 121:461-79, 1972.

Harworth, A.: Schizophrenia, hysteria and other barriers to communication. In: *Deuxieme Colloque Africain de Psychiatrie.* Paris: 1968.

Lambo, T. A.: The role of cultural factors in paranoid psychoses among the Yoruba. *J. Ment. Sci.,* 101:239-65, 1955.

Lambo, T. A.: Further neuropsychiatric observation in Nigeria. *Brit. J. Psychiat.,* 2: 1-24, 1960.

Malzberg, B. and Lee, E. S.: *Migration and Mental Disease.* New York: Social Science Research Council, 1956.

Mezey, A. G.: Personal background, emigration and mental disorder in Hungarian refugees. *J. Ment. Sci.,* 106:618-627, 1960.

MEZEY, A. G.: Psychiatric illness in Hungarian refugees. *J. Ment. Sci.*, 106:618-637.

MUHANGI, J.: Functional or organic psychosis: (Four cases of typhoid fever initially presenting as various forms of psychiatric disorder). *Afr. J. Med. Sci.*, 3:319-326, 1972.

MUHANGI, J. and GERMAN, G. A.: Patterns of child psychiatric illness in Uganda: A study of a clinic and its patients. *E. Afr. Med. J.*, 52 (8):455-461, 1975.

ØDEGAARD, O.: *Acta Psychiat. and Neuro.*, 20:247, 1945.

ØDEGAARD, O.: *Int. J. Soc. Psych.*, 2:85, 1956.

ORLEY, J. H.: Cultural correlates of mental illness amongst the Baganda. Department of Psychiatry, Makerere University, Kampala, Uganda. Mimeograph, 1968.

PRINCE, R.: The "brain fag" syndrome in Nigerian students. *J. Ment. Sci.*, 106:559-70, 1960.

RAINAULT, J.: Un aspect des psychoses transitoires en milieu African: la bouffée aigue confusionelle et anxieuse. In: *Mental Disorders and Mental Health in Africa South of the Sahara.* CCTA/CSA—WFMH. WHO meeting of specialists on Mental Health. Bukavu, London, 1958.

WITTKOWER, E. D. and HISTON, H. W.: A combined psychoanalytic and anthropological approach to magic, witchcraft and sorcery in relation to mental health and mental disorder. *Psychopathologie Africaine*, 4:277, 1968.

V

PSYCHIATRIC DISORDER AND THE WORLDS OF WORK AND CRIME

Introduction by David P. Farrington, Ph.D.

The four papers in this section are rather different in emphasis, but they all have one thing in common. They show that people who behave in a socially deviant or disapproved way in one aspect of their lives also tend to be socially deviant in other aspects. The implication of this finding is that it may be a mistake to study one kind of deviance, such as psychiatric disorder, alcoholism, poor work history, poor marital adjustment, or crime, in isolation from other kinds. It seems unlikely that any of these kinds of social deviance has a unique set of determinants different from those of any other kind.

The four papers differ in methodology and in cultural setting. In a longitudinal study of hospital patients in Iowa, Dr. Tsuang demonstrates the association between psychiatrically disturbed behavior (especially schizophrenia) and poor work and marital adjustment. In Montreal, Dr. Negrete shows that alcoholism is more closely associated with poor marital adjustment, unemployment and crime among Anglo-Protestants than among Franco-Catholics, and draws the very important conclusion that the degree of social deviance depends on the cultural context. In West Germany, Dr. Dilling and Dr. Weyerer show the relationships between somatic and mental illness and inability to work, and find that poor working conditions are related to poor work performance only among those diagnosed as mentally disturbed. In a longitudinal study of black men in St. Louis, Dr. Robins and Dr. Ratcliff demonstrate that those who were deviant in a variety of ways in childhood (in failing or being absent from school, in being arrested, in being sexually precocious, in leaving home early, and in using alcohol and illicit drugs) tend to be arrested for a variety of acts as adults (theft, violence, disturbing the peace, drug use, and gambling).

The fact that two of these papers (those by Dr. Tsuang, and by Dr. Robins and Dr. Ratcliff) report longitudinal surveys extending over a period of many years is worthy of note. In my experience, many research reports conclude by stressing the desirability of longitudinal studies, but relatively few really long-term surveys have ever been carried out. The two described here are especially noteworthy because both included a follow-up interview with their subjects. I have recently carried out a review of the literature of longitudinal surveys on crime and delinquency (Farrington, 1979), and I could only find about 25 studies which followed subjects up for at least five years, which provided information about crime or delinquency, and which included at least one direct contact with the subjects.

Moving on to consider the papers one by one, Dr. Tsuang was remarkably successful in tracing and obtaining information about his patients, especially in view of the 30-40 year follow-up period. I look forward to seeing more details of the methods used to achieve this success. The fact that the interviews with patients and their relatives were carried out blind, without any knowledge of which group the interviewee fell in, is a particularly commendable aspect of his survey. His paper demonstrates that schizophrenics, more so than manics or depressives, are unlikely to get married and likely to have long-lasting incapacitating psychiatric symptoms.

Like longitudinal research, cross-cultural research is often advocated but rarely carried out, at least on psychiatric topics. Even when cross-cultural studies are done, they lead to formidable problems of interpretation, because two societies typically differ on a bewildering number of dimensions which cannot be controlled. Dr. Negrete's paper should be welcomed, because he has carried out cross-cultural research and yet managed to avoid many of its major problems by studying two cultural groups living in the same city. His conclusions are based on small and possibly unrepresentative groups of Anglo-Protestants and Franco-Catholics, but the importance of his theory that the degree of a person's social disability depends as much on the culture in which he lives as on the severity of his illness cannot be over-estimated.

The research of Dr. Dilling and Dr. Weyerer is interesting for a number of reasons. They have studied a large representative sample of the adult population living in three different kinds of communities. They have shown that those who are unable to work tend to be those with both somatic and mental disorders, and that somatic disorders alone and mental disorders alone have approximately equal effects on work capacity. Modifying this conclusion somewhat, there was a tendency for women to be more affected by mental disorders and for men to be more affected by somatic disorders. I hope Dr. Dilling and Dr. Weyerer will continue their research to try to establish cause and effect relationships. For example, is it that certain kinds of mental disorders produce certain kinds of somatic disorders, which in turn produce an inability to work? There are other possible relationships among these three factors, and it would be interesting to try to decide among them.

I am always struck by the similarities between the results obtained by Dr. Robins and her collaborators and those obtained independently by Dr. West and myself (e.g. West & Farrington, 1973, 1977). The similarities are particularly impressive when it is remembered that Dr. Robins' and Dr. Ratcliff's paper is concerned with black males in the United States, whereas the research of Dr. West and myself is concerned with white males in England. One of our major conclusions is that a constellation of adverse family background features in childhood (including poverty, large family size, marital disharmony, inappropriate child-rearing methods, and parental criminality) produces a life style in late adolescence and early adulthood which is socially deviant in a variety of ways (including drinking, gambling, drug use, reckless driving, a poor employment history, sexual promiscuity, aggression, and delinquency). We would be in complete agreement with the argument of Dr. Robins and Dr. Ratcliff that there exists a single syndrome made up of a broad variety of antisocial behaviors arising in childhood and continuing into adulthood. We have argued that crime is one aspect of a larger phenomenon of deviance, and that the belief nurtured by some criminologists that delinquents and non-delinquents are not very different is incorrect.

In their paper, Dr. Robins and Dr. Ratcliff carefully investigate whether there are relationships between specific kinds of childhood deviance and specific kinds of adult criminal histories, over and above the relationship between general childhood deviance and general adult criminality. They find only one positive result, namely that early drug use does seem to predict adult drug arrests. Their inability to derive typologies of adult offenders agrees with our own experience in England. Whatever else a person has been found guilty of, he usually has at least one conviction for a crime of dishonesty.

We derived a measure of "antisocial tendency" at age 18 for each youth in our sample, based on heavy gambling, heavy smoking, driving after drinking, using prohibited drugs, sexual promiscuity, having an unstable job record, spending time hanging about, being involved in antisocial groups, aggressive behavior, anti-establishment attitudes, and being tattooed. Among those with at least two convictions before age 19, this measure significantly predicted those who were convicted again by age 23, even after matching for the number of prior convictions (Osborn & West, 1978). This measure of antisocial tendency also predicted those and West, 1978). This measure of antisocial tendency also predicted those sults agree with those of Dr. Robins and Dr. Ratcliff in showing the ability of a wide variety of deviant acts to predict future arrests and convictions.

The major difficulty in all these papers is to establish precise chains of cause and effect. I have alluded to this specifically in relation to the paper of Dr. Dilling and Dr. Weyerer, but similar comments apply to all four papers (and indeed to the work of Dr. West and myself). These papers are extremely valuable, if depressing, in demonstrating the associations between different kinds of social deviance. I hope they will inspire some future researcher to attack and overcome the very difficult problems of cause and effect. It is only when we know the causes that we can know how to intervene to improve the lives of those troubled by psychiatric disorder, alcoholism, poor work history, poor marital adjustment, crime, and other kinds of social deviance.

REFERENCES

FARRINGTON, D. P.: Longitudinal research on crime and delinquency. In: N. Morris and M. Tonry (Eds.), *Crime and Justice—1978: An Annual Review of Criminal Justice Research.* Chicago: University of Chicago Press, 1979.

OSBORN, S. G. and WEST, D. J.: The effectiveness of various predictors of criminal careers. *J. Adol.,* 1:101-117, 1978.

WEST, D. J. and FARRINGTON, D. P.: *Who Becomes Delinquent?* London: Heinemann, 1973.

WEST, D. J. and FARRINGTON, D. P.: *The Delinquent Way of Life.* London: Heinemann, 1977.

14

Social Effects of Schizophrenia and Affective Disorders

MING TSO TSUANG, M.D., PH.D.

This paper presents the long-term outcome of schizophrenia and affective disorders using marital, residential, occupational, and psychiatric status at the time of follow-up, 30 to 40 years after admission to the Iowa Psychiatric Hospital. The data from the present study will be used to show "The Social Effects of Psychiatric Disorder," which concurs with the main theme of this meeting.

DESCRIPTION OF THE SAMPLE

The patients were selected from consecutive admissions to the University of Iowa Psychiatric Hospital from 1934-1944. During this 10-year period, 3800 patients were admitted. Their records were reviewed and research criteria (Feighner et al., 1972; Morrison et al., 1972) for schizophrenia and affective disorders were used to select 200 cases of schizophrenia, 100 of mania and 225 of depression. Since the number of psychiatric patients in the study sample was about 500, the study has been called locally, "The Iowa 500." In addition to these psychiatric patients, 160 surgical patients were selected as controls. These surgical patients had been admitted to the same university medical center for appendectomy

This study was supported in part by grant MH 24189 from the National Institute of Mental Health. Other members of the project are Thomas Bray, M.S., Jerome Fleming, M.S., Donald Slymen, M.S., Robert Woolson, Ph.D., Lawrence Urban, M.S., Colette Brodersen, B.A., Lisa Faranda, M.A., Luke Flaherty, Ph.D., George Winokur, M.D., Raymond Crowe, M.D., and Kathleen Bucher, Ph.D.

TABLE 1

Distribution of Outcome Status and Pairwise Comparisons of Good Categories by Diagnostic Group

Diagnostic Group	Marital (%)	Residential (%)	Occupational (%)	Psychiatric (%)
Schizophrenia (N = 186)				
Good	39 (21)	64 (34)	65 (35)	38 (20)
Fair	22 (12)	89 (48)	14 (8)	48 (26)
Poor	125 (67)	33 (18)	107 (58)	100 (54)
Mania (N = 86)				
Good	60 (70)	59 (69)	58 (67)	43 (50)
Fair	7 (8)	15 (17)	7 (8)	18 (21)
Poor	19 (22)	12 (14)	21 (24)	25 (29)
Depression (N = 212)				
Good	172 (81)	148 (70)	142 (67)	129 (61)
Fair	20 (9)	39 (18)	33 (16)	37 (18)
Poor	20 (9)	25 (12)	37 (17)	46 (22)
Control (N = 144)				
Good	128 (89)	129 (90)	127 (88)	122 (85)
Fair	9 (6)	14 (10)	14 (10)	16 (11)
Poor	7 (5)	1 (1)	3 (2)	6 (4)
S:M	•	•	•	•
S:D	•	•	•	•
S:C	•	•	•	•
M:D	—	—	—	—
M:C	•	•	•	•
D:C	—	•	•	•

Pairwise Comparisons (*$p < .01$; — N.S.)

and herniorrhaphy during approximately the same time period as that of the psychiatric admissions. These surgical patients were not known to have any psychiatric symptoms. They were selected randomly within strata defined by sex, age at admission, and public or private payment status, so that the proportion in each of these categories matched the proportion among the psychiatric cases.

Mean age at admission for schizophrenia was 29, mania 34, depression 44, and controls 32. Follow-up field work (Tsuang & Winokur, 1975) of these cases and their relatives was initiated in 1974 and the field data collection was completed by the end of 1976. The index patients and relatives were interviewed blindly without knowledge of the original diagnoses or the relationship to index patients. We were able to trace approximately 97 percent of the index patients and we obtained adequate information to rate all four outcome variables of the patients traced in 95 percent of schizophrenics, 94 percent manics, 95 percent depressives, and 94 percent controls.

DEFINITIONS OF RATINGS FOR OUTCOME VARIABLES

The four outcome variables are marital, residential, and occupational status, and the presence of psychiatric symptoms at follow-up. Each variable was divided into three categories: good, fair, or poor. For *marital status,* good meant that the subject was married or widowed, fair showed that the subject was divorced or separated, while poor was given to subjects who were single, never married. *Residential status* was rated as good when the subject resided in his own home or lived with a relative, fair if the subject lived in a nursing or county home, and poor when the subject resided in a mental hospital. For *occupational status,* a good rating meant that the subject was employed, retired, a housewife, or a student, fair was given to subjects incapacitated owing to physical illness, and poor given to subjects incapacitated because of mental illness. The absence of psychiatric symptoms meant a good rating for *psychiatric status,* the presence of some psychiatric symptoms gave the subject a fair rating, and incapacitating psychiatric symptoms gave the subject a poor rating.

DISTRIBUTION AND COMPARISON OF OUTCOME STATUS BY DIAGNOSTIC GROUP

Table 1 shows the distribution of outcome status for each diagnostic group. Overall, the percent of good ratings are lowest for schizophrenia on all outcome variables, and the percent of poor ratings are highest for schizophrenics for all outcomes. The control group exhibited the opposite pattern, having the highest proportion in the good categories and the lowest proportion in the poor categories. Depression and mania differ little in proportions rated good or poor, and fall in between the control and schizophrenia groups.

To examine the differences between diagnostic groups for the distribution of outcome status, we combined the fair and poor categories. By combining them, we could make all possible pairwise comparisons between diagnostic groups for each outcome variable. The method was a chi-square with Yates correction over a number of 2 x 2 tables. Because there are four diagnostic groups yielding six pairwise comparisons for each outcome variable, the usual .05 level was divided by 6 to control the error rate for the entire set of multiple comparisons at $p < .05$, which means that $p < .01$ was required for each specific comparison for statistical significance.

The results of the analysis are shown at the bottom of Table 1. When we compared the good outcome between diagnostic groups, the schizophrenia versus the mania group showed a significant contrast for each outcome variable. The pairwise comparison between schizophrenia and depression was also significant for each of the four outcome variables. All four comparisons between schizophrenia and the control group, likewise, are statistically significant. When we compared mania to depression, we found no significant differences for the outcome variables. The mania group had a significantly lower percentage of good ratings for all four variables, when compared to the control group. Finally, when we examined the results for the depression group versus the control group, all comparisons for the outcome variables were significant, except for marital status. In recapitulation, the outcome was poorest in schizophrenia and best in the control group. Mania and depression, moreover, fell in between the schizophrenics and controls; but there was no significant difference between mania and depression.

EFFECTS OF PSYCHIATRIC DISORDERS ON OCCUPATIONAL STATUS CHANGE

In order to see the effects of schizophrenia and affective disorders on occupational status, we rated each patient's occupational status at admission according to the same criteria for rating occupational status at follow-up. For the purpose of analyzing changes in status between admission and follow-up, scores of three, two, and one were given to good, fair and

TABLE 2

Mean Admission and Outcome Scores for Occupational Status

Diagnostic Group	Admission Mean	Outcome Mean	Mean Difference (S.E.)
S	2.53	1.77	.76 (.08)
M	2.88	2.43	.45 (.10)
D	2.90	2.50	.40 (.06)
C	2.97	2.86	.11 (.04)

S = Schizophrenia; M = Mania; D = Depression; C = Control
Pairwise comparisons of mean differences: S:M† S:D* S:C* M:D M:C* D:C*
(†$p < .03$; *$p < .01$—two-sample t-test)

poor outcome ratings respectively. Table 2 shows mean admission and outcome scores for occupational status.

We can see that in comparison with admission means, outcome means dropped in all diagnostic groups. The changes, however, were greatest in schizophrenia and smallest in the control group. Pairwise comparisons (two-sample t-tests) of the mean differences between each diagnostic group showed statistical significance at less than the one percent level between schizophrenia and depression, schizophrenia and control, mania and control, and depression and the control group. The comparison between schizophrenia and mania did not reach statistical significance ($p < .03$) as defined in the present study. No significant difference was found between mania and depression. The results suggest that, in comparison with the non-psychiatric control group, schizophrenia and affective disorders have significant deleterious effects on the working status of the patients. The effects were most significant in the schizophrenia group followed by the mania and depression groups.

Although we showed that each psychiatric group has significant negative effects on working status, it is obvious from Table 1 that each psychiatric group was not homogeneous for psychiatric status at the time of the follow-up. Within each diagnostic group, 20 percent of schizophrenics, 50 percent of manics, and 61 percent of depressives fell into the good outcome category in psychiatric status, namely symptom-free at the time of the follow-up. It would be interesting to divide each psychiatric group into two subgroups, one with psychiatric symptoms and the other without psychiatric symptoms, to see whether the presence or absence of psychiatric symptoms at the time of follow-up showed any significant differences in terms of their effects on working status. We can see from Table 3 that the outcome mean scores dropped remarkably from the admission mean scores in all symptomatic subgroups, including the symptomatic controls. No such remarkable changes are seen in non-symptomatic subgroups. In fact, there is a slight increase of outcome mean scores in the non-symptomatic schizophrenic subgroup. Pairwise comparisons within each psychiatric group of symptomatic and non-symptomatic subgroups showed significant differences for the changes in admission and outcome mean scores between the subgroups. No significant difference, however, was found within the control group. The results indicate that in schizophrenia and affective disorders the presence of psychiatric symptoms had significant deleterious effects on the working status of the patient, when compared with non-symptomatic patients. In surgical control patients, the presence or absence of psychiatric symptoms seemed to show no signifi-

TABLE 3

Mean Admission and Outcome Scores for Occupational Status with or without Psychiatric Symptoms at Follow-up

Diagnostic Group		Admission Mean	Outcome Mean	Mean Difference (Out.-Adm.) (S.E.)
S				
Symptomatic	(N = 148)	2.52	1.52	-1.00 (.09)
Non-symptomatic	(N = 38)	2.58	2.76	+.18 (.12)*
M				
Symptomatic	(N = 43)	2.86	1.95	-.91 (.16)
Non-symptomatic	(N = 43)	2.90	2.90	.00 (.07)*
D				
Symptomatic	(N = 83)	2.88	2.04	-.84 (.11)
Non-symptomatic	(N = 129)	2.91	2.79	-.12 (.05)*
C				
Symptomatic	(N = 22)	2.95	2.64	-.31 (.17)
Non-symptomatic	(N = 122)	2.97	2.90	-.07 (.03)

S = Schizophrenia; M = Mania; D = Depression; C = Control
* $p < .01$ (comparison of symptomatic versus non-symptomatic—two-sample t-test)

cant difference in effect on working status.

In summary, our 40-year follow-up of schizophrenia and affective disorders shows that these psychiatric disorders had deleterious social effects, measured by marital, residential, and occupational status at time of follow-up and by change in occupational status from hospital admission to follow-up. In all categories, psychiatric patients showed poorer outcomes than did non-psychiatric surgical controls. In comparison with affective disorders, schizophrenia shows significantly greater ill effects. No significant differences were found between mania and depression within affective disorders. Preliminary analysis of the relationship between psychiatric status at the time of follow-up and the changes of working status from the time of admission to follow-up reveals that the psychiatric patients with symptoms at follow-up have a significantly greater worsening in working status, in comparison to the effect found in the psychiatric patients without symptoms at follow-up. At follow-up, symptom-free schizophrenics were as frequently employed as other symptom-free patients and controls. In the surgical control group, the presence or absence of psychiatric symptoms at the time of follow-up was not significantly related to change in working status from admission to follow-up, although the same trend appears. Thus the long-term adverse social effects of psychiatric disorder appear to depend on the continuation of symptoms. Those who lose their symptoms do not remain chronically incapacitated.

REFERENCES

FEIGHNER, J. P., ROBINS, E., GUZE, S. B., et al.: Diagnostic criteria for use in psychiatric research. *Arch. Gen. Psychiat.,* 26:57-63, 1972.

MORRISON, J., CLANCY, J., CROWE, R., et al.: The Iowa 500: 1. Diagnostic validity in mania, depression, and schizophrenia. *Arch. Gen. Psychiat.,* 27:457-461, 1972.

TSUANG, M. T. and WINOKUR, G.: The Iowa 500: Field work in a 35-year follow-up of depression, mania, and schizophrenia. *Can. Psychiat. Assoc. J.,* 20:359-365, 1975.

15

Social Disability from Alcoholism: A Cross-Cultural Perspective

JUAN C. NEGRETE, M.D.

Alcoholism is a condition frequently associated with a significant degree of social disability. A survey conducted in Buenos Aires found that alcoholics score as poorly as psychotics on a disability rating scale measuring performance at home, at work and at leisure (Tarnopolski et al., 1973). Pell and D'Alonzo compared the absenteeism record of alcoholic employees with that of matched controls within a large American firm. Suspected and confirmed alcoholics, both active and in remission, were found to miss 3.4 times more working days than the controls during the period of one year. It was also established in this study that alcoholics tend to stay off work longer when reporting sick. Periods of absence of more than 15 days at a time occur in one out of 10 controls on sick leave, as compared to one in 3 alcoholics (Pell & D'Alonzo, 1970). A review of the records of a group of male alcoholics attending a treatment center in England showed that they were off work an average of 121.7 days during the period of one year. Of that total, 86.1 days were lost because of sickness. This figure is 5.4 times greater than the 15.9 days per year recorded as a national average for working time loss due to sickness by males in that country (Glatt & Hills, 1965).

Furthermore, a study of medical records of employees in a major American company found that alcoholics were over-represented in the lower paying jobs and tended to have fewer promotions than "normal" controls. It was also observed that alcoholics gravitated to jobs which were mobile in nature—away from the more structured situations where they could be closely supervised (Trice, 1965).

Several North American and Scandinavian inquiries into the sequential development of the manifestations of alcoholism clearly indicate that poor interpersonal and social performance—that is, social disability—is an important aspect in the clinical picture of this disease (Jellinek, 1952; Park & Whitehead, 1973; Trice & Wahl, 1958).

However, Jellinek remarked that physicians in countries such as France, Switzerland and Italy have seen advanced alcoholic physical damage in "men who by their past history did not appear to be addictive drinkers or even steady excessive relief drinkers without addictive features, and whose chronic alcoholic complications came as a surprise to everybody" (Jellinek, 1960). The assumption is that these alcoholics had indulged in long-standing heavy imbibing, without making themselves noticeable because they were able to maintain an adequate psychological and social adjustment.

In an attempt at accommodating these different clinical presentations of alcoholism, Jellinek proposed a classification into five separate "species." Two of them (*alpha* and *gamma* alcoholisms) are characterized by an intermittent type of abuse and a high incidence of interpersonal and social problems. Other types (alcoholism *beta* and *delta*) typically involve regular heavy consumption and late complications of a physical nature, but much less severe behavioral disturbances than in the preceding forms of the illness. He also pointed out that these different types of alcoholism appear to be associated with cultural background, because their prevalence is not evenly distributed across different societies. The forms *alpha* and *gamma*, for example, are most frequently found in Scandinavian and Anglo-Saxon countries, whereas alcoholisms *beta* and *delta* are more prevalent among the Mediterranean wine-drinking societies. For the purposes of this discussion then, one could assume that there are basically two types of alcoholic diseases, one involving early social maladjustment and another which remains socially "disguised" until much later. Moreover, it follows that the degree of social disability shown by an alcoholic depends as much on the culture in which he lives as on the severity of his illness.

Disability is operationally defined here as the degree to which an individual is unable to fulfill his functional role in society. It is useful to separate the notion of disability from that of impairment. The latter implies *inability* to function, whereas disability is simply a measure of failure to perform adequately. It bypasses the issue of the source of that failure—whether it is inability, lack of motivation, or socially created obstacles. The individual's tasks in society vary according to role assignment. Whether disability will occur or not, therefore, depends not only on the degree of decline in previous health status but also on factors such as complexity of the expected role functions, the society's tolerance of less than optimal performance, and opportunities for role reassignment in case of failure. At an equal degree of impairment, individuals assigned more complex tasks, functioning in less tolerant environments, without opportunities for reassignment, will appear more disabled than those performing simpler functions or operating in less demanding or more open social seetings.

Alcoholism seems to be a condition particularly susceptible to these environmental influences. Since it is still a problem largely perceived as self-induced, it is frequently the target of moralistic reaction and negative social feedback. Alcoholics belonging to cultural groups where their problem is seen mainly as their own wrongdoing will not only face rejecting attitudes from their environment but, because they themselves incorporate the values of their culture, will also perceive themselves as wrongdoers and act in accordance with such self-perception. This process, described by Merton (1957), in his study of deviant behavior as the "self-fulfilling prophecy" could explain some cultural differences observed in the behavior of individuals under the effects of alcohol, and in the social consequences of their drinking. Skolnick (1958), studying the social complications experienced by college students because of drinking, found that students from religious backgrounds opposed to the use of alcohol reported more problems when drinking than did their counterparts from more tolerant affiliations. Cahalan et al. (1969), in their surveys of drinking in the U.S.A., also found that religious attitudes influence drinking behavior; groups preaching abstinence, such as Methodists, Baptists and some smaller Protestant denominations, had a larger percentage of nondrinkers than did Jews, Catholics and Lutherans. But if only drinkers are considered, the percentage of "problem drinkers" in the abstinence groups was higher than in other groups.

Social factors other than cultural beliefs may also influence the degree of disability due to alcoholism and the speed with which disability follows the onset of alcohol dependence. Within a given cultural setting, social attitudes towards the alcoholic may vary according to his position in the community. Upper social class alcoholics, for example, are believed to go undiagnosed, and presumably their behavior is tolerated for a considerably longer time than those of lower socioeconomic standing (Tamerin et al., 1971). This differential response is thought to bias surveys gathering data from official records, particularly those covering hospital admissions and work history, since upper class cases are less likely to be registered there. Even among identified cases, as was shown by Tarnopolski et al. (1973) in their household survey in Buenos Aires, alcoholics in the lower income categories tend to be rated as being more disabled than the ones in higher social positions. It would seem that the resources available to upper class alcoholics help them maintain a higher level of functioning for a longer time. In addition to such resources, it is likely that they are less subjected to what Lemert (1956) called "deviance amplifying social feedback." That is, alcoholics of lower social standing in the community are less protected against the social consequences of such a label. Thus, it can be said that the degree of disability associated with alcoholism depends on 3 major factors:

a) severity of alcohol dependence,
b) personality disturbance,
c) sociocultural setting.

It is evident that the stronger the individual's physical dependence on alcohol, the more his behavior will be determined by it. In alcoholism, as in other drug dependencies, the advanced states of the disease tend toward a homogenous set of behaviors: withdrawal symptoms, daily relief drinking, preoccupation with alcohol, and a narrowing of the spectrum of non-alcohol-related activities. This pattern is by and large the end result of the illness, regardless of the personality types and the cultural backgrounds involved. The influence of personality and culture on the social behavior of heavy drinkers is probably greater during the earlier phases of the disease, when the biological process of addiction is not yet an overriding force.

In discussing the apparent cross-cultural differences in degree of disorderly social conduct exhibited by alcoholics, Jellinek (1960) suggested that it may be the case that only in certain cultures are alcoholics predominantly individuals who suffered pre-existing personality disturbance. He proposed that in places where alcoholic beverage production is larger, and regular alcohol use socially condoned, those individuals developing alcoholism do not have personalities markedly more deviant than non-alcoholics. In societies with a tradition of temperance, alcoholics would be largely confined to the "deviant" part of the population, since the moderate drinking which precedes alcoholism is itself behavior which implies psychological alienation. Understandably, the more disturbed the individual was initially, the poorer his social adjustment will be, regardless of his drinking.

It is rather difficult to test hypotheses derived from these assumptions, for it requires quantification of both social performance and cultural attitudes. In addition, it must be done through comparative studies of at least two different sociocultural settings. Comparisons between the performance of alcoholics in two or more cultures are further complicated by differences in social structures, institutions, habits, legislation, sources of employment, medical services, etc., which do not permit the utilization of a single indicator to measure disability across them. A clear-cut index of social disability such as unemployment, for example, is linked with a large number of variables other than alcohol abuse, and it is almost impossible to hold these variables constant while exploring the association of unemployment with alcoholism cross-culturally.

One solution is that proposed here: to make a comparison between alcoholics from two separate cultural groups, but living within a single city and thus operating under the same social structure with respect to employment opportunities, law, medical services, and costs and availability of alcohol. It is assumed that in this manner, behavioral differences linked with cultural beliefs and value systems will be more clearly identified.

Source of Data

The data to be examined here originate from the files of patients treated at Senneville Lodge, a residential treatment center for alcoholic men located on the outskirts of the bi-cultural city of Montreal. This lodge is a Department of Veterans' Affairs facility which offers alcoholics a long-term in-patient rehabilitation program. Admission to the program is granted only to entitled veterans or active members of the Canadian Armed Forces. Most referrals come from other D.V.A. units providing medical and social assistance services in Montreal. The patients sent to Senneville Lodge are usually those who have failed to respond favorably to short-term or ambulatory treatment offered elsewhere. Thus, they could be described as a group selected for particularly severe impairment.

Between July 1964 and December 1966, the patients at Senneville Lodge were the subjects of an in-depth study aimed at establishing the treatment response of different types of alcoholics. This was Ph.D. dissertation work conducted by J. Ciale, then at the Department of Criminology of the Université de Montréal. Because of their free access to D.V.A., hospital, social assistance, police and court records, Dr. Ciale and his co-workers were able to gather an unusual wealth of information covering, among other things, the patients' marital, occupational, and criminal histories as well as their mental health and alcohol dependence symptomatology. Because rather strict administrative control is exercised over these patients by the Department of Veterans' Affairs, it was also possible to obtain follow-up data for most of them after their release. Details on the design, instruments and procedures of that study can be found in Dr. Ciale's final report (1968).

Subjects Selected

Only those subjects born in Canada and residing permanently in Montreal were selected. Dr. Ciale's records provided information on mother tongue, religious affiliation, place of birth and permanent address. Based on information about mother tongue, it was possible to select two groups with clearly different cultural identities: 34 whose recorded mother tongue was English, and 29 who stated French to be their primary language. Most English speaking subjects of Protestant affiliation were of British descent and will be called Anglo-Protestant (AP). All French speaking ones were French-Canadian and Catholics, and will be called Franco-Catholics (FC). All subjects had either joined the Forces voluntarily or been drafted during the Second World War, and the selection factors that played a role in their recruitment are difficult to elicit at this time. Thus, no claim can be made that these samples are representative of Anglo and French-Canadian alcoholics. However, separating them by ethnic identity and religious affiliation does permit a cross-cultural comparison that may suggest some testable hypotheses about variations in the social consequences of alcoholism in different cultures.

TABLE 1

Mean Age (± S.D.), Years of Education and Occupational Level of Anglo-Protestant (AP) and Franco-Catholic (FC) Subjects

	AP (N = 34)	FC (N = 29)
Age	49.4 ± 6.16	49.9 ± 4.79
Education		
< 11	21	22
11+	13	7
Occupation		
Manual/Semi-skilled	24	22
White collar/skilled	8	6
Professional	2	1

Since almost all of these patients are veterans of the Second World War, the groups are quite similar in age. The Anglo-Protestants show a tendency toward more formal education, but this is not statistically significant, and the distribution of the two groups by occupational level, as measured by the highest occupational status achieved by the subject in his work history, is almost identical. In summary, most subjects are middle-aged, have some high school education, and belong to the upper-lower and low-middle socio-economic strata (Table 1).

Alcohol Dependence

There could be no doubt that all these subjects were confirmed alcoholics. Not only were they required to admit to their abuse in applying for treatment at this program, but they also had many objective symptoms of alcohol dependence recorded in their medical files or disclosed during screening for admission.

As shown in Table 2, all subjects were at an advanced stage of physical dependence on ethanol. Almost all of them had become steady drinkers, regardless of an earlier pattern of periodic abuse for some. The great majority suffered from withdrawal symptoms and engaged in the vicious circle of early morning drinking in order to control them. A sizeable number had experienced at least once the severe withdrawal states characterized by delirium tremens, acute hallucinosis, or grand mal convulsions.

The subjects had been asked about the age of onset of regular drinking (use of alcoholic beverages at least once a week). The average figure for the AP group was 19.7 years and for FC's 15.9 years. This difference is statistically significant ($p < .005$), as is the higher frequency of black-

TABLE 2

Alcohol Dependence Symptoms in Anglo-Protestant (AP) and Franco-Catholic (FC) Subjects, in Percent

	AP (N = 34)	FC (N = 29)
Steady drinking	79	93
"Jitters" & "Shakes"	91	96
Morning drinking	97	90
Frequent blackouts	74	45
Delirium tremens & acute hallucinosis	44	34
Convulsions	12	7

outs among the AP's ($p < .005$). The AP's also include a higher percentage of subjects with histories of alcoholic psychoses and convulsions, but the differences in these categories do not reach statistical significance.

Psychiatric Diagnosis

Each subject received a psychiatric diagnosis when screened for admission to the Program. This was based on a clinical interview which all had with the same psychiatrist. In addition, all subjects were administered the WAIS tests by the same clinical psychologist. Although the psychiatric diagnosis was arrived at independently from these tests, the latter provided an objective measure of intelligence level and of cognitive function in the assessment of organic deficit. Though contact with a single psychiatrist and psychologist does not exclude diagnostic bias, it does ensure a certain consistency in the criteria applied. The examiners, of course, could not be blind to the language of the patients; but since no separation into cultural groups was intended at the time they were doing their work, it is safe to assume that they approached the subjects without this particular bias in mind.

TABLE 3

Psychiatric Diagnosis of Anglo-Protestant (AP) and Franco-Catholic (FC) Subjects

	None	Neurosis	Personality Disorder	Psychosis	Brain Syndrome
AP (N = 34)	11	6	14	2	1
FC (N = 29)	9	14	5	1	0

In about one-third of each group, no diagnosis other than alcoholism was found (Table 3). However, 41 percent of the Anglo-Protestants had a diagnosis of personality disorder (vs. 17 percent of the Franco-Catholics), and 48 percent of the Franco-Catholics had a diagnosis of psychoneurosis (vs. 18 percent of the Anglo-Protestants). These differences are both statistically significant ($p < .02$). As the diagnosis of personality disorder is usually made more on the basis of interpersonal and social behavior than that of psychological distress, it would appear that the AP's were cases with long-standing behavioral problems, while the FC's more frequently presented a picture of active emotional discomfort (anxiety, depression).

Marital History

Table 4 shows the subjects' marital status at the time of admission. In the married/widowed category there are only four AP subjects, and one of these had remarried after his first marriage ended in divorce. All nine FC's in this category were still living with their first wives. The difference is even more striking in the separated/divorced category.

Four out of five AP alcoholics were separated or divorced, compared with one out of three FC alcoholics. More Franco-Catholic alcoholics remain single, but if they marry, their marriage is less likely to end in separation or divorce than that of the Anglo-Protestants.

TABLE 4

Marital Status at Time of Admission of Anglo-Protestant (AP) and Franco-Catholic (FC) Subjects

	Single	Married/Widowed	Separated/Divorced
AP (N = 34)	7	4	23
FC (N = 29)	11	9	9

Criminal Record

Significantly more Anglo-Protestant subjects had a history of arrests by police (Table 5). In addition, it is noteworthy that only six subjects among the FC's were ever arrested for reason of public intoxication (public drunkenness, disorderly conduct while intoxicated, impaired driving), while 16 of the AP fall into this category ($p < .02$).

TABLE 5

Police Arrests Among Anglo-Protestant (AP) and Franco-Catholic (FC) Subjects

	Public Intoxication	Other	None
AP (N = 34)	16	9	9
FC (N = 29)	5	6	18

When only the subjects with police records are compared, there are no statistically significant differences between the groups as to average age at first arrest, average number of years of drinking prior to first arrest or average number of arrests.

Occupational Record

The occupational record is perhaps the most important item in any assessment of the disability caused by alcoholism. As expected, the majority of the subjects in both groups were out of work at the time of entering the treatment program. However, a larger number of Franco-Catholics (37 percent vs. 20.5 percent) were still employed at the time of assessment, although this tendency does not reach statistical significance.

While it could be assumed that occupational status might influence the diagnosis of personality disturbance, actually those unemployed at the time of admission were not more often diagnosed personality disorder than neurosis or no diagnosis.

The severity of alcoholism might influence the subjects' ability to maintain steady employment. To test for this possibility, patients were divided into a *severe addiction* category—subjects with a history of alcoholic psychosis and/or convulsions—and a *moderate addiction* one, containing those without such a history. No significant association of severity of alcoholism with unemployment at the time of assessment was found.

Although the numbers in this sample are small, results tend to confirm the assumption that alcoholics of higher occupational status are able to keep their employment for a longer time. The lower status occupational group (manual and semi-skilled) contains statistically significantly more unemployed subjects—40 out of 46—than does the higher status one (professionals, white collar and skilled workers), with only five out of 17 unemployed at admission ($p < .02$).

Cultural background seems to play a role in the speed with which social effects occur. Although the two groups were approximately the same age, more Anglo-Protestants among those unemployed at admission had become idle before reaching age 35 ($p < .05$) (Table 6).

Discussion

The comparison of records from these two groups appears to confirm the hypothesis that disability from alcoholism is dependent, at least

TABLE 6

Age at Time of Losing Last Steady Employment of Anglo-Protestant (AP) and Franco-Catholic (FC) Subjects

	<35	35+
AP (N = 34)	15	12
FC (N = 29)	4	14

partially, on socio-cultural factors. Indicators of poor social performance such as unemployment, marital maladjustment and law breaking are not equally experienced by alcoholics belonging to two different Canadian subcultures. The fact that almost all subjects from both groups experienced morning shakes, and were drinking early in the day to cope with it, leaves no doubt that both groups suffered from a rather advanced degree of alcohol dependence. However, the findings also suggest the possibility that cultural identity may have some influence on the phenomenology of alcoholism; Franco-Catholics less frequently reported having suffered frequent blackouts than did the Anglo-Protestants. It is not clear why this should be true. However, degree of memory interference is known to be related to drinking patterns (Tamerin et al., 1971), which probably vary by culture. The Anglo-Protestant group probably contained a larger number of lone drinkers, since a follow-up entry concerning their living arrangements six months after discharge from the treatment program indicates that only 20.5 percent of the APs as opposed to 48.0 percent of the FC's were staying with other persons (Table 7). However, whether drinking alone is associated with blackouts cannot be ascertained from records available to this study.

TABLE 7

Living Arrangements of Anglo-Protestant (AP) and Franco-Catholic (FC) Subjects, 6 Months after Discharge

	Relatives/ Friends	Alone at Fixed Address	Transient
AP (N = 34)	7	16	11
FC (N = 29)	14	5	10

The Anglo-Protestant subjects faced social difficulties such as police arrests and loss of their employment at an earlier age than did their Franco-Catholic counterparts. This would indicate that alcoholism among them is associated with disability earlier in their alcoholic careers. Most likely, these disabilities contributed to their high rate of marital disruption, since 18 of the 23 divorced or separated APs were already unemployed at the time of the marital breakdown.

The fact that the Anglo-Protestants were more often arrested by the police because of public drunkenness and disorderly conduct may also indicate cultural differences in regards to behavior under the effects of alcohol. Griffith Edwards (1974), in discussing the concept of plasticity in drug behavior, suggests it to be the result of three separate factors: a) the pharmacological effects of the drug involved, b) the personality of the individual, and c) the environment. No doubt, the stronger the pharmacological dependence, the less the importance of psychological and environmental influence. The subjects in this study were all "hard core" alcoholics, most well into middle age and with a long history of abuse. Most of them were disabled at the time of this assessment, but it is clear that their cultural identity was associated with differences in the *pace* at which disability developed, and with its final degree of severity.

The difference in police, marital, and unemployment histories of the two groups is summarized by their asymmetric distribution into psychiatric diagnosis categories. One can almost say that Anglo-Protestant alcoholics are sociopathic personalities, while French-Canadian alcoholics are neurotics.

There are some pertinent reports in the literature that may help explain the cultural differences elicited in this study. English Canadians have been found to stress independence and self-reliance in their approach to the disabled, whereas French Canadians seem to be more inclined to assign them a passive role and tolerate their dependence for a longer time (Murphy & Lemieux, 1967). A survey of attitudes among samples of these two cultures demonstrated that Anglo-Protestant respondents were more intolerant of work incompetence, and of social incompetence in general, than were their Franco-Catholic counterparts (Negrete, 1970). Moreover, community surveys on attitudes towards alcoholism conducted in Canada and elsewhere (Linsky, 1965; Pullman, 1958), found a greater tendency among Protestant respondents to perceive alcoholism mainly as a "moral" problem, as opposed to a more "medical" view expressed by Catholic respondents.

All these findings, and the fact that Franco-Catholics tend to start their regular use of alcohol at a significantly younger age, suggest that Anglo-Protestant alcoholics may face a less permissive social milieu and, accordingly, experience more severe social consequences from their illness.

REFERENCES

CAHALAN, D., CISIN, L., and CROSSLEY, H. M.: American drinking practices. Rutgers Center of Alcohol Studies, Monograph No. 6. New Brunswick, N.J., 1969.

CIALE, J.: *Treatment Response of Differential Alcoholic Patterns.* Ph.D. Dissertation, Université de Montréal, 1968.

EDWARDS, G.: Drugs, drug dependence and the concept of plasticity. *Quart. J. Studies Alcohol,* 35:176-195, 1974.

GLATT, M. M. and HILLS, D. R.: Occupational behavior patterns in samples of English alcoholic employees. *Brit. J. Addic.,* 61:71-78, 1965.

GROSS, M., LEWIS, E., and HASTEY, J.: Acute alcohol withdrawal syndrome. In: B. Kissin and H. Begleiter (Eds.), *The Biology of Alcoholism,* Vol. 3, Chapter 6. New York: Plenum Press, 1974.

JELLINEK, E. M.: Phases of alcohol addiction. *Quart. J. Studies Alcohol,* 13:673-684, 1952.

JELLINEK, E. M.: *The Disease Concept of Alcoholism.* Highland Park, N.J.: Hillhouse Press, 1960.

LEMERT, E. M.: Alcoholism; theory, problem and challenge. *Quart. J. Studies Alcohol,* 17:306-317, 1956.

LINSKY, A. S.: Religious differences in lay attitudes and knowledge of alcoholism and its treatment. *J. Scientific Study of Religion,* 5:41-50, 1965.

MERTON, R. K.: *Social Theory and Social Structure.* New York: Free Press, 1957.

MURPHY, H. B. M. and LEMIEUX, M.: Quelques considérations sur le taux élevé de schizophrénie dans un type de Communauté Canadienne Française. *Can. Psychiat. Assoc. J.,* 12 (Spec. No.):572-581, 1967.

NEGRETE, J.: Les attitudes envers le comportement des alcooliques; étude comparative dans trois sous-cultures québécoises. *Toxicomanies, Québec,* 3:192-212, 1970.

PARK, P. and WHITEHEAD, P. C.: Developmental sequence and dimensions of alcoholism. *Quart. J. Studies Alcohol,* 34:887-904, 1973.

PELL, S. and D'ALONZO, C. A.: Sickness absenteeism and alcoholics. *J. Occupa. Med.,* 12:198-210, 1970.

PULLMAN, D. R.: Some social correlates of attitudes towards the use of alcoholic beverages. *Quart. J. Studies Alcohol,* 19:623-635, 1958.

SKOLNICK, J. H.: Religious affiliation and drinking behavior. *Quart. J. Studies Alcohol,* 19:452-470, 1958.

TAMERIN, J. et al.: The upper social class alcoholic: A syndrome in itself. *Psychosomatics,* 12:200-204, 1971.

TAMERIN, J. et al.: Alcohol and memory: Amnesia and short-term memory function during experimentally induced intoxication. *Am. J. Psychiat.,* 127:1659-1664, 1971.

TARNOPOLSKI, A., LUBCHANSKY, I., and MIRENSKY, A.: Enfermedad mental e incapacitación social. *Boletin Oficina Sanitaria Panamericana,* 74:187-193, 1973.

TRICE, H. M.: Alcoholic employees. A comparison of psychotic, neurotic and "normal" personnel. *J. Occupa. Med.,* 7:94-99, 1965.

TRICE, H. and WAHL, R.: A rank order analysis of the symptoms of alcoholism. *Quart. J. Studies Alcohol,* 19:636-648, 1958.

16

Psychiatric Illness and Work Capacity

HORST DILLING, M.D.
and
SIEGFRIED WEYERER, PH.D.

"It is only in the most recent times, and imperfectly as yet, that labor has been recognized as a blessing, or, at worst, as a necessity which has great moral and social compensations, and which, if rightly understood and wisely used, brings joy and satisfaction. This can only be true, however, when labor is crowned by achievement, and that is when it is productive of wealth."

This quote from the American sociologist Sumner (1906) illustrates the fact that the concept of work has undergone a variety of evaluations from antiquity until today, from the divine punishment of work in the Old Testament to its present meaning as an indicator of social status. The high value of work and profession in today's society is important to the discussion of function of the mentally ill. Fulfillment of an occupational role is seen as an important indicator of recovery of the mentally ill. Failure to function occupationally can also be an important measure of the social costs of mental illness.

The title of this chapter emphasizes the relationship between mental illness and inhibition of work capacity. The other question, to what extent unfavorable working conditions such as overwork, monotony, etc. can cause mental disorders, has been more frequently explored, as, for example, in the classical study by Kornhauser (1965). However, we intend to explore here only questions concerning the degree to which mental illness is associated with limitations of the capacity to work.

DETERMINING WORK CAPACITY

Achievement Tests

The determination of the capacity or ability to work can be assessed in various ways. In clinical settings, achievement tests are administered to patients on the assumption that these provide a picture of actual achievement potential. Previous studies of this type were done by Kraepelin (1896, 1902), who depicted the achievement of his subjects by means of a so-called work curve. In a study inspired by him, Oehrn (1896) assessed the ability to add and memorize. Other coworkers of Kraepelin studied the effects of fatigue and its relief through introduction of pauses, for example on typewriting (Graf, 1922; Frankfurther, 1914). The Kraepelin work test was later developed into the Pauli test (Pauli & Arnold, 1951). These studies showed a great discrepancy between the work achievement of the mentally ill and the healthy. Similar recent studies include those of Schelling and Müller (1977) and Reimer et al. (1976).

Evaluation Sheets

The measurement of work achievement in rehabilitaton workshops or in work therapy within mental hospitals is usually arrived at either by counting completed items or by means of evaluation sheets which assess the quality and quantity of work done (Cheadle et al., 1967; Griffiths, 1973; Rud, 1968).

Sick-leave, Absenteeism

In large field studies the use of tests and observation is onerous or inappropriate. Another possibility, which at first appears to have no drawbacks, is to count the number of days a given subject is absent from his place of work. Absenteeism is caused primarily by an incapacity to work. However, problems can arise. In some organizations, for instance, illness absences and absences to attend courses for further education are both registered as absentee days, so that the actual number of sick days cannot be arrived at (Blohmke & Jost, 1976).

During the decade 1955-1965, the average proportion of the employed population on "absent sick" status in Germany was between 5-6 percent on any given day. Most European countries had a lower sickness absence rate for the sample year 1965. Still lower rates were reported in the United States, with 1.9 percent, and Canada, with 1.1 percent. In times of economic recession and when work is scarce, absenteeism is lower than in economic boom periods (Enterline, 1964), a hint that personal motivation influences the absentee rate. The fact that unskilled workers have more absenteeism than skilled workers, and blue-collar workers more than white-collar workers, again suggests that absenteeism may vary with attachment to work (Schaefer & Blohmke, 1978).

The sick-leave statistics probably depend not only upon the presence of physical illness, but also on the mental health of the individual, his family situation, his attitude towards work, the work climate and work demands, and finally such structural factors as health insurance matters, the state of the economy, etc. (Blohmke & Jost, 1976).

The sick-leave rate thus does not provide a direct measure of the effect on the individual of the illness. Sopp (1961) goes so far as to say that one gains the impression that "sickness" hardly has anything to do with health, but rather fulfills a sociological function, when one looks at the figures for inability to work given by the public health insurance system, and von Ferber (1977) speaks of absenteeism as a "detoured social conflict."

Furthermore, days absent are available as a measure of health only for the employed, who constitute only about one-third of the total population in highly industrialized societies (Blumenthal & Jochheim, 1976).

LIMITATION OF WORK CAPACITY

Despite all the reservations mentioned, it is interesting to ask to what degree the work capacity of the mentally ill is limited and what percentage of absenteeism is attributable to mental disorder. Here it must be remembered that ability to work is not a simple measure of the severity of mental illness: for example, a patient with a severe compulsion neurosis may continue to pursue his occupation while suffering greatly from his symptoms and losing most of his social relationships. On the other hand, patients with other neuroses may feel unable to work, and a physician may confirm their inability. Among patients, the pattern of missed work varies with the diagnosis: absenteeism among patients with manic-depressive disorder usually occurs only during the acute phase of the illness, whereas schizophrenics less often regain the ability to work.

A survey of the literature of field studies of work capacity as related to mental health produced relatively modest results. Several studies (Helgason, 1964; Lehtinen, 1975) have determined the percentage of those in their surveys suffering work handicap because of mental disorders. Because of the varying definitions of disability, studies are difficult to compare. Lehtinen says that for a total prevalence of 16 percent with mental disorders, 3 percent of all subjects showed clear work disabilities related to mental disorder, and a further 3.5 percent were completely unable to work for this reason. Helgason reports in his monograph on the determination of lifetime prevalence of mental disorder in Iceland that at the end of the observation period, of subjects aged 60, 8.1 percent were disabled for mental reason and 6.3 percent for other reasons.

The London study of general practices by Shepherd et al. (1966) is one of the few to provide more detailed data. Here, comparable to the study we will report, the incapacity to work was registered for one year and related to mental and physical illness respectively. A higher percentage of inability to work over a period of one year was found among patients with mental disturbances than among those whose only diagnosis was a physical illness. This finding applied to both men and women.

Similarly, Øgar (1977), in a study of the clientele of Norwegian general practices over a two-week period, found a severe impairment of work capacity in 32 percent of all patients with mental disorders and in 20 percent of those without mental disorders.

Several studies have been concerned with the role of mental disorder in explaining absenteeism among those employed in industry. Fraser (1947) found that 25 percent of the absenteeism among 3,000 metal workers was caused by neurotic disorders. According to Phillips (1961) and Mushlin (1962), the absenteeism of 130 workers could be assigned primarily to a mental disorder in 61 percent of cases. Mental disorder played an especially large role in women's absenteeism. This high rate emphasizes the importance of mental problems in absenteeism, since MacIver (1962) estimates that only 10-20 percent of those employed have behavioral disorders, and Blohmke and Jost (1976) quote a number of Dutch and English studies that fix the number of neuroses among factory workers at between 8-14 percent. A contrary impression is gained by Böker's 1971 study. Based on secondary statistical data, he found that among male public health insurance patients, only 0.8 percent were listed as having mental disorders that accounted for their incapacity to work. However, he believes the diagnoses given to those unable to work to be often incorrect.

It is important to note that neither physical nor mental disorders discovered are necessarily associated with an incapacity to work. For instance, studies in Baden Württemberg of insured actively working persons between the ages of 15-60 found that almost 70 percent had one or more diagnoses (von Eimeren et al., 1972). According to this study, the "ideally healthy" are rather rare, especially in the advanced age groups.

THE RESEARCH PROBLEM

The determination of inability to work within a defined period of time offers one way of estimating the influence of mental illness on the capacity to work.

The question of work capacity concerns the employed, as well as persons not involved in the work process. Work can be either of an economic or a non-economic nature. "Economic" work is paid work; non-economic work includes charitable and household work. The incapacity to work may be revealed as absenteeism from one's place of employment or as non-fulfillment of certain household functions. It is easier to determine the inability to work among the employed, where it is more visible as excessive unexcused absence and sick leave, than among persons not employed.

In the course of a survey of health and mental disorder, we asked to what extent persons were limited in their ability to do work during the week preceding the interview and during the previous twelve months. We were then able to compare those suffering from mental disorder with persons suffering from somatic diseases and with healthy persons. Further, the influence that certain variables, such as sex, age, type of community, social class, occupational status, psychiatric diagnosis, symptoms, and subjective burdens at the place of employment, have on capacity to work was ascertained.

Methods

As part of a psychiatric-epidemiological field study, psychiatric interviewers studied a total of 1,536 persons 15 years of age and older in three communities in Upper Bavaria. The three communities studied include an agricultural community (2,000 residents) with a high proportion of people occupied in farming and forestry; an industrial community (13,000 residents) with the majority of persons employed in the production process; and a service community (14,000 residents) with a high proportion of civil servants and administrative employees, as well as a high proportion of retired people.

In the interview, subjective and objective symptoms (as distinguished by Goldberg et al., 1970), social variables, and the subjective burdens at the place of employment were ascertained. Further, the complaints list constructed by von Zerssen (1976) was filled out. The test subjects comprise a random sample of the resident population. The rate of refusal was 6.8 percent.

Mental disorders were diagnosed after a psychiatric interview using the Eighth Edition of the ICD (International Classification of Diseases) and differentiated according to the degree of severity (scale 0-4; $\geq 2 =$ in need of treatment). This resulted in 18.6 percent of the subjects being classified as needing treatment. A further 22.3 percent showed milder mental disturbances. Somatic diseases were diagnosed on the basis of data provided by the subjects' general practitioner. They were classified according to the ICD and distinguished according to the degree of severity. Milder somatic disturbances (<2) were found for 24.1 percent of the subjects; disorders which needed treatment (≥ 2) for 29.3 percent. Categorization according to social class followed the method of Moore and Kleining (1960), whereby occupation is the sole criterion.

Data on capacity to work were compiled for two periods. First, the subjects were asked to what extent their capacity to work had been limited during the week prior to interview. Second, they were asked about the total length of illness-induced inability to work during the preceding 12 months.

TABLE 1

Degree of Severity of Psychiatric Disorders and Limitation of the Work Capacity During the Last 7 Days

Psychiatric diagnosis / Work capacity (last 7 days)	none	Degree of severity		Total
		< 2	≥ 2	
able	93.8	89.8	71.6	88.8
limited	3.3	4.4	16.3	5.9
unable	2.9	5.8	12.1	5.2
Total (n = 100 %)	907	343	282	1532

We wished to determine, among other things, whether mentally ill persons were more often unable to work during the 12 months preceding the psychiatric interview than somatically ill or healthy persons. Since we were assessing mental illness cross-sectionally, we cannot be certain that the illness was already present at the time of the earlier absenteeism. However, we can probably safely assume that mental disorders present at interview had been in existence for at least a year (Katschnig & Strotzka, 1977). Technically, however, since it was not possible, in a cross-sectional study to interview people at the time of an earlier inability to work, the only question we can answer is whether those suffering from mental disorders at interview have been more often unable to work in the past year than others.

RESULTS

The Week Preceding Interview

Of the 1,532 subjects for whom we obtained information (the question concerning work capacity was not answered by four persons), 11.1 percent were limited in their capacity to work or unable to work during *the week preceding the interview* (Table 1). Of the interviewees without a psychiatric diagnosis, 6.2 percent were limited in their capacity to do work or were completely incapacitated; of those with slight mental disturbances, 10.2 percent; and of those with severe mental disturbances (scores of 2+), 28.4 percent ($Chi^2 = 106.82$, 4df, $p < .001$, $r = .26$).

During the previous week 12.1 percent of the patients with severe

TABLE 2

Psychiatric (p)/Somatic (s) Disorders and Limitation of the Work Capacity During the Last 7 Days

Psychiatric/somatic diagnosis — Work capacity (last 7 days)	P+ S+	P+ S-	P- S+	P- S-	Total
able	77.9	92.3	87.3	98.8	89.2
limited	12.2	3.8	6.4	1.0	5.8
unable	9.9	3.8	6.4	0.2	4.9
Total (n = 100 %)	393	182	377	489	1441

mental disorders were totally incapacitated. The seriously mentally ill unable to work constituted 2.2 percent of all subjects, and 42.5 percent of all those totally unable to work.

Rates of disability were particularly high among subjects with *both* psychiatric and somatic diagnoses (Table 2). One-fifth of these subjects were limited in their work ability in the preceding week. The corresponding values for subjects with only mental or only somatic disturbances are 7.6 percent and 12.8 percent respectively. (The difference between these latter two groups is not statistically significant.)

The Year Preceding Interview

About two-fifths of the subjects (42.4 percent) were unable to work due to illness once or more *during the year preceding the interview* (Table 3). This figure is close to that (44 percent) found for employed persons in West Germany between the ages of 16-65 in a microcensus (Daten des Gesundheitswesens 1977). While 35.8 percent of our subjects without a psychiatric diagnosis missed at least one day of work during

TABLE 3

Degree of Severity of Psychiatric Disorders and Limitation of the Work Capacity During the Last 12 Months

Psychiatric diagnosis / Work capacity (last 12 months)	Degree of severity			
	none	<2	≥2	Total
not limited	64.2	53.4	41.8	57.6
- 1 week	14.8	17.2	12.4	14.9
- 2 weeks	7.1	11.7	7.8	8.2
- 3 weeks	3.3	4.4	5.3	3.9
- 4 weeks	2.5	1.7	4.3	2.7
- 5 weeks	1.5	1.5	3.9	2.0
- 6 weeks	1.8	2.0	2.5	2.0
more than 6 weeks	4.9	8.2	22.0	8.7
Total (n = 100 %)	907	343	282	1532

TABLE 4

Percentage of Subjects Unable to Work During the Last 12 Months, Differentiated According to Degree of Severity of Psychiatric Disorder

Controlled variable \ Psychiatric diagnosis	n	none	Degree of severity < 2	Degree of severity ≥ 2	Total	Significance (Chi^2; 2df)
Total	1532	35.8	46.6	58.2	42.4	46.50+++
Type of community						
rural	294	31.6	38.9	45.1	35.7	3.64
service	620	38.0	48.2	53.2	43.4	10.34++
industrial	618	35.7	49.5	68.0	44.5	40.91+++
B. Sex						
male	686	37.5	46.3	59.8	42.7	17.19+++
female	846	34.3	46.9	57.2	42.1	30.20+++
C. Age						
15 - 24	256	44.9	58.3	52.2	48.0	3.04
25 - 34	256	43.0	55.4	69.0	50.0	9.08+
35 - 44	273	33.6	42.3	53.5	39.2	5.95
45 - 54	245	32.8	39.6	61.8	40.8	14.64+++
55 and older	502	28.4	43.5	55.5	38.0	28.41+++
D. Social class						
I - II	253	40.1	33.3	68.0	41.1	9.84++
III	584	31.0	49.0	48.5	38.4	18.65+++
IV	549	37.5	50.9	60.8	44.4	20.20+++
V	146	42.2	50.0	65.5	52.7	6.63+
E. Occupational Status						
independent	85	29.2	25.9	50.0	30.6	0.23 (1df)
contributing family member	51	21.4	45.4	41.7	31.4	3.32 (1df)
civil servant	63	42.1	38.1	50.0	41.3	0.16 (1df)
employee	286	38.5	49.3	61.8	44.1	7.45+
worker	341	40.8	59.0	64.6	49.6	16.10+++
retiree	309	29.9	41.7	62.2	40.8	23.94+++
housewife	243	22.1	42.6	47.1	32.5	12.56++
in school	154	51.3	58.6	50.0	52.6	0.60
F. Employed						
yes	775	38.8	47.8	62.2	44.8	23.00+++
no	757	32.7	45.3	54.8	39.9	26.01+++
G. Burden at place of work						
none	124	33.3	48.9	50.0	38.7	3.34
slight	185	31.5	46.5	33.3	35.1	3.42
moderate	176	46.4	43.9	65.2	48.3	3.31
strong	118	42.9	36.4	60.0	43.2	3.00
very strong	152	43.5	61.1	72.3	56.6	9.49++

TABLE 5

Psychiatric (p)/Somatic (s) Disorders and Limitation of the Work Capacity During the Last 12 Months

Work capacity (last 12 months) \ Psychiatric/somatic Diagnosis	P+ S+	P+ S-	P- S+	P- S-	Total
not limited	47.1	51.1	58.1	69.1	57.9
- 1 week	12.5	19.2	12.7	16.6	14.8
- 2 weeks	10.2	10.4	9.3	5.3	8.3
- 3 weeks	5.3	4.4	3.7	2.9	4.0
- 4 weeks	2.8	3.3	3.2	1.6	2.6
- 5 weeks	2.0	3.3	2.4	0.8	1.9
- 6 weeks	2.0	2.7	2.1	1.4	1.9
more than 6 weeks	18.1	5.5	8.5	2.2	8.6
Total (n = 100 %)	393	182	377	489	1441

the prior year, the values for those with slight and severe mental disorders are 46.6 percent and 58.2 percent respectively. The two latter groups differed not only in the proportion missing some work but also in the duration of their illness. While 8.2 percent of the mild group were ill for more than six weeks, this was true for 22.0 percent of the severe group.

Among all subjects, 10.7 percent both missed work sometime during the last year and had, at the time of the interview, a severe psychiatric diagnosis by our criteria. The severely psychiatrically ill constituted 25.3 percent of all who missed some work during the year.

Demographic and Work-place Variables

In all three communities (Table 4), the percentage of persons unable to work (for one week or more) was higher the more severe the mental disorder ($Chi^2 = 46.50$; 2df; $p < .001$). The association was particularly strong in the industrial community. Effects were virtually identical for men and women. In general, whatever the control variable, a higher

TABLE 6

Percentage of Subjects Unable to Work During the Last 12 Months, Differentiated According to Psychiatric (p)/Somatic (s) Diagnosis

Psychiatric/somatic diagnosis / Controlled variable	n	P+ S+ (1)	P+ S- (2)	P- S+ (3)	P- S- (4)	Total	Significance (Chi^2; 1df) (2)vs(3)
Total	1441	52.9	48.9	41.9	30.9	42.1	2.68
Type of community							
rural	294	42.0	40.0	35.8	27.8	35.7	0.18
service	594	52.8	47.5	44.6	32.0	43.8	0.30
industrial	553	60.8	55.2	42.3	31.2	43.6	3.21
B. Sex							
male	645	57.1	34.7	45.8	31.1	41.6	2.93
female	796	50.2	58.2	38.9	30.7	42.5	10.93+++
C. Age							
15 - 24	247	66.7	55.1	58.1	40.9	48.6	0.18
25 - 34	245	70.2	50.0	52.4	38.2	49.0	0.19
35 - 44	255	45.9	45.7	47.9	26.0	38.4	0.18
45 - 54	222	53.4	40.0	41.7	24.6	40.1	0.00
55 and older	472	49.5	47.6	34.2	13.7	37.9	2.15
D. Social class							
I - II	234	40.4	39.4	43.9	38.6	40.6	0.19
III	548	52.6	41.2	34.7	28.5	38.5	0.84
IV	518	54.7	58.6	44.1	30.5	43.6	3.55
V	141	60.0	60.9	64.3	25.7	52.5	0.00
E. Occupational Status							
independent	81	30.4	33.3	26.3	29.6	29.6	-
contributing family member	51	37.5	57.1	23.1	20.0	31.4	-
civil servant	59	45.5	25.0	50.0	36.4	39,0	2.61
employee	267	59.6	46.3	45.3	34.3	44.2	0,00
worker	314	63.5	63.3	62.7	30.3	49.4	0,00
retiree	294	53.5	28.6	36.9	13.2	40.8	-
housewife	225	42.7	51.9	26.7	14.3	31.6	6.00+
in school	150	90.0	44.4	61.5	48.3	52.7	1.22
F. Employed							
yes	721	56.4	50.0	50.0	32.2	44.4	0,00
no	720	50.4	47.1	36.2	29.1	39.7	2.93
G. Burden at place of work							
none	118	60.9	41.2	46.2	28.8	40.7	0.40
slight	174	47.1	30.0	42.6	24.7	34.5	1.19
moderate	162	37.5	65.2	57.1	40.0	47.5	0,28
strong	113	58.3	31.8	64.7	34.0	43.3	3.78
very strong	138	67.4	66.7	47.6	36.4	54.3	1,08

percentage of subjects unable to work was noted among those needing psychiatric treatment. This held for all categories of social class, as well as for employees, workers, the retired and housewives. The relationship was especially strong for the 25 to 34-year-olds and for those over 45 years of age. When controlling for "subjective burdens at work," a significant relationship between the degree of severity of the mental illness and inability to work was found only among those with severe burdens.

Mental vs. Somatic Disorders

Having shown that subjects with mental disorders were clearly affected in their working ability, we can ask what influence mental diseases have on the capacity to work, as compared to somatic diseases (Table 5). As we found for disability within one week of interview in Table 3, persons with mental disorders had approximately the same amount of work disability in the preceding year as did those with somatic disorders, and those with both mental and somatic disorder had the highest rate of disability. The percentage of subjects with a limited ability to work in the group with both psychiatric and somatic disorders is 52.9 percent; 18.1 percent were ill for more than six weeks. Again, subjects with only mental disturbances did not differ significantly from those with only somatic illnesses.

TABLE 7

Percentage of Male and Female Subjects Unable to Work During the Last 12 Months in Three Upper Bavarian Communities; Differentiation According to Psychiatric (p)/Somatic (s) Disorders

Psychiatric/somatic diagnosis / Type of community	Male		Female	
	P+ S-	P- S+	P+ S-	P- S+
rural	27.8	41.2	52.9	31.9
service	34.3	48.0	57.8	41.7
industrial	42.1	45.6	60.4	40.0
Total	34.7	45.8	58.2	38.9

While there was little difference in the impact of psychiatric as compared with somatic illness overall, psychiatric illness seemed to affect women more than men (Table 6). This result was consistent in all three communities (Table 7). Women were the only group among whom the effects of mental illness on work differed markedly from the effects of somatic illness.

Psychiatric disorder had a strong impact on women's housework, as well as on their paid work, but housework was not uniquely affected, since disability rates for housewives with mental but no somatic disorder (51.9 percent) were no higher than for all women with mental but no somatic disorder (58.2 percent).

Specific Symptoms

Thus far, we have judged psychiatric diagnoses only on interview information. When we draw upon other indicators to determine mental disorders, such as subjective assessment of the individual's health, the score of the Goldberg interview, and the list of complaints according to von Zerssen, we continue to find a highly significant positive correlation (Table 8).

We analyzed individual symptoms from the Goldberg questionnaire to determine which had the strongest association with the duration of

TABLE 8

Correlation Between Indicators of Mental Health and Duration of Inability to Work Within the Last 12 Months

State of health (subj.)	.37+++
GOLDBERG - Score (subj.)	.31+++
GOLDBERG - Score (obj.)	.25+++
GOLDBERG - Score (total)	.32+++
Complaint lists (v. ZERSSEN)	.32+++
Degree of severity of mental disorder	.27+++

TABLE 9

Correlation Between Psychiatric Symptoms According to Goldberg and Duration of Inability to Work in the Last 12 Months

SUBJECTIVE SYMPTOMS		OBJECTIVE SYMPTOMS	
1. Somatic symptoms	.21^{+++}	1. Slow	.17^{+++}
2. Fatigue	.36^{+++}	2. Defensive	.07^{++}
3. Sleep disturbance	.23^{+++}	3. Histrionic	.04
4. Hypnotics	-.01	4. Depressed	.27^{+++}
5. Irritability	.17^{+++}	5. Anxious	.21^{+++}
6. Lack of concentration	.25^{+++}	6. Elated	.01
7. Depression	.27^{+++}	7. Flattened	.07^{++}
8. Anxiety	.23^{+++}	8. Delusions	.09^{+++}
9. Phobias	.02	9. Hallucinations	.05
10. Obsessions and compulsions	.06^{+}	10. Intellectual impairment a) Organic brain syndrom b) Mentally retarded	 .12^{+++} .04
11. Depersonalisation	.06^{+}	11. Excessive concern with bodily functions	.10^{+++}
12. Alcohol	.04	12. Depressive thoughts	.28^{+++}

inability to work. Fatigue and depression were the two symptoms most highly correlated with longer-lasting disability (Table 9). Similarly, in the evaluation of the list of complaints according to von Zerssen, lack of energy and rapid exhaustion were most correlated (>.30) with long-lasting disability. However, we also find significant relationships for most of the other symptoms on the von Zerssen complaint list (for 60 of 65).

Specific Diagnoses

Presentation of the relationship between diagnosis and work incapacity is limited to a rough classification (Table 10), since each of the diagnostic groups, with the exception of the neurotic and psychosomatic disorders, contains only a small number of cases.

For each diagnostic group considered, the percentage of subjects unable to work at least one day in the last year lies above the value for those with

TABLE 10

Percentage of Subjects Unable to Work During the Last 12 Months. Differentiation According to Types and Degree of Severity of Psychiatric Disorders

	Degree of severity		
Psychiatric Diagnosis	< 2	≥ 2	Total
(pre)senile dementia, other organic psychiatric disorders, Oligophrenia	41,2 (n = 34)	40.0 (n = 45)	40,5 (n = 79)
Functional psychoses	0.0 (n = 5)	69,2 (n = 26)	58,1 (n = 31)
Neurotic and psychosomatic diseases, Personality disorders	48,4 (n = 275)	62,8 (n = 183)	54,1 (n = 458)
Alcoholism/Drug addiction	44.8 (n = 29)	46,4 (n = 28)	45,6 (n = 57)
Total	46.6 (n = 343)	58,2 (n = 282)	51.8 (n = 625)

neither a psychiatric nor a somatic diagnosis. We find especially high rates of disability among the severe functional psychoses and the group with severe neuroses and personality disorders. Only the organic psychiatric diseases did not differ significantly from the total.

Our results are similar to those of Taylor (1968), who studied the mental well-being of male employees of an oil refinery. He showed that workers with longer-lasting illnesses had a much higher average score (22.5 points) for neurotic behavior measured with the Eysenck questionnaire than did subjects never ill during the period of the study (12.2 points). Howell and Crown (1971) also found higher than average absenteeism for the group with the highest scores on the Middlesex Hospital Questionnaire, a self-rating scale to determine psychoneurotic tendencies. The absenteeism of subjects with neurotic, psychosomatic, or psychotic disorders all lay significantly above the average for their total population.

TABLE 11

Correlation Between Subjective Factors of Burden at Place of Employment and Duration of Inability to Work During the Last 12 Months

Factors of burden at place of work	No psychiatric diagnosis	Psychiatric diagnosis	Total
overly long working time	-.07	.03	.00
rush	-.02	.10	.05
low salary	..12+	.11	.12++
unfavorable working climate	.04	.12+	.09+
competition	.08	.07	.08+
physically very demanding	.04	.17++	.12++
minimum possibilities for advancement	-.01	.09	.03
noise, dirt, unfavorable working conditions	.03	.20+++	.13+++
fear of loss of job	-.01	.15++	.10++
mentally very demanding	-.01	.07	.04
monotony	-.03	.11	.04
to long a commute	.00	.08	.05
long absences from home	.01	.08	.06
Score	.02	.23+++	.14+++

The Workplace

Persons offering complaints about their place of work and the nature of their job had more work disability than others ($r = .14$, $p < .001$) (Table 11). However, when we separate subjects into those with and without a psychiatric diagnosis, it is apparent that the association between complaints about the workplace and attendance at work applies only to subjects with mental disorders ($r = .23$, $p < .001$). Those with mental disorders who objected to noise and dirt ($r = .20$), physically very demanding work ($r = .17$), fear of loss of job ($r = .15$) and unfavorable working climate ($r = .12$) had been most frequently absent.

The results of Pierloot et al. (1962) are of interest in this connection. They show that workers incapable of working because of functional mental disorders were much more critical of their working situations than were members of a group unable to work for purely physical reasons. Between the groups there was especially great disagreement on "interest in work."

SUMMARY

Persons with mental disorders show an increased incapacity for work during the previous 12 months, compared to those without such symptoms. However, the percentage of subjects unable to work who had mental disorders without somatic illness (48.9 percent) is only slightly higher than the rate for those with somatic diseases but no mental illness (41.9 percent). This result shows that it is important to consider the influence of somatic disorders in any study of the relationship between mental disorders and incapacity for work.

Mental disturbances have a particularly marked effect on the working capacity of women. Neurotic and personality disorders are especially associated with incapacity for work. Incapacity for work correlates especially strongly with the symptoms of lack of energy, fatigue, and depression. A strong positive correlation can also be found between the subjective burdens at the place of employment and the duration of incapacity for work, but only among subjects with mental disorders.

It is desirable that this study, based on information from subjects in an epidemiological field study, be expanded through a corresponding study in industry and business. Such a study, using attendance records, could overcome one possible source of bias in the current study—that persons with mental disorders are more likely to report missed work than are other subjects.

REFERENCES

BLOHMKE, M. and JOST, K.: Krankenstand, medizinische Sicht. In: M. Blohmke, C. v. Ferber, K. P. Kisker, and H. Schaefer (Eds.), *Handbuch der Sozialmedizin,* Bd. III. Stuttgart: Enke, 1976.

BLUMENTHAL, W. and JOCHHEIM, K.-A.: Begriff, Abgrenzung, interdisziplinäre Zusammenarbeit der medizinisch-sozialen Rehabilitation. In: M. Blohmke, C. v. Ferber, K. P. Kisker, and H. Schaefer (Eds.), *Handbuch der Sozialmedizin,* Bd. III. Stuttgart: Enke, 1976.

BÖKER, K.: Entwicklung und Ursachen des Krankenstandes der westdeutschen Arbeiter. In: W. F. Haug and Chr. Müller-Wirth (Eds.), *Das Argument,* 13:901-927, 1971.

CHEADLE, A. J., CUSHING, D., DREW, C. D. A., and MORGAN, R.: The measurement of the work performance of psychiatric patients. *Brit. J. Psychiat.,* 113:841-846, 1967.

v. EIMEREN, W., SELBMANN, H. K., and ÜBERLA, K.: Modell einer allgemeinen Vorsorgeuntersuchung im Jahre 1969/70. Ministerium für Arbeit, Gesundheit und Sozialordnung Baden-Württemberg: Stuttgart, 1972.

ENTERLINE, P. E.: Sick absence in certain western countries. *Industr. Med. Surg.*, 33: 738-741, 1964.

v. FERBER, C.: Soziale Konflikte—Welche Bedeutung haben soziologische Aussagen zum Krankenstand? In: M. Blohmke and U. Keil (Eds.), *Gesundheit—Krankheit—Arbeitsunfähigkeit.* Schriftenreihe Arbeitsmedizin—Sozialmedizin—Präventivmedizin, Bd. 64. Stuttgart: A. W. Gentner, 1977.

FRANKFURTHER, W.: Arbeitsversuche an der Schreibmaschine. In: E. Kraepelin (Ed.), *Psychologische Arbeiten.* Leipzig-Berlin: Wilhelm Engelmann, 1914.

FRASER, R.: *The Incidence of Neurosis Among Factory Workers.* London: HMSO, 1947.

GOLDBERG, D. P., COOPER, B., EASTWOOD, M. R., KEDWARD, H. B., and SHEPHERD, M.: A standardized psychiatric interview for use in community surveys. *Brit. J. Prev. Soc. Med.*, 24:18-23, 1970.

GRAF, O.: Über lohnendste Arbeitspausen bei geistiger Arbeit. In: E. Kraepelin (Ed.), *Psychologische Arbeiten.* Berlin: Julius Springer, 1922.

GRIFFITHS, R. D. P.: A standardized assessment of the work behavior of psychiatric patients. *Brit. J. Psychiat.*, 123:403-408, 1973.

HELGASON, T.: Epidemiology of mental disorder in Iceland. *Acta Psychiatrica Scandinavica,* Suppl. 173, 1964.

HOWELL, R. W. and CROWN, S.: Sickness absence levels and personality inventory score. *Brit. J. Industr. Med.*, 28:126-130, 1971.

KATSCHNIG, H. and STROTZKA, H.: Epidemiologie der Neurosen und psychosomatischen Störungen. In: M. Blohmke, C. v. Ferber, K. P. Kisker, and H. Schaefer (Eds.), *Handbuch der Sozialmedizin,* Bd. II. Stuttgart: Enke, 1977.

KORNHAUSER, A.: *Mental Health of the Industrial Worker.* New York-London-Sydney: J. Wiley & Sons, 1965.

KRAEPELIN, E.: Die Arbeitskurve. *Wundts Psychol. Studien* 19, 1902.

KRAEPELIN, E.: Der psychologische Versuch in der Psychiatrie. In: E. Kraepelin (Ed.), *Psychologische Arbeiten.* Leipzig: Wilhelm Engelmann, 1896.

KRAEPELIN, E.: *Psychiatrie.* Leipzig: Johann Ambrosius Barth, 1915—8. Auflage.

LEHTINEN, V.: Psykiatrisen hoidon ja kuntoutuksen tarve sekä mielisairauteen kohdistuvat asenteet. Turku: Kansaneläkelaitoksen Julkaisuja, 1975.

MACIVER, J.: *Industr. Med. Surg.* 31:11, 1962. (zit. nach McLean 1963).

MCLEAN, A. A.: Occupational psychiatry. *Amer. J. Psychiat.*, 119:633-637, 1963.

MOORE, H. and KLEINING, G.: Das soziale Selbstbild der Gesellschaftsschichten in Deutschland. *Kol. Ztsch. Soziol. Soz.-Psychol.*, 12:86-119, 1960.

MUSHLIN, H. R.: *J. Occup. Med.*, 4:256, 1962. (Zit. n. McLean 1963).

OEHRN, A.: Experimentelle Studien zur Individualpsychologie. In: E. Kraepelin (Ed.), *Psychologische Arbeiten.* Leipzig: Wilhelm Engelmann, 1896.

ØGAR, B.: Pasienter i norsk almenpraksis. Oslo: Universitetsforlaget, 1977.

PAULI, R. and ARNOLD, W.: *Der Pauli-Test.* München: Johann Ambrosius Barth, 1951.

PHILLIPS, A. M.: *J. Occup. Med.*, 3:575, 1961. (Zit. n. McLean 1963)

PIERLOOT, R., GELISSEN, L., and REYNDERS, M.: Psycho-soziale Faktoren bei chronischem Arbeitsausfall wegan Krankheit in der Industrie. *Psycho-som Med.*, 8:205-213, 1962.

REIMER, F., MÜLLER, P. O., SCHELLING, U., and WILLIS, E.: Erste Ergebnisse einer Untersuchung über Leistungsausfälle bei chronisch psychisch Kranken. In: G. Huber (Ed.), *Therapie, Rehabilitation und Prävention Schizophrener Erkrankungen.* Stuttgart-New York: Schattauer, 1976.

RUD, J.: Attføringsavdeling for psykiatriske pasienter. *T. norske Laegeforen,* 88:1563-1570, 1968.

SCHAEFER, H. and BLOHMKE, M.: *Sozialmedizin.* Stuttgart: Thieme, 1978.

SCHELLING, U. and MÜLLER, P. O.: Erste Ergebnisse einer Untersuchung über Leistungsausfälle bei chronisch psychisch Kranken. In: F. Reimer (Ed.), *Arbeitstherapie—Praxis und Probleme in der Psychiatrie.* Stuttgart: Thieme, 1977.
SHEPHERD, M., COOPER, B., BROWN, A. C., and KALTON, G. W.: *Psychiatric Illness in General Practice.* London: Oxford University Press, 1966.
SOPP, H.: Sozialanalyse des Krankenstandes. *Psycho-som. Med.,* 7:204-207, 1961.
SUMNER, W. G.: *Folkways.* Boston: Ginn & Co., 1906.
TAYLOR, P. J.: Personal factors associated with sickness absence. *Brit. J. Occup. Med.,* 25:106-118, 1968.
v. ZERSSEN, D.: *Die Beschwerden-Liste.* Weinheim: Beltz, 1976.

17

Childhood Conduct Disorders and Later Arrest

LEE N. ROBINS, PH.D.
and
KATHRYN STROTHER RATCLIFF, PH.D.

In recent papers (Robins, 1978; Robins & Ratcliff, 1979), we attempted to test the validity of the concept that there exists a single syndrome made up of a broad variety of antisocial behaviors arising in childhood and continuing into adulthood. We compared data from three studies in which I have been engaged, a follow-up of child guidance clinic patients, a follow-up of normal young black men, and a follow-up of Vietnam veterans, and found that each study substantiated the argument that deviant behavior of varied types does form a syndrome which virtually always begins in childhood and which tends to continue, although in only about half the cases, into adulthood.

The argument for a syndrome was based on finding, first, that each type of childhood deviant behavior was independently correlated with the overall level of adult deviance; second, that each type of adult deviant behavior was predicted by the overall level of childhood deviance; third, that the overall level of childhood deviant behavior was a better predictor of the level of adult deviance than was any particular childhood behavior; and finally, that these relationships did not depend on the continuation of the same behavior from childhood into adulthood. Al-

This work was supported in part by U.S.P.H.S. grants DA 00013, MH 18864, MH 16477, MH 31302, and AA 00539.

though there was continuity from childhood to adulthood with respect to behaviors sharing the same domain—such as drinking before age 15 and adult alcoholism or juvenile delinquency and adult crime—persons *without* the childhood behavior in that domain still had an increased risk of the adult behavior if they had experienced other types of childhood deviance.

Evidence that the syndrome of antisocial behavior frequently terminated before adulthood lay in our finding that no matter how severe we required the childhood syndrome to be, no more than 40 to 50 percent of any definable extreme group showed the syndrome as adults. On the other hand, the *absence* of the syndrome in childhood virtually precluded its appearance in adulthood.

Lest we make the evidence for the existence of a syndrome continuing from childhood into adulthood more simple than it really is, let me add that we found two possible exceptions: in our original study of child guidance patients, we found that boys (but not girls) who were referred for sexual behavior (usually "indecent exposure") were usually only trivially deviant in other ways, and very unlikely to be antisocial adults. Further, we found in our second study, the study of young black men, that adolescent drug use was not associated with early school problems, and therefore was different from other types of adolescent deviant behavior. Nonetheless, drug use was closely associated with other forms of adolescent deviance and was a more powerful predictor of the level of adult deviance than was any other juvenile behavior.

With these two exceptions, there was strong evidence that deviance did in fact act as a syndrome extending from early childhood into adulthood, rather than as a set of correlated but essentially independent behaviors, each with its own set of determinants. This view of deviance as a syndrome has relevance to some of the popular arguments about adult criminality and its relationship to antisocial personality disorder. Our finding of an antisocial syndrome rather than a set of independent but intercorrelated antisocial behaviors would seem grounds for questioning the existence of the discrete criminal types described in the literature (Peterson et al., 1962).

If behaviors as different as poor job performance and wife desertion share childhood predictors, it would seem likely that those who commit different crimes may also share a common set of predictors. Nonetheless, Hare (1978) applied global ratings for psychopathy to felons and has concluded that psychopathy was more common in property and violent offenders than in drug offenders. This is an interesting echo of our own observation that the early school histories of drug users were less troubled than the school histories of other deviant children, although adolescent drug users were at least as likely as other deviants to become involved in adult criminality and thus to be found in penal institutions. Hare's results would lead us to expect that drug offenses might be less well predicted by childhood conduct disorder than are other types of offenses.

Another body of research which suggests indirectly that it may be possible to distinguish among criminals on the basis of childhood conduct disorders is the adoptive study of criminals by Hutchings (1972). In comparing the criminality of biological fathers of criminal male adoptees as compared with the criminality of biological fathers of noncriminal adoptees, he found larger contrasts between fathers of property criminals and fathers of controls than between fathers of violent criminals and fathers of controls. The rate of criminality among biological fathers of property offenders was almost five times the rate among fathers of control cases, while the rate of criminality among biological fathers of men guilty of assault was only about one and a half times that of controls. Hutchings also found that person offenses had a somewhat later onset than property offenses. To the extent that criminality in the father is evidence for a syndrome which can be transmitted genetically to his son, in whom it would be initially displayed as a conduct disorder of childhood, and to the extent that early onset suggests continuity with childhood behavior problems, we would expect that property offenders will more often have a childhood history of conduct disorder than will assaultive offenders.

A similar expectation might be drawn from the work of Megargee and Hokanson (1970). He argues that seriously assaultive delinquents are typically *over*controlled persons. Their extreme behavior is the result of chronic inhibition of their aggressive impulses, which eventually break through the dam of inhibition in an uncontrolled fashion. His evidence is somewhat tenuous and based on a very small sample—nine juvenile delinquents charged with murder, assault, or beating, whom he compared with less seriously assaultive delinquents and with delinquents charged with theft or incorrigibility. In the institution in which they were detained, the seriously assaultive delinquents were observed to be less aggressive than other delinquents and a review of their official records showed that they had had fewer prior offenses, supporting his view. Unfortunately, the effort to demonstrate that they were in fact less aggressive individuals through psychological testing foundered; no difference was found on test scores. The results of this study would seem to reinforce the expectations based on Hutchings' study that assaultive prisoners should less often have a history of conduct disorder than other offenders, although this message is not clear, since Megargee found these results only among the *severely* assaultive delinquents. Those moderately assaultive appeared not to differ from other delinquents.

A study of Japanese recidivist delinquents by Doi and Sugimoto (1967) found that recidivists who were property offenders had more often had a history of truancy and had begun their delinquent careers earlier than did recidivists who were violent offenders. In addition, the number of repeated offenses of property offenders was greater—40 percent having at least two subsequent arrests compared with only 16 percent of violent offenders. These observations would seem consistent with the implications of Megargee's and Hutching's work that property offenders should have more deviant early histories than violent offenders.

It is not clear, however, how that inference fits with the review by Gross (1971) of studies showing an association between violence and abnormal electroencophalographic findings. Unless the brain pathology was consequent to recent injury or illness, it might have existed in childhood and been associated at that time with various types of impulsive behavior diagnosable as conduct disorder. The same supposition would apply to the reported association between the XYY chromosome and violence, since a genetic defect would certainly have been present in childhood. It is probable, however, that the proportion of violent offenders with either abnormal EEG's or XYY chromosomes is small. There are no available figures for the proportion of violent offenders with abnormal EEG's, but a recent systematic investigation by Witkin et al. (1978) has gone a long way toward answering the question of the extent to which the XYY genotype contributes to criminality. This study shows that there is indeed an elevated rate of criminality in XYY men, but that their offenses are almost entirely restricted to petty theft, not violence, and that in any case, the XYY male is so rare that even if all were violent, they could not make a significant contribution to the population of violent criminals.

In contrast to the studies cited which suggest that different types of offenders may have different rates of conduct disorder in their childhoods, there are many studies which have tried but failed to distinguish between types of prisoners on the basis of any kind of underlying psychological or psychiatric differences. Gynther (1961) gave the MMPI to prisoners hospitalized for observation. He confirmed the work of others showing no significant differences in MMPI profiles by offender type, but he did find differences in F scores. However, elevated F scores occurred both among prisoners charged with rape and those charged with theft. Low F scores were found both for drunk drivers and for those charged with assault. There seemed to be no clear violence vs. property distinction. Both types appeared at both ends of the F score spectrum.

As part of their follow-up study of the Cambridge-Somerville project, the McCords tried to distinguish childhood family variables that could account for the choice of crime among those boys who went on to develop a criminal record. Their results speak strongly for the difficulties of making such distinctions. They used four types of offense—property, person, sex, and drunkenness—and were able to find nothing that distinguished among them in terms of parental neglect, paternal personality, the mother's role model, the paternal role model, type of discipline, quarreling in the home, quality of the neighborhood, or IQ. They found a slight association between broken homes and both person crimes and drunkenness, and a small association between having a cruel father and committing person crimes, but the similarities were much more striking than the differences.

The studies cited thus far have had various deficiences such as being confined to special populations or looking only at a current offense. Wolfgang et al. (1972) have looked at the complete juvenile offense history of a birth cohort, overcoming both of these objections. They carefully studied transitions from one type of offense to another in an effort to find out whether committing an offense of one kind predicted committing the same kind of offense the next time. They were unable to find evidence for offense careers that could be described as belonging to separate property or violent offender typologies. A boy charged with assault had approximately the same likelihood of committing a property offense for his next crime as did a boy charged with burglary or theft, and the chances of each committing *some* further offense were also about equal. Wolfgang's work argues for there being an increased risk of offense of some kind the more past offenses there have been. While property offenses occur two to three times as often as assaults, the selection of offense type seems relatively independent of prior type of offense.

Wolfgang's conclusion that criminality is a unitary phenomenon rather than a collection of offender typologies would seem consistent with the Jessors' (1977) finding of strong correlations between a general deviance measure, which included truancy, breaking and entering, theft from parents, and threatening teachers, and other behaviors disapproved for high school students, drug use, alcohol problems, and early sexual intercourse. Whenever any of these behaviors occurred, the chances were enhanced that any of the others that had not yet been tried would occur soon. The order of occurrence seemed unimportant. All these behaviors seemed to belong to a common adolescent process.

The literature, then, presents data on both sides of the argument that offender types should differ with respect to childhood history. Certainly the findings by the McCords and Wolfgang would seem to confirm our own impressions that various types of offense, like other aspects of deviance, are part of a common syndrome. Still, in the interest of exploring our data as far as it will allow us to go, and because of suggestions in the literature that conduct disorder may predict property but not person offenses, or property and person offenses but not drug offenses, and because of our own anomalous findings about the tangential attachment of adolescent drug use and sexual deviation in boys to the remainder of childhood conduct problems, we decided to see whether we could differentiate offenses in terms of their relationship to childhood deviance, using data from our follow-up study of young black men. We will explore the relationship between childhood conduct disorders and type of adult crime, asking whether conduct disorder does indeed predict one type of adult crime rather than another. Next we will ask whether there are any specific types of childhood deviance associated with particular types of crimes. As we did in the paper referred to earlier, when we find any positive results, we will attempt to verify these by replication in another study, our follow-up of Vietnam veterans.

METHODS

A. *Data Sources*

Our sample of young black men was collected in 1965-66. The study was a follow-up of men whose names were chosen from the St. Louis public school records of the late 1930's. All were born in St. Louis and were of average or better IQ (85+). The men were followed at the ages of 30 to 35 by interview and record searches. The sample, being urban, male, black, and in its thirties has important advantages for the study of the relationship of childhood deviance to adult arrest types. Both childhood deviance and adult arrests occur at a high rate in such an inner-city sample. Further, the fact that the men were in their thirties at the time of study means that they had passed through most of the period of high risk for arrest. In all probability, most of those who would ever have committed a particular type of offense had already done so. The sample may be unique in the degree to which it combines complete school records, complete juvenile and adult police records, records from a host of social agencies and medical services, and from the armed services and the Veterans Administration, with personal interviews. The data that we will use come both from records and from interviews.

Childhood deviance will be assessed by counting how many of nine behaviors occurred:

1) failure in elementary school despite an adequate IQ, as indicated by repeated assignments to the same grade level in elementary school;
2) excessive absence in elementary school, as indicated by school attendance records showing presence on less than 80 percent of days in five or more out of 32 elementary school quarters;
3) dropout from elementary or high school for at least a semester, as indicated by school records;
4) arrest or referral to juvenile court before the age of 18, as indicated by police or juvenile court records;
5) sexual intercourse before age 15, as reported in interview;
6) drinking before age 15, as reported in interview;
7) leaving the parental home before age 18, as reported in interview;
8) illicit drug use before age 18, as reported in interview;
9) alcohol problems before 18, as reported in interview.

Adult police records serve as the source of our information about both the number and types of arrest. The arrest types we will consider are "theft," including burglary and larceny; "violence," including assault, aggravated assault, battery, murder, attempted murder and forcible rape; "peace disturbance," including drunk and disorderly, "drugs and possession of narcotics," which was in fact often only possession of marijuana; and "gambling," which included running numbers, playing poker and craps, "making book" on horses.

B. *Our Method of Answering the Question*

A difficulty in trying to answer the question of whether childhood conduct disorder is more closely associated with one type of crime than another lies in the fact that a given person may commit many crimes, and the more crimes he commits, the greater are the chances that he will have committed any particular crime. Further, some types of offenses are much more common than others. Therefore, as the number of his crimes increases, the chances of having committed a relatively rare crime at least once increase more dramatically than do the chances of having committed a relatively common crime at least once. The corollary of these observations in that if conduct disorder in childhood predicts that *more* crimes will be committed, then it inevitably also predicts that the rarer offenses will be committed. In order to overcome these difficulties, we will first ask whether the number of childhood antisocial symptoms and the number of adult offenses both do predict the occurrence of particular types of adult offense. If both do, we will then inquire as to whether the number of childhood offenses also predicts the number of adult offenses. If this relationship also occurs, we will need to control on the total number of adult arrests when evaluating whether childhood conduct disorder does indeed predict the choice of crime.

RESULTS

1. *The Association between Conduct Disorder and Type of Offense*

Table 1 looks at the relationship between number of childhood deviant behaviors and particular offenses for which arrests occurred. At every level of childhood deviant behavior, theft and peace disturbance were the two most common offenses. If we regard those with five or more forms of juvenile deviance as having "conduct disorder," we find that among those who had conduct disorders as children, violence and drug use were next most common (both were about half as common as peace disturbance) with gambling following close behind. For those with relatively little deviant behavior in childhood, gambling was the third most common offense. Except for gambling, the popularity of offenses was much the same across categories of childhood deviance.

The rate of each type of offense was much higher in men with a history of conduct disorder than in the remainder of the sample. Since conduct disorders of childhood predicted *each* type of offense, it was not clear that there was any special affinity between conduct disorder and any *particular* offender type. Results seemed consistent so far with a unitary view of

TABLE 1

Childhood Conduct Disorders as a Predictor of Particular Arrests

	Number of Childhood Deviant Behaviors			
	None (24)	1-2 (79)	3-4 (171)	5+* (57)
	%	%	%	%
Theft	10	23	13	63
Peace Disturbance	7	22	10	55
Drugs	0	1	5	29
Violence	0	8	6	27
Gambling	7	13	3	22

* Conduct Disorder

criminality as one aspect of adult deviance, although we note that drug and violent offenses were virtually absent in men who had been only mildly deviant children. However, that could simply reflect the fact that these were relatively rare offenses. They might occur almost exclusively in men with conduct disorder simply because these men are the only ones with a sufficient number of arrests to have a substantial rate of these rare offenses.

To see whether such an argument was plausible, we examined the relationship between number of arrests and type of offense.

2. *The Association of Number of Arrests with Type of Offense*

Table 2 shows that the chance of committing any particular offense goes up dramatically with the total number of arrests. At least three arrests were required to have a reasonable probability of being arrested for drugs or violence. Virtually every man who had six or more arrests had had at least one property offense, and at least half had had each of the other types of offense. Since thefts were universal in the group with six or more offenses, it follows that *every* violent offender, drug offender, disturber of the peace, and gambler in this group was also a property offender. One could simply not find violent offenders to contrast with property offenders among men with a large number of arrests—there were only property offenders with and without offenses for violence (or peace disturbance, or drugs, or gambling). Thus, if conduct disorder predicted *number* of arrests, that might well explain the fact that it predicted the likelihood of each of these arrests and was virtually *necessary* to having an arrest for drugs or violence.

TABLE 2

Chances of Committing Any Particular Offense Increase With *Number* of Offenses

Percent with a Least One Arrest for:	Number of Non-Traffic Adult Arrests 1 %	2 %	3-6 %	6+ %
Theft	21	47	64	99
Peace Disturbance	25	36	65	73
Drugs	1	2	11	52
Violence	0	4	34	50
Gambling	3	31	5	50

TABLE 3

The Role of Childhood Deviance in Predicting Number of Adult Non-Traffic Arrests

	Child Deviance			
Adult Arrests	None (24) %	1-2 (79) %	3-4 (171) %	5+ (57) %
None	76	55	47	9
1-2	12	29	20	22
3-5	7	9	14	32
6+	5	7	19	37
Total	100	100	100	100

3. *The Association between Number of Childhood Symptoms and Number of Adult Arrests*

Table 3 shows that childhood deviance was indeed an excellent predictor of the number of adult arrests of young black men. Men who had none of the types of deviance we have explored before the age of 18 were also almost always totally free of adult arrests, and only 12 percent of them had at least three arrests. On the other hand, young black men who as children had had five or more of the nine juvenile behaviors we explored were almost all arrested as adults, and two-thirds of them had three or more adult arrests. Having a conduct disorder virtually guaranteed having an adult arrest of some kind.

Because conduct disorder predicted *number* of arrests as well as each individual type of offense, it is necessary to control on number of arrests to learn whether there was an affinity between conduct disorders and particular offenses. We cannot expect to separate our sample into pure offender types, since it was so rare to find any other offense in the *absence* of property offenses, but we can at least explore whether childhood conduct disorder predicts the *addition* of one kind of offense rather than another to property offenses.

4. *Conduct Disorder and Type of Offense, Controlling on Number of Offenses*

Figure 1 presents the association between conduct disorder and type of offense at three levels of adult arrests.

Men who had only one or two arrests had approximately the same rate of each type of arrest whether they had or had not had conduct disorder in childhood. Among men with a moderate number of arrests, three to five, there was also similarity between those with conduct disorder and

CONDUCT DISORDER OF CHILDHOOD AND ADULT OFFENSE

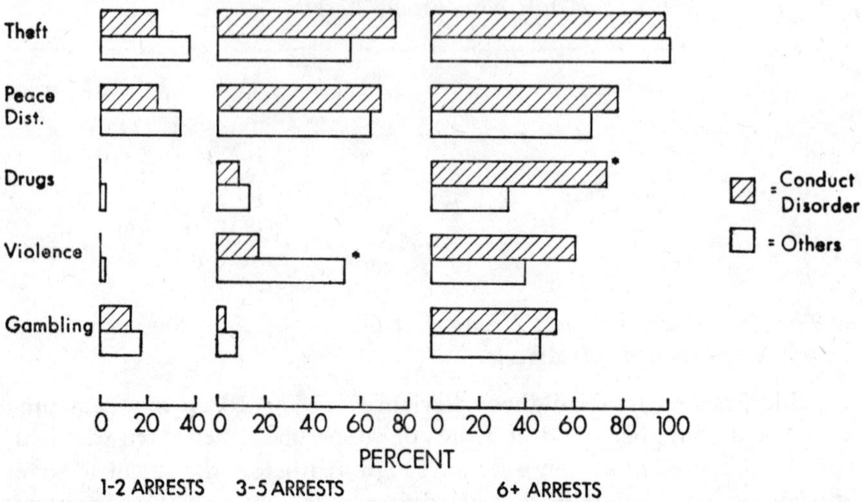

FIGURE 1

*Significantly greater.

others in frequency of peace disturbance, drug use and gambling. Theft was somewhat more common in those who had a history of conduct disorder, but not significantly so, while violence was more common in those who had not had conduct disorder. This result would seem consistent with the results of Megargee and Hokanson (1970), Hutchings (1972), and Doi (1967), which would suggest that the violent offender was "more normal" as a child than the property offender. However, when one moves then to the group with a very large number of arrests, this finding no longer applies. Men with a history of conduct disorder who had six or more adult arrests had *more* arrests for violence than others, as well as more arrests of all other types except theft, which we noted to be universal among men with so many arrests. Their excess is significant only for arrests for drugs. Before we are impressed by this finding, however, we need to remember that our upper interval is an open-ended one. It may well be the case that men with conduct disorder and six or more adult arrests had a substantially higher average number of arrests than did other men with six or more arrests. If this were the case, we still have not adequately controlled for the total number of adult arrests when we compare the two groups. Certainly men with conduct disorder showed no special affinity for drug arrests when they had had *fewer* than six arrests.

Our results, in short, seem compatible with our earlier belief that conduct disorder in childhood predicts number of arrests in adulthood, but does not predict any specific type of arrest. The fact that all men with a large number of arrests had at least a property offense, along with whatever other offenses they also had, seems to conform with Wolfgang's finding that there are no offense specialists, i.e., that the more arrests a person has, the greater the chances that he will have any particular type of arrest.

5. *Particular Problems in Childhood as Predictors of Particular Offenses*

We have shown that if we assume that childhood deviance is a syndrome, then it powerfully predicts number of adult arrests but it has no power to differentiate among types of offenses. One question remains. Have we made an error in assuming that conduct disorder itself is a unitary phenomenon? Perhaps the specific childhood behaviors of which it is composed do indeed predict specific types of arrest. To demonstrate this, however, we will again need to control on total number of arrests, as we did when we treated the syndrome of conduct disorder as a whole. In addition, we have a further problem. Each particular childhood behavior becomes more probable the more deviant the child. Thus we need to control not only on adult arrest levels, but on levels of childhood deviance as well. Needing to control on levels of deviance in childhood as well as number of adult arrests strains our small sample size excessively, even in a sample at high risk of both childhood deviance and adult arrest. It is also staggering to realize how many correlations we would need to look at to answer the question exhaustively as to whether there is any association between particular forms of childhood deviance and particular types of adult arrests. We have nine forms of childhood deviance, each of which might be associated with five types of adult arrest ($9 \times 5 = 45$ correlations), and each association should be examined at four levels of childhood deviance and four levels of adult arrest (or $45 \times 16 = 720$ comparisons). To attempt to approach the question in this fashion is clearly unreasonable in so small a sample. We need, therefore, to limit our pursuit to the relationships we think are most plausible.

It seems reasonable to expect that behaviors in childhood which if continued into adulthood can lead to arrest are the best candidates, i.e., that early drinking might lead to drunk arrests, early drug use to drug arrests, and early sexual experience to arrests for rape. To reduce the number of relationships with which we need be concerned to those most likely to be fruitful, we will restrict ourselves to men with three or more adult arrests, since those with fewer arrests will have few arrests for the particular offenses in which we are interested, and to those with some childhood deviance, since those with none would have no chance of showing the particular form of childhood deviance we are considering. We will divide those with some childhood deviance into those qualifying for conduct disorder, i.e., five or more forms of deviance, and those not so qualifying. Table 4 shows the results.

Men with three or more arrests who had used drugs before 18 were significantly more likely to have a drug arrest than those without early drug use, but with other childhood deviance. The same pattern appears both in those who did and who did not qualify for conduct disorder. With respect to arrests for peace disturbance and drunkenness, however, no effect of early drinking can be seen. Nor did early sex experience predict arrest for rape. Indeed, if anything, the relationship was the reverse—those without early sex experience were more frequently involved in rape. Although not statistically significant, this finding does recall the innocuousness as a predictor of adult deviance of early male sexual behavior as compared with other forms of deviance in our first study, the follow-up of child guidance clinic patients.

At last we have one positive finding that seems consistent across sub-

TABLE 4

Do Specific Forms of Childhood Deviance Predict Offenses?
(Men With Some Childhood Deviance and 3 or More Adult Arrests)

	Total		Less Dev. as Child[a]		Conduct Disorder[b]	
			Percent Arrested For: Drugs			
Drugs before 18	(43)	51*	(16)	56	(27)	50
No	(40)	21	(29)	19	(11)	25
			Drunk, Peace Disturbance			
Drank before 15	(28)	69	(3)	87	(25)	67
No	(40)	77	(27)	72	(13)	88
			Forcible Rape			
Sex before 15	(52)	9	(18)	5	(34)	11
No	(17)	21	(12)	22	(5)	19

[a] 1 to 4 types of childhood behavior
[b] 5 or more types of childhood behavior
* $p < .01$

TABLE 5

Specific Forms of Childhood Deviance as Predictors of Offense Types Among Vietnam Veterans Arrest Since Return

	Total		Less Dev. Before Service		More Dev. Before Service	
			% Arrested For: Drugs			
2+ Drugs before service	(60)	36	(17)	43	(43)	33
No	(123)	24	(60)	25	(63)	23
			Drunk, Peace Disturbance			
Drunk before 15	(92)	43*	(14)	32	(78)	45
No	(93)	30	(62)	23	(31)	43
			Assault, Murder			
Fought before service	(87)	7	(5)	5	(82)	7
No	(98)	5	(71)	3	(27)	9

* $p < .10$

groups—very early drug use does seem to increase the risk of later drug arrests. We therefore attempted to replicate this finding in our Vietnam veteran sample (Table 5). The veterans studied are 571 men who left Vietnam in September, 1971, who were interviewed first when they had been back in the States 8 to 12 months and again three years after their return. They were asked which of five classes of illicit drugs they had used before entering service—marijuana, amphetamines, barbiturates, narcotics, and others (tranquilizers, cocaine, or hallucinogens). Those who had tried at least two of these classes of drugs were considered pre-service users. In both interviews, they were asked about reasons for arrest since their return. Deviance before service was determined by their score on a scale adding one or two points for degree of fighting, arrests, school truancy, early drunkenness, and school dropout and expulsion. Those considered only moderately deviant had scores of 2 to 4, those more deviant had scores of 5 or more.

Testing the effect of pre-service drug use on the later arrest for a drug offense in Vietnam veterans is somewhat confounded by the extraordinary exposure of these young men to heroin while they were in Vietnam. Nonetheless, as we have shown (Robins et al., 1977), pre-service drug experience played an important role in determining their post-Vietnam drug use. Now we shall a chance to see whether pre-service drug experience forecast their drug arrest as well. Table 5 shows that the association between early drug experience and later drug arrests is modestly supported among Vietnam veterans, although the relationship is below statistical significance. It is noteworthy that for veterans, like young black men, early drug use has some predictive power both when these men had been highly deviant and when they had been moderately deviant in adolescence.

We also tested our finding that early drinking did *not* forecast drunk arrests. In veterans, unlike young black men, we did find some relationship, perhaps because we used as our criterion *getting drunk* before 15, rather than simply drinking. But this relationship held only for the less deviant group. It did not apply to veterans who could have been considered to have conduct disorders in childhood.

Our interviews with Vietnam veterans did not ask them about early sex experience, and so we cannot see whether the negative finding with respect to rape holds for veterans (and in any case, we had too few cases of rape among veterans to study), but we do have information on early fighting, and can learn whether that correlates with arrests for violence. Fighting before service did *not* predict arrests for assault. Vietnam veterans rarely were arrested for violence, whether or not they had been fighters before service, and whether or not they had been highly deviant in other ways.

Having a modest replication of our one significant finding, we have some tenuous but suggestive indication that early drug use may indeed be different from other aspects of behaviors that make up conduct disorder. Not only is it not predicted by early school problems, but it leads a somewhat independent life in predicting drug arrests. Johnston (1973) and Lukoff (1977) have shown that illicit drug use is adopted both by the most promising as well as the least promising adolescents in terms of IQ and school achievement. Other deviant behaviors, by contrast, are much more common among students with school problems and dropouts. Therefore there is indeed reason to think that drug use in adolescents may be an independent predictor of later difficulties, particularly drug arrests, difficulties that could not have been predicted on the basis of other indicators of a predisposition for deviance.

With the exception of early drug use, however, we find no childhood behavioral predictors of particular types of offenders. We have no evidence that violent offenders are less (or more) pathological than property offenders. Men with only a few arrests seldom have an arrest for violence, but when they have multiple arrests, half or more of them will have at least one offense of a violent nature, as well as one or more property arrests. Type of offense seems a better indicator of the *severity of the adult arrest history* than of having had a childhood history suggestive of psychiatric disorder.

REFERENCES

DOI, T. and SUGIMOTO, I.: Juvenile recidivists: Property offenders and violent offenders. *Int. Crim. Police Rev.*, 22 (204):24-28, 1967.

GROSS, M. D.: Violence associated with organic brain disease. In: J. Fawcett (Ed.), *Dynamics of Violence*. Chicago: American Medical Association, 1971.

GYNTHER, M. D.: The clinical utility of "invalid" MMPI F Scores. *J. Consult. Psychol.*, 25:540-542, 1961.

HARE, R. D.: Psychopathy and crime. Paper presented at the Colloqium on the Correlates of Crime and Determinants of Criminal Behavior. Washington, D.C., March 30-31, 1978.

HUTCHINGS, B.: Environmental and genetic factors in psychopathology and criminality. Thesis submitted for the degree of M.Phil., University of London, 1972.

JESSOR, R. and JESSOR, S. L.: *Problem Behavior and Psychosocial Development: A Longitudinal Study of Youth*. New York: Academic Press, 1977.

JOHNSTON, L.: *Drugs and American Youth*. Ann Arbor, Michigan: Institute for Social Research, The University of Michigan, 1973.

LUKOFF, I. F.: Consequences of use: Heroin and other narcotics. In: J. D. Rittenhouse (Ed.), *The Epidemiology of Heroin and Other Narcotics*, NIDA Research Monograph 16, Washington, D.C.: U.S. Government Printing Office, 1977.

MCCORD, W. and MCCORD, J.: *Origins of Crime: A New Evaluation of the Cambridge-Somerville Youth Study*. New York: Columbia University Press, 1959.

MEGARGEE, E. I. and HOKANSON, J. E.: *The Dynamics of Aggression*. New York: Harper & Row, 1970.

PETERSON, R. A., PITTMAN, D. J., and O'NEAL, P.: Stabilities in deviance: A study of assaultive and non-assaultive offenders. *J. Crim. Law, Criminol. Police Sci.*, 53 (1): 44-48, 1962.

ROBINS, L. N.: Sturdy childhood predictors of adult outcomes: Replications from longitudinal studies. In: J. Barret (Ed.), *Stress and Mental Disorder*, Raven Press (in press); *Psychol. Med.*, 8(4):611-622, 1978.

ROBINS, L. N., DAVIS, D. H., and WISH, E. D.: Detecting predictors of rare events: Demographic, family, and personal deviance as predictors of states in the progression toward narcotic addiction. In: J. Strauss, H. Babigian, and M. Roff (Eds.), *Origins and Course of Psychopathology: Methods of Longitudinal Research*. New York: Plenum Press, 1977.

ROBINS, L. N. and RATCLIFF, K. S.: Risk factors in the continuation of childhood antisocial behaviors into adulthood. *Int. J. Ment. Health*, 1:96-116, 1979.

WITKIN, H. A., MEDNICK, S. A., SCHULSINGER, F., BAKKESTROM, E., CHRISTIANSEN, K. O., GOODENOUGH, D. R., HIRSCHHORN, K., LUNDSTEEN, C., OWEN, D. R., PHILLIP, J., RUBIN, D. B., and STOCKING, M.: *Biosocial Bases of Criminal Behavior*. New York: Gardner Press, 1977.

WOLFGANG, M. E., FIGLIO, R. M., and SELLIN, T.: *Delinquency in a Birth Cohort*. Chicago: The University of Chicago Press, 1972.

Subject Index

Italic page numbers indicate material in tables and figures.

Name Index

Italic page numbers indicate material in tables and figures.